Communication
in Management

Communication
in Management

THE THEORY AND PRACTICE
OF ADMINISTRATIVE COMMUNICATION

By Charles E. Redfield

REVISED EDITION

 THE UNIVERSITY OF CHICAGO PRESS

CHIGAGO AND LONDON

Library of Congress Catalog Card Number: 58-11955

THE UNIVERSITY OF CHICAGO PRESS, CHICAGO 60637
The University of Chicago Press, Ltd., London W.C. 1

211501

Foreword

ONE of the most remarkable developments of recent years in the business world has been the growing concern of business managers with the problems of communication. This is a relatively new interest. While no one can pinpoint a date and say with assurance that businessmen then began to recognize the problems of communication, my own observation is that, in general, concern with communication goes back not more than twenty-five years and perhaps less. Before that time, few businessmen thought of communication as a problem.

This change in attitude is a reflection of the change in the environment of business. In the pre-1930 world, business as an institution was generally admired and respected. Mr. Coolidge spoke for the millions when he said, in 1925, "The business of America is business."

Correspondingly, the groups with whom the businessman was concerned were not numerous, and his relationships with them were straightforward and simple. He was preoccupied then, as now, with the customer, with whom he communicated through advertising and personal contact. He was interested in his share-owners, but dividends were lush, taxes low, extra dividends frequent, and the "problem" of stockholder relations had not yet appeared.

Employees were not organized into unions, except in particular industries. Their interest in and support of the enterprise for which they worked could be and was taken for granted. The immense flowering of specialization in business was then only at its incipience, and the problems of communication within business—for example, between line groups and staff groups— were scarcely visible.

v

Finally, the prevailing basic attitude conceived of business as an intensely private affair. Any inquiry by government, by the press, or by citizens of the plant community into the policies or activities of a particular business was looked upon not merely as improper but as verging on impertinence. The average corporation president of those years would no more readily discuss his business affairs than his family affairs in public.

How radically all this has changed is familiar to everyone beyond the age of forty. The depression of the early 1930's; the gigantic growth of government and of regulatory official bodies; the rise of the mass labor unions, active, vocal, and frequently hostile—these and other developments shattered forever the calm private world in which the earlier businessmen had functioned. The sociological changes affecting business have been even more far-reaching than the technological changes.

Executives discovered that silence was not golden; that misunderstandings flourished in an atmosphere of secrecy; that business, like other institutions in a democracy, could progress only as far and as rapidly as it could carry with it the consent of the people, whether those people were acting in their capacities as voters, as employees, as share-owners, as suppliers, or as neighbors.

So management people in their turn began to try to communicate. They improved their systems of order-giving. They instituted employee newspapers or magazines. They conducted meetings or made speeches. They wrote letters, published pamphlets, produced slide films and motion pictures.

There were many mistakes, many false starts, as business began to try to communicate. At the outset, little was known by executives about the available techniques, the psychological and other problems involved, or the attitudes of the groups with which communication was sought.

This was not surprising, since little in the background of an engineer, a manufacturing executive, or an accountant prepares him for the problems of communication. Executives with a background in sales were perhaps slightly better off, not because they knew more than the others, but chiefly because most of them had acquired the habit of listening, of observing the customer, of trying to detect his interests and gauge his probable reactions.

The whole field of business communication bristles today with unsolved problems. Some have not been solved because research has not yet produced reliable answers. Others continue because solutions which do not work are still being applied out of custom or habit.

Meanwhile, the communication activity has attracted wider and wider interest. The colleges and universities are active in it. They conduct seminars and institutes on the subject. They carry on research projects. The semanticists, the social psychologists, the sociologists, the anthropologists, and other scholars are prospecting these hills with pick and shovel. Professional societies—notably those in the fields of industrial relations and public relations—have made communication one of their primary concerns.

All these activities are good. But they are also confusing to the business executive. The senior executive who has risen through the grades in a particular sphere of activity—such as manufacturing—suddenly finds himself confronted as a new vice-president or president with activities which he may only dimly understand and problems with which he has little or no experience. He is in approximately the position of a man who has come into the theater in the middle of a movie—an exciting movie, full of fast action and sudden shifts of scene—who has to guess at what came before and the meaning of what he sees happening now.

This executive needs help. Above everything, he needs orientation. His responsibilities for communication are identical with his other responsibilities, in the sense that they involve the three classic executive duties of planning, organization, and control. But, before he can discharge these functions, he must get a grasp of the general field of communication, of the available techniques, of the particular communication problems of his own business. He must know enough about the fundamentals of communication so that he can set realistic goals and evaluate the results.

Where is he to turn for the help he needs? There are many answers to that question, of course. But one of the quickest and easiest answers, in my judgment, is this book of Mr. Redfield's.

Here the executive will find, in an orderly and systematic presentation, the fundamentals he needs to know about the problems of communication, about the techniques which have been usefully employed, about the basic difficulties involved, about the areas of certainty and the areas of doubt.

No book, of course, can provide the specific answers needed for particular problems in communication. But this book will repay reading by business managers through helping to steer them past the pitfalls of uncritical imitation, on the one hand, or the adoption of unsound programs, on the other. It can give them—and this I take to be its purpose—a sense of direction, a knowledge of the past, and a view into the probable future of business communication.

JOHN L. McCAFFREY
Director, International Harvester Company

Preface to the Second Edition

FIVE years ago, when *Communication in Management* first appeared, the study of administrative communication was a novelty in the field of management. Today communication is among the most popular subjects in the United States. The managers of business firms, government departments, and nonprofit institutions of all kinds share this new interest.

Hardly a day passes in modern organizations, large and small alike, without someone identifying and tackling one or another communications problem—perhaps a problem of stating a new policy, preparing a new manual or employee handbook, setting up a reporting system, or devising a scheme for the interchange of information among research scientists and engineers.

Communication is rarely omitted now from management development programs, supervisory training courses, and meetings of professional societies. This is true not only for professional management groups but also for engineers, physical scientists, health and welfare officials, educators, and many others. This new interest in the United States has had its parallel in Great Britain, Canada, Japan, Latin America, and elsewhere throughout the world.

The constantly expanding interest has spawned many new articles and some new books. The National Society for the Study of Communication is a young group made up originally of teachers of composition, speech, and drama; today the Society has a section devoted to the specialty of communication in business and industry. In the recent literature there have been many excellent items, and we have tried to add the very best of these to our reading lists at the end of each chapter. We have added two entirely new chapters: chapter ix on employee publications and chapter x on communication and control. In chapter xv, we have added a new section on communication in scientific and industrial research.

There is no doubt that the continuing growth of giant organizations is still a major factor behind the interest in administrative communication. But size alone does not explain the ever widening interest. The increasing complexity of modern civilization—technologically, geographically, financially—is a highly important factor. Closely related to complexity is the factor of rapid change, which is a signal characteristic of the present time and of the foreseeable future. Rapidly changing conditions require ever new decisions, with new implementing policies and procedures. Making decisions, and implementing them, depends very heavily on an optimum system of information-handling throughout the organization.

C. E. R.

The Arrangement of This Book

THIS book is arranged in four parts. Part I orients the subject, describes the types of information communicated, and establishes certain guiding principles for more effective communication. Part II treats communication downward and outward—from superior to subordinate and from central headquarters to branches and field offices. The most important downward-flowing activity is, of course, order-giving. In Part III the emphasis is on communication upward and inward. Reporting is the most important activity in this category, though attention is given to other upward-flowing processes as well. Part IV emphasizes the horizontal elements, with particular attention to the processes of clearing, reviewing, and conferring.

At the end of each chapter is a list of selected readings covering the items which we believe to be the most pertinent.

A Memo to the Busy Executive Who "Cannot Read Everything"

A good overview of our subject can be gained from reading only a portion of the book. We suggest that priority be given to the first five chapters plus chapters x and xi.

Table of Contents

xiii

ACKNOWLEDGMENTS

NOTES

INDEX

PART I / *Communication:*
            Its Role in Administration

Organizations are created to get work done—efficiently. Communication has an important role in the achievement of that objective. This must be the starting point for a study of administrative communication.

Administrative communication—the combining of communication and administration—is distinguished by its concern with information of certain types and the various ways of preparing, disseminating, and responding to it. These aspects of the subject are discussed here, along with a presentation of certain principles which guide and measure success in the field.

I / Introduction

> The first executive function is to develop and maintain a system of communication.
>
> CHESTER I. BARNARD[1]

WITHIN recent years, management groups in America and throughout the world have been engaged in a historic program of self-evaluation and improvement. Today there is great promise of carrying this program forward through an improvement in communication. By communication we mean here the broad field of human interchange of facts and opinions and not the workings of the telephone, telegraph, radio, and the like.

Producing, distributing, and service organizations—no matter what their endeavor—are made up of individuals and groups whose work is related to the work of other individuals, groups, and the organization as a whole. The process of getting all the different work routines to move along together smoothly calls for the highest order of decision-making, programming, controlling, and reappraising. All these activities depend heavily, sometimes crucially, on communication.

WHAT IS ADMINISTRATIVE COMMUNICATION?

The Basic Process

Communication is, in the first instance, the process of transferring a selected bit of information (a message) from an information source to a destination. There are many examples of information sources: a radio studio is one; the brain of a lecturer, writer, or painter is another.

The selected messages may be transmitted as spoken or

written words, pictures, or in some other form. In oral communication, the transmitter is the voice box; in telegraphy it is the telegraph key which codes the message into dots and dashes. The receiver decodes the message, as transmitted, into a form understandable to the information destination. The receiver may be, for example, the mechanism of the ear, which converts sound waves into a form recognizable to the brain; a television receiver decodes the electromagnetic waves into recognizable visual representations.[2]

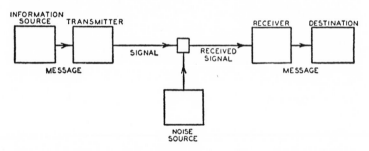

Fig. 1.—The basic communication process. (From Claude E. Shannon and Warren Weaver, *The Mathematical Theory of Communication.* Copr. 1949, The University of Illinois Press. Reproduced by permission.)

This model of the communication process, developed originally for physicists and mathematicians by Shannon and Weaver, identifies yet another important element—noise. "Noise" is their generic term for the distortions, additions, and errors (not necessarily auditory) which adversely affect the message-signal en route from transmitter to receiver. Static is an example; so is the movement of a train when a person is trying to read. Noise, in short, impairs the ideal communication process, makes it less efficient than it would be in the absence of noise.

Relating the Shannon-Weaver diagram to communication in management, one can visualize an executive's brain as the source, an order as the message, and a subordinate's brain as the destination. Indeed, the executive has long been the typical communicator and the subordinate the typical communicatee. It has been the boss's function to tell his employees what to do, and theirs to listen and do it. This is one-way communication, in which information passes from one part of an organization to another without response, without feedback from the communicatee to the communicator.[3]

Communication in Management

In management we are not dealing with one-way communication, of which commercial radio, television, motion pictures, newspapers, and other mass media are examples. Instead we are concerned with bilateral communication, in which information passes in both directions, from superior to subordinate, or vice versa, and back again in a continuous (albeit often interrupted) cycle. In conventional public opinion polls, members of the public furnish a pollster with answers to the polling questions, and that concludes the relationship between the pollster (communicatee) and the respondents (communicators). In employee opinion polls, however, management cannot avoid responding to the respondents; a notification, some other action, or even inaction—employees recognize these as being responses to the polling results.

Administrative communication can best be regarded as a form of social or human communication in which there are these five elements:

A *Communicator* (a speaker, sender, issuer) who
   Transmits (says, sends, issues)
      Messages (orders, reports, suggestions) to a
         Communicatee (addressee, respondent, audience) to influence the behavior of the communicatee, as seen in his
            Response (reply, reaction).

In Lasswell's popular paradigm, it is a question of "*Who* says *what* in *which channel* to *whom* with *what effect?*"[4]

Administrative communication can be analyzed in terms of any of these five elements, although ultimately all of them are involved. One's role as a communicator, whether superior or subordinate, depends on who he is, what he is, and where he is. Individuals at work are total personalities, but their positions involve only segments of their personalities. A look at the communicatee reminds us of the many problems of perception and cognition: What does he hear when he listens? What does he see when he looks? What does he remember when he reads? And what does he believe? Questions such as these, and similar ones applying to processes of transmission, to messages, and to the element of response or feedback, occupy much of the substance of this book.

Because communication is concerned with the interactions of people, individually and in groups, the subject is interwoven with semantics, sociology, anthropology, psychology, education, and administration. Communication is the tool of the advertiser, the movie producer, the radio broadcaster, the newspaper editor, and the politician. The administrator draws on all communication resources in his day-to-day work, with his organization serving as a communication proving ground.

The Organizational Setting

Organizations abound with social communication. Some of the communication is overt, while much of it is unverbalized—in gesture, imitation, and social suggestion. *Nonverbal Communication* is the title of a book published in 1956, by Ruesch and Kees, the former a psychiatrist and the latter a photographer. In this volume one is reminded of the meaningfulness of countless non-verbal expressions, as, for example, when a person cups his hand behind his ear, or when one person lays a reassuring hand on another's shoulder.[5]

In the course of a day there occur many contacts among workers, and between workers and supervisors, during which ideas and information, orders and reports, are communicated from one to the other. The communication may be conveyed by a nod or a glance, a frown or a smile, or simply by the knowledge that both parties are physically present in the same room. An industrial relations director in Chicago says that one of his subordinates insists on at least *seeing* him once a week even if no trace of overt communication takes place.

This book is concerned with those segments of social communication within a formal organization that are institutionally determined by that organization. A business, a government department, or a labor union establishes and maintains certain communication processes for use primarily within its own organization. These processes are intended to apply primarily to persons who are members of that organization, or subject to that organization's authority and control, and represent what we call "administrative communication." Communications between union members as union members while they are at work (for example, when a shop steward solicits dues) are administrative communications of the labor union; they are not administrative communications of the plant or factory. When a customer gives his order to a waiter, that is not administrative communication. (The customer is not a member of the organization.) But when the waiter gives the order to the chef, that is.

Although administrative communication is essentially internal to the organization that prescribes it, there are instances where administrative communications overflow the organizational borders. Some employee publications that were originally set up for internal distribution have acquired external audiences that far outnumber the employee audience. Financial reports prepared for today's meeting of the board of directors may appear in tomorrow's *Wall Street Journal*.

Administrative communication is concerned not only with communication but also with administration. Problems of communication in an organization cannot be divorced from such problems as compensation, working conditions, the quality of supervision, organizational structure, and work methods. If there were two distinct fields of human endeavor—administration and communication—administrative communication would fall more logically under the former than under the latter.

Positional Communication

A formal organization starts with a broad purpose or plan; this is subdivided into activities, and the activities are assigned to positions. Structural relationships are established between Position A and Position B, not between Mr. Smith and Miss Jones. Since communication is the vehicle for carrying on relationships between positions, we find in any formal organization a phenomenon which can be designated as positional communication. The entire organization, as it appears on an organization chart (p. 9), can be referred to as a positional communications network.

Positional communication is upset in practice, however, because positions are staffed with human beings with total personalities. The relationship between Position A and Position B does not exist apart from the relationship between Joe and Gertrude and the other folks in the office. Yet, although it is impossible completely to insulate a position from the incumbent's personality, administrative communication depends most of the time on positional behavior, including positional communication. People in positions are required to communicate in accordance with their positional roles to a certain extent, and in connection with some matters they do so to a surprisingly great extent. For instance, an office manager rejects an employee's request for an afternoon off, saying, "If this were just a matter between you and me, I would tell you to go ahead. But it would set a bad example. So, as office manager, I must say 'No.'"

Just as his position may affect the way a person communicates, so an individual can and often does affect pure positional communication. Take the case of the first sergeant who posts his KP list for the next morning. The first four names on the list are Anderson, Bennett, Costello, and Dennison—all of them privates whose names appear on the company roster in that

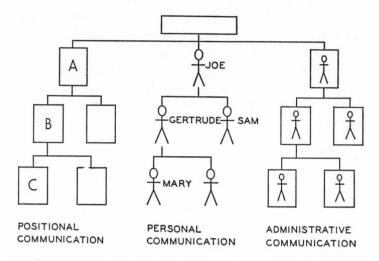

POSITIONAL
COMMUNICATION

PERSONAL
COMMUNICATION

ADMINISTRATIVE
COMMUNICATION

order. Despite the fact that names are used, this is clearly an example of positional communication from a first sergeant to four privates. But the fifth and final name on the KP list is Zilch. Obviously something outside the scope of positional communication has caused the first sergeant to put Private Zilch's name next on the list.

FORMAL COMMUNICATION AND
INFORMAL COMMUNICATION

Administrative communication is identified with formal organizations, but more than one system of administrative communication may exist in the same environment. It is enough to note that an organization such as a labor union uses many of the same communicative processes as does an industrial establishment or government department. Some unions are even beginning to use opinion polls to get information from their members.

Informal communication is identified with informal organizations. In any work group the working code may be communicated in a highly articulate manner through hints, gestures, and even silences.[6] Once a machinist opened his locker at noon and found his lunch box painted yellow. He understood that his co-workers were telling him not to work so hard and so fast. But, if painting lunch boxes yellow were an established communication device of a labor union, it could no longer be regarded as informal communication. Melville Dalton has suggested that we might better use the adjective "explicit" for "formal" and the adjective "implicit" for "informal."

Some of the communicative processes within a formal organization appear to be informal when in fact they are formal. A good example would be the so-called informal contacts that supervisors make with their subordinates at work. Some companies require their supervisors to make these contacts; certainly most managements look on them with favor. A program to make the contacts even more formal would provide each supervisor with mimeographed lists of his subordinates and require him daily to check off the names of the employees contacted and periodically to review the lists to see which employees had been missed.[7] Perhaps this is not bad as a communication technique, but the communication that would take place under such a system could hardly be thought to be informal.

The Grapevine

A classic example of informal communication is the so-called grapevine, which can be thought of as the "rumor network."

Since this network is not firmly structured and follows different directions in different situations, there are several or many grapevines, rather than just one, in every organization.

Let us assume that a secretary in the personnel director's office is a link in the formal channel for receiving requisitions for personnel. This girl may also be a link in a grapevine to other girls throughout the organization. When a requisition comes to her, she may process it to her superior in the proper fashion or, instead, use her grapevine to secure candidates for the vacancy before notice of it reaches her superior. Here we have an example of informal communication at work, provided the personnel director is unaware of what has transpired. But if he condones her continued use of the grapevine, and accepts her candidates in lieu of using established recruiting methods, that grapevine is no longer informal; it has become a part of the organization's formal communication mechanism.

The grapevine is a most undependable means of communication. According to Allport and Postman, one cannot predict with assurance the direction, speed, or final substance of a message transmitted via grapevine. The processes of leveling, sharpening, and assimilation impinge on a rumored message to abbreviate it, to magnify what remains of it, and to restructure it to conform to the needs and interests of the individual rumorers.[8] Thus no extensive, complex, or vital instruction or report can be intrusted to the grapevine. It is so difficult to get full and accurate information to the right person at the proper time through formal mechanisms that it seems unwise even to attempt using informal mechanisms.

The emphasis on formal communication in these pages is not intended to depreciate the amenities of working together; good manners and consideration for others are certainly important. Indeed, expressions of personal and social feeling often pave the way for directive and informative communication, the stuff of which administrative communication is made.[9]

COMMUNICATION, MORALE, AND EFFICIENCY

The subject of communication first appeared on the managerial horizon during and immediately after World War II. At that time the thinking went something like this: "The efficiency of our operation can be increased if we can only improve the morale of our employees. We can do this by improving communication with them. So let's communicate."

This line of reasoning—that we need to communicate to improve morale, which, in turn, will increase efficiency—held sway for about ten years. Today it is seldom encountered at all. At least three lines of inquiry and thinking have caused the picture to change.

First, it was found that morale was a much more complex phenomenon than had been believed theretofore. Morale was not something that you could measure very easily, nor was it, speaking crudely, something that you could turn on and off like a faucet. Morale, it was decided, was a very delicate, fragile, and unpredictable property, like the changing moods of a child (which are so hard for adults to understand). There were many instances in which men with so-called poor morale were doing a competent day's work. It was found, too, that many of the roots of poor morale lay outside the factory gates, where management could not be very effective. The whole area became so tenuous that the very word "morale" tended to retreat in favor of the term "job satisfaction," which has a much more limited connotation.

Another development was the appearance of experimental evidence negating the assumed relationship between communication and morale. Bavelas and Barrett, two researchers at Massachusetts Institute of Technology, building on the earlier work of Leavitt and other experimental psychologists, found that communication is a variable that can affect both morale and efficiency, but not necessarily in the same direction. Thus one system of communication may be more effective in improving morale than efficiency, while another system may improve efficiency and worsen morale. A group at the University of Minnesota's Industrial Relations Center tested the relationship between communication and morale in five firms. They concluded that "there is no significant relationship between employees' attitudes toward the company and their knowledge about the company." Interestingly, they found consistent, though not statistically significant, negative correlations between information and attitude for supervisory groups in all five firms.[10]

Finally, the statements of theorists in the field vigorously challenged the earlier assumptions. P. H. Cook, an Australian personnel expert, suggested that the efforts to improve morale through improved communication were entirely misdirected. Morale, he said, does not depend on communication. Instead communication depends on morale. In other words, there has to be an atmosphere favoring rather than interfering with successful communication. In support of Cook's position, T. M. Higham, an English psychologist, asserted that "the pathetic notion that you can improve communications by giving more and better information should surely be allowed to die a natural death; you will not get any reception if you are not trusted; but if relations are good, then there is a good chance that what you say will be received, and that you will get cooperation in return."[11]

These developments have forced a retreat to a more conservative position. The subject of administrative communication must primarily be concerned with communication and efficiency, more or less shunting aside the matter of morale. Communication needs to be improved because, very plainly, there is a need to improve efficiency and productivity. Administrative communication accepts as one of its variables the general problem of the atmosphere for communication, but not the specific problem of employee morale. It will have to be assumed that someone else is taking care of that; hopefully, that everyone is!

Selected Readings

BOOKS AND MONOGRAPHS

BARNARD, CHESTER I. *The Functions of the Executive.* Cambridge: Harvard University Press, 1938.
Observations of far-reaching influence on the role of communication, formal and informal channels within an organization, and barriers to more effective communication.

CHISHOLM, CECIL (ed.). *Communication in Industry.* London: B. T. Batsford, Ltd., 1955.
Collected papers on British practice.

DOOHER, M. JOSEPH (ed.). *Effective Communication on the Job.* New York: American Management Association, 1956.
Reprints of articles from *Personnel,* plus some new training materials from industry.

HARTLEY, EUGENE L. and RUTH E. *Fundamentals of Social Psychology.* New York: Alfred A. Knopf, 1952. Part I, "Communication—the Basic Social Process."
A significant treatment, summarizing both theoretical and experimental data. Bibliography.

HERON, ALEXANDER R. *Sharing Information with Employees.* Stanford, Calif.: Stanford University Press, 1942.
A pioneering study of techniques for the dissemination of general information to employees.

Human Relations in Metal Working Plants, Report II: *Metal Trades Committee, Fourth Session, Geneva, 1952.* Geneva: International Labour Office, 1952. Pp. 67–71, 94–104.
An authoritative review of communication as a facet of management-employee relations.

PFIFFNER, JOHN M. *The Supervision of Personnel: Human Relations in the Management of Men.* New York: Prentice-Hall, Inc., 1951. Chap. ix, "Communication."
The "why" of administrative communication.

PIGORS, PAUL. *Effective Communication in Industry.* New York: National Association of Manufacturers, 1949.

Comprehensive statement of theory and practice. Bibliography.

SHANNON, CLAUDE E., and WEAVER, WARREN. *The Mathematical Theory of Communication.* Urbana: University of Illinois Press, 1949.

Profound analysis of the technology of transmission, with long-term implications in the area of social communication.

SIMON, H. A.; SMITHBURG, D. W.; and THOMPSON, V. A. *Public Administration.* New York: Alfred A. Knopf, 1950. Chap. x, "Securing Teamwork: The Communication Process."

A generalized statement on communication and co-ordination. Bibliography.

WHYTE, WILLIAM H., JR., and the EDITORS OF "FORTUNE." *Is Anybody Listening?* New York: Simon & Schuster, Inc., 1952.

Critical review of modern communication activities. Reprinted from a series of *Fortune* articles.

ARTICLES

BAVELAS, ALEX, and BARRETT, DERMOT. "An Experimental Approach to Organizational Communication," *Personnel,* Vol. 27 (March, 1951), pp. 366–71.

How different communication routes affect morale and efficiency.

COATES, R. H. "Human Communication," *British Management Review,* Vol. 13 (October, 1955), pp. 255–62.

An engineer's analogy of information handling to materials handling.

COOK, P. H. "An Examination of the Notion of Communication in Industry," *Occupational Psychology,* Vol. 25 (January, 1951), pp. 1–14.

A theory that communication is a part and a result, rather than a determinant, of social relationships.

CORSON, JOHN J. "Management—Tongue-tied, Deaf and Blind?" *Advanced Management,* Vol. 11 (September, 1946), pp. 101–4.

———. "The Role of Communication in the Process of Administration," *Public Administration Review,* Vol. 4 (Winter, 1944), pp. 7–15.

Two articles on the importance of communication in a large government bureau.

CROWNFIELD, A. C., and GRANT, E. S. "Communication Techniques in Labor-Management Relations—Their Development and Application," *Mechanical Engineering*, Vol. 72 (May, 1950), pp. 392–96.

On the importance of making communication a part of every supervisory job.

DAVIS, KEITH. "Communication within Management," *Personnel*, Vol. 31 (November, 1954), pp. 212–18.

How staff personnel and the grapevine affect communication within the management group.

DORSEY, JOHN T. "A Communication Model for Administration," *Administrative Science Quarterly*, Vol. 2 (December, 1957), pp. 307–24.

A theory that all administration is a communication process.

GUEST, ROBERT H. "Tell It to the Boss!" *Personnel*, Vol. 34 (July–August, 1957), pp. 8–15.

Effective communication requires, above all, competent general management.

HIGHAM, T. M. "Basic Psychological Factors in Communication," *Occupational Psychology*, Vol. 31 (January, 1957), pp. 1–10.

Emphasizing the need for more knowledge about the communicatee and his environment.

HOVLAND, CARL I. "Social Communication," *Proceedings of the American Philosophical Society*, Vol. 92 (1948), pp. 371–75.

Problems and possibilities of scientific research in the field of social communication.

LEYTON, A. C. "Communication Training: A Progress Report," *BACIE Journal* [of the British Association for Commercial and Industrial Education], Vol. 7 (November–December, 1953), pp. 213–19.

On the training of business managers in communication skills.

———. "Operational Definition in Communication," *British Management Review*, Vol. 12 (October, 1954), pp. 267–76.

Outline of a theory of communication, including the concept that there are only degrees of approximation of understanding.

REDFIELD, CHARLES E. "Communication: The Lifestream of Every Organization," *Office Management*, Vol. 18 (March 15, 1957) (yearbook issue), pp. 30–32, 152 ff.

Expanded treatment of the relationship between communication, morale, and efficiency.

SAPIR, EDWARD. "Communication," *Encyclopaedia of the Social Sciences*, Vol. 4, pp. 78–80. New York: Macmillan Co., 1937.

Communication's place among the social sciences.

SCHRAMM, WILBUR. "How Communication Works," pp. 3–26 in *The Process and Effects of Mass Communication*, ed. WILBUR SCHRAMM. Urbana: University of Illinois Press, 1955.

Up-to-date description of the process in general and mass communication in particular.

WEAVER, WARREN. "The Mathematics of Information," pp. 97–110 in *Automatic Control*. ("Scientific American" series.) New York: Simon & Schuster, Inc., 1956.

Refinement and advancement of his earlier paper in *The Mathematical Theory of Communication*.

II / What Administrative Communication Deals With

EVERY process or activity involving two or more people in an organization has an element of communication in it. There are a number of aspects of administration where success depends to a great extent on the mastery of communicative abilities and techniques. Mere mention of such subjects as training, supervision, and leadership reminds us that they require effective communication. But administrative communication cannot be said to take in every endeavor that involves communication; the activities and subjects that undeniably fall under that heading are great enough in number.

To support the structure and basic workings of a formal organization, certain essential information must move in three directions—down, up, and horizontally. The term "down" should be understood to mean "downward *and outward*," because in most organizations there is a dimension of distance-away just as there is one of distance-below. Relations between central headquarters and branch offices are affected significantly by distance-away. By the same reasoning, the term "up" implies "upward and inward."

A general's decision to attack is empty until the men in the front-line companies move into action: an order for the attack has to be issued, transmitted to designated units, and complied with. The underlying decision and the resulting order are based on information contained in previous reports that have come in (and up) from the front. The soundness of that decision and that order, as well as the formulation and issuance of the next ones, can be determined only after the receipt of further reports.

Sometimes an organization can be made to move as a team using only the reciprocal processes of downward and upward communication. The decision-maker and order-giver, whether he is a quarterback or simply acts like one, must be close enough to the situation to be able to blend all the separate acts into co-ordinated group activity. However, most situations require co-ordination at one or more levels below the top. Cast in terms of an organization chart, this co-ordination is horizontal in nature, and it is carried on by means of horizontal communication.

THE DOWNWARD FLOW

Types of Information Transmitted

Orders: policy and procedure.—The downward flow is dominated by orders, of which the greatest number deal with policy and procedure. Policies are guiding principles that furnish an underlying and continuing basis for taking specific action; they may appear as formalized statements, or simply exist as conventional understandings. Policies are characteristically rigid— once they are established, divergence is not easy—and they are necessarily issued at a high level relative to their point of application. Policy is to an administrator what a theme is to a symphony conductor, what a law is to a judge, or what a campaign platform is to a candidate for public office.

Procedure differs from policy in that it represents in detail the specific steps, methods, or routines to be followed in carrying out established policies. "Procedures," according to one writer, "are policy dressed in work clothes and with tools in hand."[1]

For instance, a board of directors might indorse the principle of seniority to govern company-wide personnel policy. In this situation, *especially from the standpoint of the policy-makers,* the application of the seniority principle to specific questions of layoff, re-employment, or promotion would be procedural.[2] If the policy-makers disapprove of the way the subsidiary procedures work out, they may either order a change in the procedures or refashion their policy.

There is no single rule that will always differentiate policy from procedure. On the contrary, it is frequently impossible to say where policy stops and procedure begins. When, asked a Greek legend, do grains of sand become a sand pile? When, we might ask, do procedures become policy?[3]

Let us say that top management issues an order that all safety requirements are to be met. This is certainly policy, and in conforming with it one foreman may prohibit smoking, while the foreman in a neighboring department does not. Top management properly regards both actions as procedural—simply specific steps in carrying out top policy. But the workers in the two departments are equally correct in looking on a smoking or no-smoking order as policy at their levels.

Organization.—Orders are given on the subject of the organization itself, focusing attention on structure, responsibilities, authority and the limits thereof, and relationships between positions and units in the organization. In smaller companies and departments, where there is little to say about organizational structure and related matters, the subject of organization is likely not to be treated separately.

General information.—There is a constant downward flow of information that does not directly order anything. Management issues factual material to increase general knowledge about the organization and its work, one objective being to increase the employees' sense of belonging. In much the same way management disseminates opinions on various subjects, such as politics and economics, with the object of influencing employee opinion. Also illustrative of general information are notices of Red Cross and Community Chest campaigns, employee gatherings, group insurance matters, and references to technical and professional articles and meetings.

Besides being not directly instructional, general information is likely to be transitory in nature, as are notices of charitable campaigns and the like. Although general information is not transmitted in the form of an order, it does have potential influence, sometimes in very important and effective ways.

Methods for Transmitting Information Downward

In any cross-section of business and government almost every conceivable oral, pictorial, written, and symbolic method is being used for the downward transmission of information.

Information is transmitted orally in face-to-face contacts or in meetings; by telephone, motion picture, plant broadcast or telecast, and tape recording. General Electric's Electric Housewares Division has used two-way closed-circuit television between the Bridgeport home office and its field force, and the company's Apparatus Sales Division has introduced semimonthly newsreels as the medium for acquainting its officials with new products and manufacturing methods.[4]

The Borden Company has been a pioneer in the systematic use of the oft-neglected bulletin board, which served as the principal communication channel for the company's centennial anniversary contest for employees in 1957. Under the title "Why," the Rogers Corporation publishes a daily bulletin-board feature on company affairs of the previous day.[5] In every office and shop we find a variety of posters and signs, some of which say only "No Smoking" or "Think." And sometimes information is transmitted downward and outward through liaison personnel or by the transfer of personnel out of the central office.

Today great emphasis is placed on written media, including individual messages, circulars and bulletins, manuals, handbooks, and employee handbooks. The most common media for information on organization are organization charts, job descriptions, duty statements, and job instruction sheets. Evidences of rank or status, whether a corporal's stripes, a machinist's overalls, or an executive's private office, serve to govern many structural relationships.

Throughout the United States and Canada there are about six thousand company publications addressed to employees. Some are newspapers, others magazines, and altogether they represent an annual expenditure of approximately three hundred million dollars.[6] About fifteen hundred companies have followed General Motors' lead in setting up self-service reading racks at accessible locations within their plants and offices, with employees voluntarily taking from them more than a million booklets a week. The booklets cover a wide variety of subject matter, ranging from sports, hobbies, and health, to safety, citizenship, and economics.[7] Many companies issue annual reports to employees, and many more, including Allis-Chalmers, Electric Auto-Lite, and Minneapolis-Honeywell, sponsor regular or occasional letters to employees, most often directly to their homes. Some organizations limit their letters to one or more groups of managers or supervisors.[8] The lowly pay envelope antedates most other media as a vehicle for notices to factory employees.

Training is a major communicative activity, supplementing administrative communication in varying degrees. Whenever a newcomer is assigned to a job, the line supervisor may either repeat all the instructions he has issued in the past or send the novice to a training program. In the latter case, training supplements the supervisor's order-giving authority and responsibility. The distinction between training and ordering is clearer when, as in the California Department of Employment, an organization issues training materials separate from its written orders. The orders are probably more effective *as orders* without any training slant, while the training releases can be used most profitably by skilled training people.

THE UPWARD FLOW

Types of Information Transmitted

Flowing upward are reports dealing with statistics: units produced or distributed; periods or distances operated and materials and man-hours consumed; personnel newly employed, discharged, currently employed, and turnover. Other reports are cast in financial terms: increases, decreases, and balances in cash, investments, accounts receivable and payable, and inventories; income and expense; budget accounts, costs, and profits or losses. In narrative form come items of general information: exceptional events, anticipated problems, professional and technical developments; interpretations of statistical and financial data; and commentaries on a host of other matters that do not lend themselves to precise statistical or financial treatment.

Also flowing upward are opinions, ideas, and suggestions; and complaints, grievances, gripes, and rumors. Opinions, it should be noted, are overt expressions that presumably mirror attitudes. There is always some doubt, however, whether an expressed opinion is as directly related to a particular attitude as at first glance it appears to be. Suggestions are generally held to be constructive, which is not the case with complaints and gripes. Grievances are complaints that travel upward through established grievance procedures and generally demand solution.

Methods for Transmitting Information Upward

Information is communicated upward through written reports, face-to-face contacts, in conferences of all sorts, and at social gatherings. Staff personnel are often able to secure information that would not flow up through channels. Management engineers, liaison men, expediters, inspectors, and staff conference leaders can all gather worthwhile information incidental to their work. A big part of the interviewer's job in his conduct of counseling and exit interviews is to secure information from employees. Information is also transmitted upward and inward through the transfer of field and plant personnel to the central office. Pitney-Bowes shuts down its plant each month for a short period to allow employee work groups to air their complaints. The foreman and an elected employee alternate as chairmen of these groups, and unresolved problems are taken up with department heads.[9]

Some of the thousands of employee periodicals carry question-and-answer features, and many print letters from subordinate employees along with management's replies. The president of United Air Lines states that he will reply personally to any letter addressed to him by an employee. Ford, General Motors, and the Illinois Central Railroad have all conducted letter-writing contests on such subjects as "Why I Like My Job," while Aldens has conducted similar contests on the subject "What I Dislike Most about the Company."

Within the supervisory hierarchy, from bottom to top, a most important medium of communication is the activity (or administrative) report. There are thousands of suggestion systems, some of which also accept complaints, and both rumor boxes and gripe boxes. One company has experimented with tape recorders installed in "telephone booths" in its plant. Employees can complain or gripe anonymously on tape. A committee made up of workers and supervisors regularly hears the playback and decides what actions to take, if any.[10] Grievance procedures are designed as systems for upward communication entirely or partly through unions, but union representatives are able to pass along much additional information outside the established grievance machinery.[11] Employee opinion polls rank high among the newer methods for upward communication.

THE HORIZONTAL INTERCHANGE

Some of the most persistent and acute problems of administration, especially in large or decentralized organizations, stem from deficiencies in horizontal communication—still a relatively unexplored field. One of the principal roles for many staff people, such as management engineers and expediters, is to transmit information among positions and units at the same level. Current interest in the conference process, as evidenced by research reports and other writings, indicates that serious attention is being given to this method of horizontal interchange. The conference-type telephone hook-up is growing in use, with as many as twenty-five different offices linked together by phone at one time.

Managerial and supervisory newsletters, mentioned earlier in connection with the downward flow, move information horizontally as well. Ford Motor Company's management and employee information department publishes, among other things, an *Executive Information Bulletin* (circulation: one thousand) and a *Management Information Bulletin* (circulation: fifteen thousand). *The Sears World,* initiated as a quarterly in 1957, is primarily a medium of interchange for the company's eleven thousand executives scattered throughout this country and abroad, many of whom never get to Chicago.[12]

Information is also exchanged horizontally through face-to-face contacts outside the conference room, by telephone, and through procedures for the clearance and review of written material. Copies of letters, entire files of letters, and reports are circulated from reader to reader, usually according to the list on an accompanying routing or "buck" slip.

Management is constantly expanding its range of communicative activities, devices, materials, and techniques. There is a concomitant widening of the scope of information being transmitted, while developments continue apace in training and other fields of administration that incorporate significant elements of communication. Here we must emphasize again the importance of the truly informal communication that occurs within an organization, although our primary concern is with the overt, formal processes of administrative communication.

Selected Readings

BOOKS AND MONOGRAPHS

BAKER, HELEN. *Company-wide Understanding of Industrial Relations Policies.* Princeton: Princeton University, Industrial Relations Section, 1948.

Survey of methods used to inform supervisors and employees about industrial relations policies.

BAKER, HELEN; BALLANTINE, J. W.; and TRUE, J. M. *Transmitting Information through Management and Union Channels.* Princeton: Princeton University, Industrial Relations Section, 1949.

Communication methods in Johnson & Johnson Company and Esso Standard Oil Company.

Care and Feeding of Bulletin Boards. New York: The Borden Company, Public Relations Department, 1948.

Informational and procedural booklet for Borden's plants and offices.

MARSTON, E. C.; THOMPON, L. M.; and ZACHER, FRANK. *Business Communication.* New York: Macmillan Co., 1949.

PETERS, RAYMOND W. *Communication within Industry.* New York: Harper & Bros., 1950.
Survey report, with special attention to practices in the Esso Standard Oil Company. Bibliography.

ARTICLES

BARLOW, WALTER G. "Measuring the Effectiveness of Communication," pp. 3–13 in *Key Problems in Human Relations.* ("General Management Series," No. 181.) New York: American Management Association, 1956.

Comparative statistics on various media.

FRANKLIN, W. H. "Reporting to Employees," pp. 28–43 in *Reporting to Employees and the Public on Profits and Productivity.* ("Financial Management Series," No. 88.) New York: American Management Association, 1947.

How to make annual stockholders' reports suitable for employees.

LULL, PAUL E.; FUNK, FRANK E.; and PIERSOL, DARREL T. "What Communication Means to the Corporation President," *Advanced Management,* Vol. 20 (March, 1955), pp. 17–20.

Survey by Industrial Relations Research Staff at Purdue University of the one hundred largest corporations in the United States.

MCKEAND, CHARLES A., and VAN NOSTRAND, RALPH. "Employee Information from A to Z," *Personnel Journal,* Vol. 28 (December, 1949), pp. 254–61.
What to tell and methods of telling it.

MUMBLOW, MILTON E. "Employee Communications—a Number One Job: The General Motors Story," pp. 14–21 in *Developments in Office Personnel Administration.* ("Office Management Series," No. 127.) New York: American Management Association, 1950.

Case study, describing, among other aspects of General Motors' program, its self-service book racks.

Title, Monroe M. "Getting Information to Employees—Effectively," *Hospital Management*, Vol. 81 (January, 1956), pp. 50–51, 116 ff.

Inventory and description of media used at Brent General Hospital, Detroit.

III / Some Guiding Principles

THERE are already so many methods for carrying on administrative communication, and so many new ones are being introduced, that, whenever either an existing or a proposed method is discussed, management must decide whether it is worthwhile. The trial-and-error approach is not all bad; on the contrary, out of experimentation comes success as well as failure, and the user of communication devices is constantly gathering new ideas and refining old ones. But we need a yardstick, beyond trial and error alone, that will help us appraise a particular communicative act or an entire system of communication.

In our search for a practical yardstick we can draw on an abundance of material from the writings on administrative communication. Certain principles derived from this material serve as guides for effective communication in almost any administrative situation. The following check list presents seven such principles:

> Clarity
> Consistency
> Adequacy
> Timing and timeliness
> Distribution
> Adaptability and uniformity
> Interest and acceptance

CLARITY

In the administration of utopia every communicator always says what he means and means what he says, and every communicatee always understands exactly what the communicator

29

intends to convey. We have no such utopias today and encounter instead one failure after another because someone did not say what he meant or because someone else did not understand what he heard or read.

"Clarity," the poet Lloyd Frankenberg said one time, "is a beautiful word. It sounds like a precise word. Anything is clear that we can see easily, that we can hear without straining. It makes us think of bells and cloudless skies, of a good telephone connection. When we apply it to ideas, the physical association that comes with it is a sensation of effortlessness. Clear directions are those we can follow with the least trouble, three blocks to the right, two to the left, number 29. The right facts in the right order: a Paris policeman can do it with gestures."[1] This concept of clarity is the least common denominator; it is important, but it is not, of course, the be-all and end-all.

Clear Language

The quest for clarity is primarily a striving for better manipulation and comprehension of language. Language pervades all aspects of administration, and much attention has been given to it in recent years. Formulas have been devised for computing readability, human-interest value, and other factors. Short sentences, short words, and a quota of proper names and personal pronouns will give a high rating to an order or report on the various scales that have been established.

Out of the many commentaries on the use of readability formulas, two points stand out: one, that they are tests of the written word after it has been written, not tools of the writer; and, two, that a high score on the tests is not the final measure of quality, or even understandability.[2] "The cat sits on the mat. The cat sees the mouse," scores better than "The cat, sitting on the mat, sees the mouse." But where (except perhaps in a first-year reading primer) would the former be preferable, on any basis, to the latter?[3] Indeed, Rudolf Flesch, himself the author of the best-known of all readability measures, has noted that they will not tell whether the written material is nonsense. Understandability is more important than readability, and the one does not necessarily correlate with the other.[4]

The speaker or writer can go only so far, however—with or without formulas—in improving his use of language; the members of his audience must improve their language facility also. There is no doubt that people of low intellectual attainment are poor communicators and communicatees.[5] Many others are also. Some firms have introduced reading-improvement programs to upgrade this area of communicative ability among their personnel.[6] Other communication training programs have the same objective in other areas, for example, in letter-writing, conferring, and interviewing.

The sometimes peculiar language of administration, variously labeled "businessese," "officialese," "federalese," or "gobbledygook," has been the butt of a good deal of friendly and not-so-friendly ribbing. This comment by the editors of *Fortune* is typical:

Almost invariably, businessese is marked by the heavy use of the passive construction. Nobody ever *does* anything. Things *happen*—and the author of the action is only barely implied. Thus, one does not refer to something, reference is made to; similarly, while prices may rise, nobody *raises* them. To be sure, in businessese there is not quite the same anonymity as is found in federal prose, for "I" and "we" do appear often. Except when the news to be relayed is good, however, there is no mistaking that the "I" and "we" are merely a convenient fiction and that the real author isn't a person at all but that great mystic force known as the corporation. . . .

A businessman who castigates government bureaucrats, for example, is at the same time apt to be activating, expediting, implementing, effectuating, optimizing, minimizing and maximizing—and at all levels and echelons within the framework of broad policy areas. Similarly, though he pokes fun at the long-hairs and the social scientists, he is beginning to speak knowingly of projective techniques, social dynamics, depth interviewing; . . . and sometime soon he will probably appropriate the hallmark of the sound sociological paper, "insightful." Businessese, in fact, has very nearly become the great common meeting ground of the jargons.[7]

Every organization has its jargon, a language of its own that is particularly strange and unintelligible to the new employee. Jargon is often a necessary evil. Professional and technical language characterizes many fields of endeavor. (Administration

PEANUTS •   By Schulz

Reproduced by permission. Copr. 1954 United Feature Syndicate.

and communication are no exceptions.) People working in such specialized fields understand each other well enough, but outsiders and newcomers hear only an unintelligible dialect. For them it is necessary that the knowledgeable communicators explain the meanings of terms being used, either explicitly or by checking for understanding.[8] Or perhaps the jargon-users can, to some extent, substitute terminology that is more generally understood. In this connection we might recollect these lines written by the late Arthur Kudner for his son:

> Never fear big long words,
> Big long words mean little things,
> All big things have little names
> Such as life and death, peace and war
> Or dawn, day, night, hope, love, home.
> Learn to use little words in a big way,
> It is hard to do
> But they say what you mean.
> When you don't know what you mean
> Use big words—
> That often fools little people.

We are often handicapped by language when we attempt to convey certain aspects of problems that occur in an organization, particularly those problems involving people rather than things. A situation may be vibrant with the stresses and strains of human relations and yet become, in an order or report, a cold statistic or cryptic generalization. At the risk of injecting even more jargon into administration, we probably do need either some new language symbols or some better ones.[9]

Understanding is made more difficult because of the barriers of administrative distance. Often a member of a management group will interpret a situation differently from the way it is interpreted by members of other work groups. He may perceive an emergency requirement but fail to communicate that perception to the subordinates whom he asks to act quickly. Moreover, subordinates are at a serious disadvantage in their upward communication because they lack the necessary insight into managerial interests and predispositions. These barriers to communication are least pronounced between adjacent levels. This is one of the best reasons for communicating through channels, giving intermediates at each level the opportunity to interpret as required.

Comparisons

Comparison is an aspect of clarity that is almost unique to administrative communication. Although a few executives still insist that there are absolute rights and wrongs in administration, the truth is that things can only be better or worse. A change is ordered in a manufacturing process not because the new method will be 100 per cent efficient but because it is comparatively better than what has been done in the past. Thus the order putting a change into effect must be understood in the context of the situation.

The understanding of reports depends greatly on the comparisons they afford the reader. Production is either more or less efficient than it was last month or last year, or complaints are greater or fewer than they were during a previous period. Such records of experience during a previous period can be regarded as historical standards. Comparisons can also be made against other standards, some developed from the experiences of comparable organizations and others based on theoretical potentialities. Neither language nor administration is absolute; thus the language of administration depends on comparisons, which may be explicit or may simply be understood by persons familiar with the situation.

CONSISTENCY

Messages must be consistent with one another. There should never be an order to perform a task in a certain way while there is another order to perform it in a different way. Orders must also be consistent with the known objectives of the organization and with its other activities, including its reports.[10] Since an order reflects management's interest in a certain subject, management must interest itself in reports about that subject.

It would be inconsistent to tell a visiting nurse that she can save some time on each visit by not washing her hands. It would be inconsistent to set up a suggestion system and then not have the best possible machinery for investigating suggestions. The assurance of an open-door policy in an employee handbook requires that the door really be open and not barricaded by secretaries, lines of callers, or even by expensive furnishings that frighten subordinates into not entering or overwhelm them into saying nothing when they do enter. The president of one firm has gone so far as to get rid of his desk, which he calls "the great dais that important men sit behind."[11] (Ultimately, of course, the absence of a desk may become the very status symbol that he seeks to avoid.)

There are often distracting inconsistencies in punctuation, capitalization, and forms of address. The "Mr. Jonas" in the first paragraph becomes simply "Jonas" or even "Hans" later in the same written message. Commas and semicolons are often used inconsistently. References to the "Goodyear Tire & Rubber Co." may appear later as "The Goodyear Tire and Rubber Company," or some variation thereof.

Enforcement

Enforcement is the most important point at which management can achieve the desired unity and consistency. One can go just so far in stating that an order is mandatory, or that it is not just "for the record." An executive demonstrates his consistency, not only in the way he issues orders, but ultimately in the way he enforces orders and responds to reports. It is not enough for him simply to acknowledge reports; he should follow them up, seek out more information, and send his final interpretations back down the line in support of either existing or new instructions.

Exceptions

Exceptions, which are in effect inconsistencies, deserve special mention. For, no matter how artfully exceptions are provided for or permitted, they tend to establish precedents that will, if they accumulate, establish new rules. Since it is impossible to anticipate every contingency, an order-giver should provide for any exceptions at the outset. Only then can he permit them—even encourage them—later when they become necessary. But he will insure that the exceptions supplement rather than undercut his basic instructions; and he will revise his instructions promptly to incorporate exceptions that have become the rule.

The foregoing points are embodied in this statement from the initial policy bulletin of the Cherry-Burrell Corporation:

> Necessity for deviation from policy is bound to arise occasionally.
> Where possible deviation can be foreseen, the steps to be taken to secure approval will be outlined in the individual Policy Bulletins.
> There will likely be cases where deviation from policy on a one-time or temporary basis will be considered necessary or advisable. An appeal should be addressed to the President by the Group Head, or by the Division Manager with a copy to Vice President—Operations.

ADEQUACY

The goal in administrative communication is to insure an optimum flow of information—neither too little nor too much —enough to cover but not so much as to smother. The only point where the adequacy of communication can be measured is in the mind of the recipient. Dean Kapp of the Engineering Faculty of London University has in mind the concept of adequacy when he cites the confusion between what is needed to *express* a meaning and what is needed to *convey* it. "Tell the young scientist by all means not to use more words than are needed to convey his meaning. But if he is restricted austerely to the bare number needed to express it he may commit the error of overcrowding, which is just as bad an error as verbosity."[12] We seem to need a modest amount of redundancy to make our essential communication effective.

Advertising men often assert that comprehension and acceptance can be increased to some extent by saying the same thing over and over again. But the field of mass communication is a competitive one, with the audience free to select the material it wants to see or hear repeatedly. Such competition and selection are to be avoided in the field of administrative communication. Organizational audiences are captive audiences; presumably they hear and read everything transmitted to them. The fact is, they do pick and choose—and therein lie the roots of many failures.

Brevity is often cited as a virtue, but brevity may be interpreted by a communicatee as curtness. Policemen are brief; they say "Stop," "Move on," "Don't do that." It is interesting to observe that superiors characteristically use fewer words in talking or writing to subordinates than subordinates use in talking or writing to superiors.

Quantity

There is an anecdote about a utility installer who, laden down with tools, arrived at a new building to make an installation. His foreman berated him for not bringing along the pertinent technical instructions and told him to bring them the following day. The next morning the installer arrived laden down with manuals and standard practice instructions. This time, however, he had no tools—for he could not possibly carry both.

The first consideration is the total quantity of communications received and used. The new policy statement from the board must be compounded with the reports that accumulated while the individual was away for several days; and to these must be added the technical advice he received that very hour in a conference with some visiting consultants; and on top of all these are the shelves of manuals, bulletins, and handbooks that serve as permanent guides for all phases of his work.

Detail

The second consideration is the size of any single message —the amount of detail, the appended forms and charts, the length and bulk. It is possible for a few lengthy and complex instructions and reports to be more overwhelming than a greater number of shorter ones.

In any large organization, information must be interpreted and digested from time to time and at different points in its transmission. Yet, the same item will vary in significance as it passes from level to level. Communication that is entirely clear between a subordinate and his boss may be unclear to persons at other levels above and below. Furthermore, the material passed along may not even be necessary or useful. The question in a large organization is not *whether* to interpret and digest administrative communications but, rather, *how*. This is a problem to which we give more attention later.

According to the exception principle in reporting, the things to report are not the normal items but the exceptional ones. If a subordinate can focus his reports on exceptions occurring within his area of delegated authority, much detail can be omitted. Normally a superior can accept a performance that conforms within reasonable limits to established standards. It is assumed that the standards exist and are known, and also that subordinates will unfailingly report the occurrence of exceptions. Either the lack of known standards or a lack of forthrightness will make the exception principle inoperable.

TIMING AND TIMELINESS

Timing

The same message will be received or responded to differently by different individuals and groups at the same time or by the same individuals and groups at different times. Even in an emergency one dare not overlook the situational and technical aspects of timing.

The experts who conduct employee opinion polls know that a poll can be seriously affected if the timing is bad, and they try to avoid taking polls just before or just after labor disputes or immediately after the announcement of a wage increase or benefit program. Every message is subject to influences of the same sort, with individuals and groups absorbed in activities and thoughts quite different from, and oftentimes as important as, the substance of the latest message.

In the two-party relationship of a superior and a subordinate both parties should be alert to the attendant psychological factors. Some executive and supervisory training today is concerned with teaching people to be more aware of behavioral differences among their subordinates. A person may or may not know why psychological differences exist, and seldom will he be able to overcome them, but he should have sufficient knowledge to be able—time permitting—to minimize their effect. He may delay transmitting an order or report for a while, or he may present it in a special way. The immediate superior or immediate subordinate is in the best position to perceive the psychological factors and to time the transmittal of a message successfully.

Dean Kapp offers two metaphorical propositions to dramatize the importance of timing. The first relates to the music-hall comedian, the greatest expert of all in the art of timing. "Are pace and timing less important to the presentation of technical information? A little less important perhaps, but surely still of considerable importance. If a scientific fact or argument is presented at a moment when the person addressed is thinking about something else it will fail to reach its mark. And if something fails to reach its mark in a learned Society it certainly does not matter less than if something fails to do so in a music hall."

The second relates to the pilot who in nasty weather has no time for small talk with a passenger. "Only when he sees the ship of your discourse glide past the beacon that marks the entrance to harbour and still water does he find the leisure for mental note-taking." So it is a part of a communicator's duty to provide "moments of harbour and still water. The things said during these moments must be designed for the one and only purpose of aiding memory." They should be judicious repetitions, restatements and summaries, spaced and timed at "quiet moments" amid the onrush of new information.[13]

Timeliness

Out-of-date information is as bad as or worse than none at all. But organizations do not hold still while instructions are being prepared or after they are issued. Tactical information for the use of small combat units on land or sea becomes obsolete in a matter of hours; for air defense, in a matter of minutes, even seconds.[14]

Reports exist primarily to facilitate the exercise of administrative control by the recipient. If a report is delayed in preparation or transmission, it ceases to be a control medium and becomes a historical document instead. (Of course, some reports do have historical value, as in the substantiation of a patent.) Every organization should try to insure that new instructions, changes in work, and reports of changes are as nearly simultaneous as possible. No one of them should lag unduly behind either of the others.

Orders once issued, and reports once made, tend to achieve a permanent status, even when it is known at the outset that they will be only temporary. Order-givers and reporters are inclined to feel that their responsibilities begin and end with the issuance of an order or the writing of a report. It is necessary to review and revise instructions and reporting systems periodically to eliminate or forestall obsolescence, regardless whether the obsolescence is in form (a faded mimeographed page or a format since superseded) or, as is more commonly the case, in substance.

DISTRIBUTION

The most skilfully prepared message may be undercut in its transmission. From initial source to ultimate recipient exists a succession of hazards that can destroy any promise of effectiveness. One of the most frequent causes of miscarriages in administration is the failure of information to reach the correct destination.

One December day in 1956 the control tower at a Dutch airport sent out a signal: "Henk, your plane is on fire." Several thousand feet up Pilot Henk heard the signal, checked his parachute, and bailed out. As he drifted to earth at the airport he saw his plane (not afire) crash in a field nearby. He also saw a plane afire on the airport runway. This second plane, he learned a few minutes later, had also been piloted by a man by the name of Henk.

The message, "Henk, your plane is on fire," was perfectly clear. But no matter how clear a message may be, it must reach the proper person in the proper position before it can be properly effective.

Applicability

Communicators in any organization, whether they are executives or first-line supervisors, have something to learn from advertising experts who constantly ask themselves, "What audience do I want to reach?" There are many audiences in an organization, although the principal audience, of course, is the entire organization. The central office, branch offices, and other portions of the organization make smaller audiences. A message may be intended for certain positions (for example, the comptroller, the medical officer, or new employees), for certain units (for example, foreign branches, personnel offices, or machine shops), or for certain designated individuals.

Thus the audience must be determined before a message is transmitted. *Who* is to be told is often just as important as *what* is to be told, since the question of *who* will determine largely *how* the telling is to be done. Sometimes it is only necessary to adjust the wording, for example, by adding a "please" to an order where the relationship with the recipient requires such an amenity. At other times there will be major problems concerning the *how* of communicating, as in devising methods of transmission or selecting media, both of which are discussed later.

The person receiving a message should always know its purpose—he has been addressed either because he has the authority or responsibility to act, because he may profit from the information, or for some other reason. The important thing is that there be a reason. If there is none, people who receive messages may not know why they received them; some may be frustrated at not being able to do anything in response, while others may be inundated with so much inapplicable material that their essential work suffers. The flow of information can be governed in the first instance by the "horizon concept," which dictates that an individual should receive information essential to his position (that is, within its horizon) and no more.[15] Other information, or the same information to other audiences, should be recognized (and even labeled) for what it is—general information.

Transmission

A message can be transmitted most quickly and surely if it moves directly from the issuing source to its destination. This is most readily possible in a two-party relationship. Supervisory hierarchies are intermediate transmitters that act to slow down transmission and distort it. In order to circumvent delays and distortions, management tends to disregard supervisory channels, as, for instance, when it transmits an order through a public-address system or introduces a conventional suggestion system.

Despite the dangers of delay and distortion, as Chester Barnard put it, "a communication from the head of an organization to the bottom should pass through every stage of the line of authority."[16] This rule applies to upward communication also. In 1814, the War Department issued orders to subordinate commanders, bypassing Major General Andrew Jackson, then commanding the Division of the South. Jackson complained to the War Department that such a practice "tends to disorganize all the plans of the Superior, without his knowledge or consent." Jackson first warned the Department that all orders had to come through his headquarters and then forbade his subordinates to obey any command that did not.[17]

This bypassing of channels not only violates the formal organization structure, as Jackson maintained, but also creates resentment and interferes with the duty to keep next-level superiors and subordinates informed.[18] The communicator who bypasses intermediates in the chain of command is telling them, in effect, that they are not competent or honest enough to pass along orders, reports, suggestions, opinions, even general information; or, as Lent Upson once said, "making privates believe they are majors and majors believe they are nothing at all."[19] One of the prerogatives of a middle-management position is the control of information flowing through it.

When channels become chronically ineffective, top management must correct the trouble, either through training or by changing personnel. And one can always use the clearance process or other techniques to enlist the participation of intermediates in preparing orders before they are issued. These methods will be discussed later.

ADAPTABILITY AND UNIFORMITY

One of the most difficult assignments for management is to achieve a happy balance between adaptability and uniformity in administration. By adaptability we mean flexibility, individuality, and suitability; uniformity is the opposite of adaptability, and it is not entirely separable from our earlier principle of consistency.

Uniformity

The smooth operation of every organization depends to a certain extent on uniformity. The mass-production industries have been built on standardization, and uniform instructions and reports have proved their worth in securing a maximum degree of standardization. Budgeting, too, is an activity that depends on uniform orders and reports.

Adaptability

There is a striking dissimilarity, however, in the enforcement of uniformity among five hundred workers on an assembly line and the enforcement of the same degree of uniformity among a lesser number of more skilled eployees working in separate offices and shops throughout a nation or a state or in different parts of a large city. This is dramatically true among even a small number of executives where each is in charge of a decentralized operation within a single large organization. Uniformity must give way to adaptability in such cases because of the inherent differences in the situations and in the individuals involved. Systems of uniform orders and reports may fail to achieve their objectives simply because these differences are overlooked.

Take the case of the company that issued uniform instructions on the location of a portrait of its president in all its offices. It was specified that the portrait "be placed directly behind the desk—five feet from the floor and centered by the breadth of the desk." In one office, as might have been expected, there was a window at the specified spot.[20] In another case a state agency notified its district offices that they could close during the afternoon preceding an impending holiday, provided someone was on hand to receive messages. Again one office did not fit the pattern because the manager of that office worked alone.

Business and government bureaucracies alike tend to enforce uniform reporting requirements and to institutionalize them through the use of standard report forms. Unless a reporting system provides some opportunity for adaptation, subordinate reporters will abjectly follow the authoritative and uniform format, even to the point of omitting essential information or conducting their work with the view to making a better showing on the report. In some cases, they may actually fabricate the report.

Uniform Coverage

Systems of orders and reports must be uniform in their coverage of common problems and in the extent of their coverage of all departments and operations. No department or operation should be made to bear a disproportionate burden of orders or reports, nor should any be partially or wholly uncovered.

INTEREST AND ACCEPTANCE

Interest and acceptance are contributory to effective communication. Speaking a bit loosely, we can say that in downward communication morale must be good, and in upward communication the boss must be a good listener.

The purpose of any communication is to secure a positive response. Some responses occur immediately, as when troops are ordered to advance. Other responses are delayed; indeed, some are delayed so long that they are not directly traceable to a particular stimulus. The ultimate response—no matter how remote or how minute—will, mathematically speaking, be a function of the receiver's interest in and acceptance of the message.

The Effect of Authority

Authority is a factor to be reckoned with in communication, above all in gauging acceptance. As noted earlier, organizational audiences are captive audiences; subordinates in particular can never wholly insulate themselves and reject what they are told. An order-giver can depend solely on authority to secure varying but passable degrees of acceptance, often with little or no accompanying interest. The power element of authority has been in a downward trend (in civilian organizations) as a result of the expansion of labor unions and civil service, and continued full employment. But the basic concept of authority in organizational life is still valid.[21]

Upward-flowing messages flow against the tide. Thus it is difficult for many upward communications to elicit interest (which is vital here) and to secure acceptance. A likely exception, of course, is the report that a superior is particularly interested in, or one for which he has made a special request. Such reports flow upward with the same overtone of authority that caused them to be made.

The Atmosphere for Communication

Aside from authority, interest and acceptance depend on two things. The first is a well-devised communicative act or system of communication. To achieve this, a communicator can utilize the six preceding principles—clarity, consistency, adequacy, timing, distribution, and adaptability. The second is a broad, aggregate factor, and we can describe it simply as a good atmosphere for communication. This is evidenced by a feeling of mutual trust and respect. The parties to a communicative act need to understand and share a common concern for the success of their joint endeavors. The way these two elements relate to interest and acceptance looks like this:

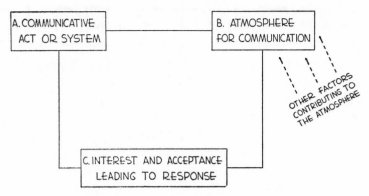

The challenging thing about this three-part relationship is that it works in several directions. *C* is an element of *B* (interest and acceptance improve the atmosphere for communication), and *C* is also an element of *A* (interest and acceptance improve the technical efficiency of a communicative act or system). A subordinate submits a report (*A*), to which the superior responds (*C*), which improves the atmosphere for communication between him and the subordinate (*B*). This improvement in *B* improves the efficiency of *A* (whether it is an existing communication or a subsequent communicative act).

Or take an adverse situation: a superior has issued a number of instructions (*A*) which were unadaptable or were only for the record. The atmosphere for communication (*B*) has been adversely affected, which pretty well precludes any wholehearted interest and acceptance (*C*) preliminary to response.

There are serious barriers in many situations that limit the degree to which the atmosphere for communication can be improved and the degree to which interest and acceptance can be secured. These barriers form the subject matter of books and courses on human relations and social psychology. It is enough for us to note that interest and acceptance represent an important principle of communication in management.

The manner in which a discussion of interest and acceptance carries us somewhat afield is itself an indication that the subject of administrative communication is not just a certain number of communicative processes or activities, even though this approach is sometimes recommended by individuals and organizations that have a communicative device or program to sell. "What you need," an executive may be told, "is a good manual of policies and procedures" (or a suggestion system, or greater readability and interest-value in the employee handbook, or a reading course for supervisors, and so forth).

There is an interrelationship among all the communicative activities, and they are related in turn to other activities that do not fall under the heading of communication at all. Communication is not separable from such factors as organizational structure, office and plant layout, the quality of supervision, and a host of others. Communicative activities comprise a unity with the organization and the people in it.

Selected Readings

BOOKS AND MONOGRAPHS

Flesch, Rudolf. *The Art of Plain Talk*. New York: Harper & Bros., 1946.

———. *The Art of Readable Writing*. New York: Harper & Bros., 1949.
Two books on the measurement of readability and human interest value.

Gowers, Sir Ernest. *Plain Words*. London: H.M. Stationery Office, 1948.

———. *Plain Words: Their ABC*. New York: Alfred A. Knopf, 1957.
Important guides on good writing.

GUNNING, ROBERT. *The Technique of Clear Writing.* New York: McGraw-Hill Book Co., 1952.

Measuring readability according to a scale ("fog index") and according to school grade.

KAPP, REGINALD O. *The Presentation of Technical Information.* London: Constable & Co., 1949.

"Functional English" for scientists and engineers.

KLARE, GEORGE R., and BUCK, BYRON. *Know Your Reader: The Scientific Aproach to Readability.* New York: Hermitage House, 1954.

Historical and comparative treatise. Bibliography.

MORTON, HERBERT C. *Putting Words To Work.* Hanover, N.H.: Dartmouth College, Amos Tuck School, 1955.

Advocating the establishment of writing-improvement programs.

PIGORS, PAUL and FAITH. *Understanding as a Condition for Success in Order-giving.* Cambridge, Mass.: Industrial Relations Associates, Inc., 1945.

Suggestions for better communication, based on a psychological analysis of order-giving.

ROETHLISBERGER, F. J. *Management and Morale.* Cambridge: Harvard University Press, 1941. Chap. vi, "Of Words and Men."

Semantics in industry.

SHIDLE, NORMAN G. *Clear Writing for Easy Reading.* New York: McGraw-Hill Book Co., 1951.

WHYTE, WILLIAM H., JR., and the EDITORS OF "FORTUNE." *Is Anybody Listening?* New York: Simon & Schuster, Inc., 1952. Chap. iii, "The Language of Business," and chap. iv, "The Prose Engineers."

On businessese and, also, on the bad effects of oversimplification.

ARTICLES

BARZUN, JACQUES. "Not Gobbledygook—But Plain Words," *New York Times Magazine,* August 21, 1955, pp. 25, 60.

Commentary on the plain-words movement.

FLESCH, RUDOLF. "A New Readability Yardstick," *Journal of Applied Psychology,* Vol. 32 (June, 1948), pp. 221–33.

HOSLETT, SCHUYLER D. "Barriers to Communication," *Personnel,* Vol. 28 (September, 1951), pp. 108–14.

Understanding and acceptance depend on improved face-to-face contacts and require an "atmosphere of approval."

LOCKMAN, ROBERT F. "A Note on Measuring 'Understandability,'" *Journal of Applied Psychology,* Vol. 40 (June, 1956), pp. 195–96.

MACHAVER, W. V., and BORRIE, W. A. "A Reading Improvement Program for Industry," *Personnel,* Vol. 28 (September, 1951), pp. 123–30.

Johnson & Johnson's program for increasing executives' reading speed and comprehension.

MCLEAN, ALAN. "An Industrial Psychiatrist Looks at Employee Communications," *Personnel Journal,* Vol. 33 (February, 1955), pp. 340–43.

How management's failure to communicate causes feelings of anxiety among employees.

NEUBERGER, S. R. "An Introduction to the Concept of Readability," *British Management Review,* Vol. 12 (October, 1954), pp. 292–306.

Comparative analysis of the various readability formulas. Bibliography.

POLLOCK, ROSS. "Word Usage in Position Classification," *Public Personnel Review,* Vol. 4 (October, 1943), pp. 266–73.

A criticism of the methods of writing up job descriptions.

STRYKER, PERRIN. "A Slight Case of Overcommunication," *Fortune,* Vol. 49 (March, 1954), pp. 116–17, 150 ff. (Reprinted in PERRIN STRYKER and the EDITORS OF "FORTUNE," *A Guide to Modern Management Methods* [New York: McGraw-Hill Book Co., 1954], pp. 177–86.)

Illustrating the principle of adequacy.

WHYTE, WILLIAM F. "The Semantics of Industrial Relations," *Human Organization,* Vol. 8 (Spring, 1949), pp. 4–10.

Organizational barriers to conveying intended meanings.

PART II / *Communication Downward*
and Outward

To get work done, executives must issue orders and transmit downward some general information. Since understanding and acceptance are not guaranteed, order-givers must make their communication as effective as possible.

Executives use, for their downward communication, individual messages, circulars and bulletins, manuals, handbooks and employee handbooks, employee publications, and a host of other media. Each medium has its particular potentiality, and yet all of them are interrelated.

IV / Telling Others What To Do

> Orders are the things which make a business tick. They are given when the office boy is sent to get stamps, when the girl from the typist pool is required to take down a letter, when a planning clerk sends a schedule of work to a machine shop, when a sales clerk sends a customer's order to a production department. At all these times, orders are given, just as I give an order if I go into a shop and ask for a box of matches.
>
> V. W. Oubridge[1]

THE NEED FOR ORDERS

THERE is an abundance of downward-flowing information in any organization: part of it is essential to operations, another part is indirectly related to operations, and some of it bears no discernible relationship to operations at all. Because there has been such a fashion recently for the less essential types of information, we need to be reminded that "the business of business is business."[2] No matter how ingenious an organization may be in its use of indirect methods of influencing subordinates, it dare not rely entirely on the exercise of *indirect* influences. The successful functioning of even a perfectly designed and staffed formal structure depends, basically, on the effectiveness of its instructional system.

Orders are absolutely necessary; they tell individuals how to act in their formal positions. Because of their personality differences and their identification with a variety of groups, people are motivated to act in a variety of ways, or they may be impelled not to act at all. If orders are incomplete or defective, subordinates are likely to act in a manner inconsistent with, or contrary to, the organization's established objectives.

Subordinates represent a type of captive audience that cannot refrain from listening to orders, receiving them in writing, or seeing them displayed as signs and posters. Whether or not compliance follows is another matter. Conversely, superiors are responsible for issuing and enforcing orders, and their responsibility for the behavior of subordinates cannot be avoided or reduced by not ordering or not instructing. On the contrary, a superior's silence or inaction communicates approval of whatever his subordinates may be doing—even if they are doing nothing! In other words, you can "pass the buck" up, or across, but you cannot pass it down.

Andrew Jackson was vigorously aware of the superior's responsibility for order-giving. Said Jackson:

> An order, generally, to perform a certain service, or effect a certain object, without specification of the means to be adopted, or the limits to govern the executive officer—leaves an *entire discretion* with the officer, as to the choice and application of means, but preserves the responsibility, for his acts, in the authority from which the order emanated. Under such an order, *all* the acts of the inferior are the acts of the Superior. . . .[3]

Too many executives and supervisors are reluctant to accept the responsibility for order-giving, and for other downward communication as well. No doubt many of the things that need saying are unpleasant, and everyone seeks to avoid as many unpleasant occasions as he can. The importance of an individual to his position is often likely to depend more on his controlling information than on his communicating any.

This reluctance to communicate downward seems to vary at different levels in an organization. The individual who believes he is on the way up lives with an eye toward the top. He is eager to communicate upward, but he sees no reason for communicating downward.[4] Indeed, he may even prefer to dissociate himself from subordinates whom he has left behind.[5] For the latter, at the lowest levels of supervision, giving orders (often excessively) may be a symbol of unhappy status.

PROBLEMS IN ORDER-GIVING

Clarity, consistency, and the other principles described in chapter iii apply to downward communication, including order-giving. One encounters certain practical problems, however, that seem to be unique to the giving of orders, and these problems tend to cross the artificial boundaries separating one principle from another. Even brief mention of these problems here will make clearer why, in succeeding chapters, certain practices are recommended in the use of actual order-giving media—manuals, handbooks, and the like.

Policy and Procedure

It is difficult, as was pointed out in chapter ii, to distinguish precisely between policy and procedure, but an order-giver can clarify his intention by himself perceiving, and then communicating, whatever distinction is possible. This involves breaking down and classifying the contents of each order or collection of orders under separate headings, "policy" and "procedure."

In the Works Public Relations Manual of the International Harvester Company an attempt has been made to present each major subject under three subheadings: *general, policy,* and *recommendations.* Under *general,* we find brief introductory statements that set the stage for the policies and recommendations that follow. Under *policy,* in statements ranging from a few sentences to several pages, are expressions of the corporation's public-relations requirements imposed on all works managers. Under *recommendations* appear the suggestions, the bits of worthwhile information, the "tips" that may be helpful to a works manager in carrying out the policy requirements.

Quite different, according to Ernest Dale, was the situation in the General Motors Corporation during the early days when

Will Durant was president and Walter Chrysler general manager. Chrysler, upset at the constant shifts and changes, beseeched Durant for some firm policies. As Chrysler told it:

> I remember I went to see him once and said, "Billy, for the love of ――― please, now, say what your policies are for General Motors. I'll work on them; whatever they are, I'll work to make them effective. Leave the operations alone; the building, the buying, the selling and the men—leave them alone, but say what your policies are."
>
> Billy laughed at me. "Walt, I believe in changing the policies just as often as my office door opens and closes."[6]

Durant was succeeded in the General Motors presidency by Alfred P. Sloan, Jr., a serious student of administration. One of Sloan's major innovations was to establish a body of corporate policies, of which the major one was stated to be "to produce a car for every purse and purpose . . . just as a general conducting a campaign wants to have an army at every point at which he is likely to be attacked." The corporation was never again to skirt the bankruptcy which almost befell it in 1921.[7]

Substantive policy and procedure.—Both policy and procedure can be further delineated. There is, first, substantive material; that is, material dealing with the mission of the organization. The mission could be to manufacture valves of a certain type, to be distributed in a particular way—possibly through jobbers—or it could be to carry out a reforestation program. For the word "substantive" we can generally read "operating," or we can refer to more specific policies or procedures, such as sales or manufacturing.

Institutional policy and procedure.—There are, second, policies and procedures on institutional or administrative matters, such as purchasing and accounting or administrative communication. An important example of institutional policy and procedure is the body of personnel rules governing employment, hours of work, safety, vacations, and similar items—items that have traditionally dominated most employee handbooks.

Until recently, institutional or administrative matters could be identified as staff functions, but now many of them are being performed by line officials. Within subsidiary units of an organization, also, the identity of substantive and institutional policies and procedures may shift. The conduct of a suggestion system, for example, is an institutional activity, but the suggestion department may have its own internal operating policies and procedures.

The need for procedure.—If some people are allergic to policy, many more bristle at procedure. To them it means regimentation and red tape. We must put the lie to this misapprehension, for, as Lawrence A. Appley says, "in its truest sense a procedure is a history of the finest experience to date. It is a record of the best available know-how of predecessors on the job or of experts who have studied the job. A procedure should indicate to an individual the way others have found best for doing this job and therefore the way it should be done until he or someone else finds a better way. When a better way is found, procedure should then be changed and the know-how in relation to this job increased and improved."[8]

Mandatory and Discretionary Orders

The necessary distinction between mandatory and discretionary orders is partly a matter of clarity and partly one of adaptability. Expressions such as *must, shall, will,* and *is to* are alike in the way they order action, while expressions such as *may, wherever practical,* and *it is recommended* do not clearly order anything. The word *should* is on the border line. Whether one uses mandatory or discretionary terminology depends on the problem being dealt with, the competence of the personnel and their identification with the organization, and the meanings that words seem to have within a particular organization.

Is it essential that columns of figures be subtotaled at the foot of each page? Must a salesman know that a customer has a satisfactory credit rating before he writes an order? Can a person qualify for a pension before he attains a certain age? There is seldom any need for discretion in matters like these. Direct or mandatory orders are indicated, and we can assume that they will be welcomed.

But should an employee be dismissed because he is six minutes late getting to work, when five minutes' tardiness is the maximum allowed? He *may* be if the superior—in his discretion—believes that this violation, on top of others, justifies such drastic action. Should an auditor make a complete count of all inventories, or should he make spot-checks only? Under certain circumstances a complete count is *recommended*, but under other circumstances spot-checks are to be *preferred*. In cases like these, discretionary orders are more suitable than mandatory ones.

Unless order-givers recognize the need for distinguishing between mandatory and discretionary instructions, subsequent enforcement becomes confused or breaks down entirely. Many administrative failures can be traced to discretionary orders to which absolutely strict compliance was expected. In February, 1944, when the Allies landed at Anzio, Winston Churchill was distressed because no attempt was made to occupy the high ground overlooking the beachhead during the first twenty-four hours after the Allies' unopposed landing. The British theater commander-in-chief explained his position by saying that "there was no lack of urging from above." Churchill immediately sent word to General Marshall in Washington that "senior commanders should not 'urge' but 'order.'" Furthermore, to General Alexander, commanding the Anzio operation, Churchill wrote:

I have a feeling that you may have hesitated to assert your authority because you were dealing so largely with Americans and therefore *urged* an advance instead of *ordering* it. You are however quite entitled to give them orders, and I have it from the highest

American authorities that it is their wish that their troops receive direct orders. They say that their Army has been framed more on Prussian lines than on the more smooth British lines, and that American commanders expect to receive positive orders, which they will immediately obey. . . .[9]

In 1956 the world was shaken by the news of the Hungarian revolt against Soviet control. The surprising thing was that so many Hungarians were able to flee across the Hungarian border. What had happened, according to the New York *Herald Tribune,* was that the Hungarian border guards had been ordered by their superiors to "dissuade" fugitives but not to use force. Their interpretation of the order, coupled with their own feelings, was to negate the former border controls and thus allow more than one hundred thousand refugees to escape.[10]

Employees at all levels are constantly performing a variety of tasks, some mandatory, others discretionary, and still others partly one and partly the other. Frequently the determining factor is the stage of technical development. When an activity is first undertaken, there may be many uncertainties, requiring considerable discretion, as, for example, in the conduct of research and development work; but, as work is refined over a period of time, much discretion gives way to mandate. In some situations, particularly those involving professional people, the only thing that can be made mandatory is the exercise of discretion.

Command and Operational Orders

We rightfully assume that an order-giver is a superior and that an order-taker is a subordinate. But this is not to say that the former is *the* superior, i.e., the "commander," of the latter. A weapons-bearer is truly subordinate to his platoon sergeant and is directed in his activities by the sergeant's many "command" orders. Similarly, a nurse in a doctor's office is subordinate to the doctor and is governed by his command orders. But in a hospital we have an entirely different story. The nurses' superior is the director of nursing, and her superior, in turn, is the hospital superintendent, who may be a physician or a lay person. The physicians and surgeons on the medical staff are not subordinates of the hospital superintendent, nor are they superiors of the nurses. Yet they issue "operational" orders without challenge to the nurses. In like manner, stock-chasers in a machine shop are not subordinates of the machinist who gives them many orders. If the hospital nurses refuse to obey the orders of the physician or surgeon, or if the stock-chasers refuse to obey the orders of the machinist, they are disobeying the superintendent who engaged them, for he is indeed their superior. As a condition of their employment he has, in effect, commanded them to obey authentic operational orders.[11]

This concept of command and operational orders, originally developed by V. W. Oubridge, is not to be confused with the dualism of command and technical orders. The latter stem from technical or special staff officers at a higher echelon to their counterparts below. Personnel and budget officers are examples in business as are ordnance and quartermaster officers in the military.

"Going on Record"

A serious problem arises when instructions are used simply as a means for "going on record." This is a practice traditionally encountered in large government departments, but business officials are also subject to the pressures of the courts, labor unions, and other organized groups—pressures which may cause an order to be given with no intention that it be complied with. The more sophisticated employees take a wait-and-see attitude. "Does he mean it," they ask, "or is it simply for the record?" If the latter, the order does not mean what it says.

An example is the typical prohibition in expense accounts against reimbursement for tips, or for tips beyond a certain modest percentage. Most experienced salesmen and civil servants alike interpret such prohibitions not to mean that reimbursement is impossible, but, instead, that some or all of their tips have to be included under other expense headings. One company tried a policy of authorizing only one drink per person at meals; and the salesmen followed the rule to the letter—including all non-drinkers at the table. In another example, throughout a large factory there are signs prohibiting smoking —but many people smoke. Commented one of the employees, "The company must put up those signs for the insurance company and the fire department."

Instructions "for the record" endanger the processes of order-giving on at least two counts. First, the new employee comes to the organization unaware of such a practice. Once he has had to turn to his more experienced co-workers for their interpretation, his attitude toward future instructions will be skeptical, if not negative. Second, employees are placed in an untenable position. By failing to comply they are ostensibly remiss and their formal status is imperiled, but compliance is impossible if it runs counter to the behavior pattern of the work group with which a satisfactory relationship must be maintained. The organizational setting is soon characterized by a situation where compliance is withheld until the members of the various employee groups agree among themselves that compliance is indicated.

Quantity and Detail

Several solutions have been advanced to combat the problem of quantity beyond the most elementary one of limiting the number of instructions issued.

Consolidating orders.—It is possible, periodically, to consolidate instructions which, over the years, have grown beyond usable dimensions. Some organizations have rewritten their manuals simply to reduce bulk, and others have developed abbreviated handbooks based on their authoritative but lengthier manuals, with the latter assigned to a reference status.

In 1954 the Post Office Department issued a new Postal Manual; in 268 pages it covered the same points that had been covered in manuals and circulars comprising more than 4,000 pages of fine print. The New York Telephone Company furnishes abstracts of some of its technical instructions for the use of fully trained workers on the job, believing that a highly detailed instruction has maximum usefulness only for training purposes.

A written instruction that has been amended by a series of partial revisions needs to be consolidated whenever the basic instruction with all its addenda becomes too difficult to assimilate. Understanding can be made easier, and probably surer, if the entire instruction is issued anew.

A line of demarcation for detail.—A device for limiting detail calls for the establishment of a hypothetical line of demarcation to apply to both superior-subordinate and headquarters-field relationships. Above the line is the area of responsibility of the issuing authority; here are the minimum instructions that are vital to the objective, and only essential details would be included. Below the line are the alternatives and the discretionary instructions that are subsidiary to the essentials, and authority is delegated to subordinates to fill in details in this area. A procedure might require that the blue cable be soldered to the blue post, since the mechanism will not operate properly otherwise. But there are varied and equally acceptable ways to do the soldering, and every operator has developed techniques that may indeed be the best for him.

The location of the line of demarcation for detail may vary among different activities or for a single activity at different times or in different locations. Accounting and purchasing are typical activities where the line is usually low and little discretion is permitted. Recruiting, on the other hand, is an activity where the line is likely to be quite high, permitting subordinates wide latitude in their recruiting procedures. Specific decisions in this matter will depend largely on the organization's general policy in delegating authority.

The horizon concept.—At Pratt and Whitney, the authors of the foreman's manual applied the horizon concept to their audience by asking: "Where does he get the thing as it comes to him over the horizon; what does he do with it while he has it; when he finishes with it, in which direction does he start it out over his horizon in order for it to go through the proper channels?"[12] The horizon concept was translated into four specific standards which were used to determine the inclusion or exclusion of details:

1. Does the foreman have to know about this?
2. What are his responsibilities in this connection?
3. What action does he have to take about this?
4. What tools or paper work does he need to take action?
    a) Where can he get them?
    b) Exactly what does he do with them when he gets them?
    c) To whom does he give them when he has done his part?

Through the use of these standards, 1,600 pages of draft material were cut to 275 pages.[13]

In many instances, such as a change in an accounting code or in a metallurgical standard, it is quite simple to determine whether an instruction falls within or beyond the horizon of a certain position. But there are cogent reasons for considering not only the limited horizon of an employee's immediate position but the broader horizon of his section, department, or even the entire organization. How can foremen develop into managers if they are never given any information beyond that which is strictly required for their current work? Handbooks (discussed in chap. viii) offer one answer; employee publications (discussed in chap. ix) offer another.

Secondary and Non-subordinate Audiences

There are situations where an audience is not truly subordinate to the order-giving authority, possibly because it is a secondary or incidental audience. Sometimes, for example, an order-giver has some measure of power to prescribe (short of ordering) certain standards for a non-subordinate organizational unit or person. These standards may deal with policy, as when a manufacturer requires dealers to market his items on an exclusive basis. Or they may deal with procedure, as when a professional society prescribes certain forms of records for member organizations carrying on that type of work. Under the Constitution the states are not subordinate to the federal government, so the latter must resort to the use of standards rather than conventional orders to control state activities (highway construction and welfare, for example) to which the federal government makes financial contributions.

Standards are delicate devices, and there is still much to be learned about their use. We find some standards that are mandatory, others that are discretionary or advisory; frequently it is difficult to determine just how binding they actually are.

A typical secondary, or incidental, audience is the housewife who uses the maintenance instructions which a washing-machine manufacturer issues primarily for his maintenance crews. Treasury Department regulations apply primarily to Treasury officials and employees, but they apply also to taxpayers. The Postal Manual of the Post Office Department applies primarily to postal employees, but many mail users find that they must have their own copies. These are examples of administrative communications overflowing their normal boundaries, and we encounter the same phenomenon later in our discussion of administrative reports.

The Order-giver's Attitude

Attitudes are always conveyed along with orders; that is to say, *an* attitude is conveyed, although it may not be the attitude that the order-giver intended.[14] Attitudes may be wholly non-verbal, but they are communicated nonetheless. One of the easiest ways for an intermediate to sabotage an order is to transmit it with a here's-another-one-of-those-central-office-orders-you-are-supposed-to-follow attitude.

An order-giver, like a salesman, must believe in his product (which is always easier if the product is a good one), and he must get that belief across. If any transmitter of an order, even one far down the line, is not sold on it, he will do a poor job of selling it. Attitudes become grossly apparent when orders are discussed, especially in the explanations of why they are necessary. Such explanations are important, of course, if subordinates are to see that an assignment is not an unthinking demand by a higher authority but a necessity for the organization's success. (This is Mary Follett's "law of the situation.")[15]

Problems such as these, involving at the same time technical, sociological, and psychological factors, recur in every system of orders and even in single orders. They may be less noticeable in a small organization than in a large one, but they seem to come up everywhere sooner or later.

It can be asserted that the greatest single cause of inefficiency is poor downward and outward communication, of which orders are by far the most important segment. The inescapable objective of all orders is to secure compliance, which can be more confidently expected if all the technical aspects of an order are sound and if all the accompanying social and psychological elements of acceptance are cultivated.

PRELIMINARIES TO BETTER ORDER-GIVING

A variety of devices is available for testing orders before they are issued. One such device, particularly useful when the subject matter deals with procedure, is that of the spot-test or pilot installation. The pretesting may be done in any typical operating unit, making sure that the unit is neither the best nor the worst. The testing process may be quite elaborate, involving a series of pilot installations and revisions in instructions, until a satisfactory combination of practice and procedural instructions is worked out. One management engineer advocates the use of a methods development laboratory, pointing out that by using a laboratory instead of an operating unit he avoids upsetting the work of the regular employees.[16]

Another device is that of clearance and review. This involves sending draft instructions out to the operating people for comment before their final preparation and release, as described in chapter xv. Worthwhile information on the soundness of projected instructions can be gained from the experiences of other organizations; other sources are the meetings and publications of business and professional associations.

The knowledge and experience of rank-and-file employees can be tapped through interviews, suggestion systems, and employee opinion polls. A practice being viewed with increasing favor is that of securing representative participation from all echelons in the early development of instructions. The concept of participation envisioned here gives the participants a greater degree of control over the work than would attend the use of clearance procedures or any of the other conventional methods for tapping employee thinking. Participation, to be effective, must get under way early, since, at or near the time of order-giving, the likely participants—as subordinates—are already being *told* how to act.[17]

Some managers have been known to have their orders read for understandability by a person in their immediate office before issuing them. Legend has it that one Captain Morgan was able to retain his place on General Grant's staff solely because of his suitability for this assignment. Recently the manager of a New York bank used this pretesting device for his very last time. He had chosen one of his subordinate employees to follow a new written procedure for escaping from the vault, which was assumed to have been inadvertently locked behind him. After the employee had validated the procedure by "escaping," he confided to the manager that he knew why he had been selected for the test—"because you think I'm the most stupid man here."

A most important prerequisite is that the order-giver have a mature understanding of the persons at the receiving end of his messages. Those in business who are responsible for initiating communications can be certain, according to Sir Geoffrey Vickers, "that the activities which their words awaken will not be exactly the same as those to which they correspond in their own minds. They will be lucky if the resemblance is close enough to have the desired effect; and they cannot know whether it has had even that degree of success, except by watching what happens, and guessing."[18]

The watching and listening for responses must be done with an open mind. Open-mindedness is demonstrated—at the upper levels particularly—by allowing some discretion and by listening to suggestions for changes. There must be provision, of course, for confirming, correcting, and commending discretionary actions and for adopting meritorious suggestions without delay.

Selected Readings

BOOKS AND MONOGRAPHS

BARNARD, CHESTER I. *The Functions of the Executive.* Cambridge: Harvard University Press, 1938. Chap. xii, "The Theory of Authority."
Relationship between authority and communication and seven "controlling factors" in communication.

[FOLLETT, MARY PARKER.] *Dynamic Administration: The Collected Papers of Mary Parker Follett*, ed. HENRY C. METCALF and L. URWICK. New York and London: Harper & Bros., 1942. Chap. ii, "The Giving of Orders."

The importance of orders to the success of the organization, the attitudes of subordinates toward them, and the improvement of these attitudes through employee participation in the planning of orders.

GILBRETH, LILLIAN M., and COOK, ALICE R. *The Foreman in Manpower Management.* New York: McGraw-Hill Book Co., 1947. Chap. ii, "Arts of Communication."

The important communication role of the foreman in order-giving, training, interviewing, and reporting.

ARTICLES

GOTTSCHALK, O. A. "Standardization of Procedures," *Public Administration Review*, Vol. 4 (Autumn, 1944), pp. 287–97.

The extensive pretesting of procedures in the Army Service Forces.

HENRY, WILLIAM E. "The Business Executive: A Study in the Psychodynamics of a Social Role," *American Journal of Sociology*, Vol. 54 (January, 1949), pp. 286–91. (Reprinted in HOWARD BRAND [ed.], *The Study of Personality* [New York: John Wiley & Sons, 1954].)

Stereotype of the executive, with insight into his communicative behavior.

JOYNT, JOHN B. "Policy Formulation," *Systems and Procedures Quarterly*, Vol. 3 (December, 1952), pp. 4–6, 23, and Vol. 4 (February, 1953), pp. 17–20, 25–26.

Policy and procedure: their characteristics, development, and application.

MAYNARD, H. B. "Installing a Methods Program," *Advanced Management*, Vol. 11 (June, 1946), pp. 57–61.

Testing and perfecting new procedures in a separate "methods development laboratory."

OUBRIDGE, V. W. "Delegation of Authority in the Medium-sized Company," *British Management Review*, Vol. 12 (July, 1954), pp. 199–213.

Command and operational orders—a new concept especially applicable to non-unitary organizations, such as hospitals, and to line and staff relationships.

Roy, Donald. "Efficiency and 'the Fix': Informal Intergroup Relations in a Piecework Machine Shop," *American Journal of Sociology,* Vol. 60 (November, 1954), pp. 255–66.

How the operating employees, aided by staff units, had to ignore managerial directives in order to get the work out.

Simon, Herbert A. "The Fine Art of Issuing Orders," *Public Management,* Vol. 27 (July, 1945), pp. 206–8.

Seven principles of order-giving.

Vickers, Sir Geoffrey. "Human Communication," *British Management Review,* Vol. 12 (January, 1954), pp. 71–79.

Order-givers need to improve their understanding of subordinates.

Waldo, Dwight. "Government by Procedure," in *Elements of Public Administration,* ed. Fritz Morstein Marx. New York: Prentice-Hall, Inc., 1946.

Institutional and substantive procedures and policy-making versus procedure-making.

V / *Oral or Written Instructions?*

SUITING THE MEDIUM TO THE AUDIENCE

BEFORE transmitting any message, communicators must determine what audience they want to reach and how to reach it most effectively. They must ascertain what they know about the audience—its interests and reactions and the competition for its time and attention. What first appears to be one audience is no doubt several audiences, suggesting that the message be transmitted in more than one way. "Given this particular message to get across, and this particular audience, and this particular objective, and given certain reasonable limitations on time and budget and manpower—then what medium or combination of media is likely to do the best job?"[1]

Seldom has there been a more dramatic and tragic demonstration of the importance of the medium of transmission than the train wreck at Woodbridge, New Jersey, on February 6, 1951, when eighty-five people were killed. After the wreck the conductor testified that, when he started the day's work, he had received special oral orders to slow down for the temporary trestle that the railroad had erected to pass over some highway construction at Woodbridge and that, at the time of the wreck, he had the railroad's written instructions in his pocket. In addition, the conductor said that he had checked these orders with the engineer who had acknowledged them.

Both the engineer and the conductor had been working for another railroad, one whose warning system for temporary construction consisted of yellow flags and lights ("yellow board" in railroad parlance) along the right of way. The engineer was watching for yellow flags and lights when the train suddenly left the trestle and crashed to the ground below.[2]

The orders covering the Woodbridge trestle were both oral and written, but these two media were not adequate for a train crew that was alert to a third medium—the visual symbol, yellow board. Eighty-five lives might have been saved if the form of instructions had been more skilfully determined in terms of this unique two-man audience. (At the time, the New Jersey Public Utility Commission held that the engineer had been responsible for the wreck. Subsequently, he brought suit against the railroad for back pay and compensation for his injuries, contending, among other things, that the company had been at fault in not setting up the proper signals; but the court held against him.)

THE RANGE OF MEDIA AVAILABLE

Although there is potentially a great variety of media available to the order-giver, he is generally forced to choose from among a few existing ones that have nothing more than tradition in their favor. When certain media have become established, all subsequent material is made to fit them. If, for example, an organization has a personnel manual, it becomes the pattern to announce through a routine revision of the manual even those changes that may be of immediate and crucial interest to the employees. A change in the design of an application form will not elicit widespread interest, but a new system for computing vacation allowances is bound to be intensely interesting to everyone. Such differences in interest value are important factors in the proper selection of media, but the media must be available to choose from.

In Figure 2 we illustrate the range of instructional media available and in current use. By far the majority are of two types—the oral and the written. Actually, as seen in our diagram, the two basic forms are the audial, which includes both oral and symbolic media, and the visual, which includes written, pictorial, and symbolic media, as well as combinations of them.

Several years ago John J. Corson, one of the pioneers in administrative communication, raised some important questions about the use of different media, the relative efficiency of oral and written orders, and their respective degrees of distortion.[3] There has not yet been sufficient time to gather the scientific data that would answer his questions. We do not know enough, for example, about individual variations in sensory acuity. Many persons are reached most effectively through the

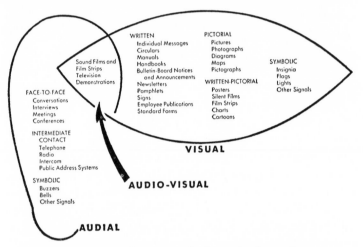

FIG. 2.—Typical forms or media for issuing instructions

visual sense. But within this group are some who are word-minded, others who are figure-minded, and still others who are picture-minded. There are persons whose audial perception is better than their visual, so that they best absorb things that they hear. Still others possess acute tactile ability and learn best by working with their hands with actual materials. But in most cases management does not know which of these many classifications apply within a particular employee group, under what circumstances they apply, and with respect to what subject matter.

This is not to suggest that there are no effective means of order-giving. On the contrary, one sees or hears occasionally of highly ingenious methods of transmitting orders. Before the First World War the Russians had drafted many ignorant peasants who did not know their left foot from their right. It was impossible to teach these men how to drill and march. But a drill sergeant tied some straw on their left boots. Thereafter, instead of shouting the command, "Left, left, left," which the peasants found so difficult to remember, he said, "Straw, straw, straw." This communicative device was so successful that the American Army adopted it in 1918 for the young men who were drafted from some of the backward areas of the United States. A marching chant entitled "Hayfoot, strawfoot" came out of this experiment and persisted throughout the War.

At a point north of Harmon, New York, the New York Central tracks pass through an underpass where, painted in bold letters on the concrete wall, is the sign—DO NOT RAISE THESE TRACKS. What better way could there be to get this order to every future work gang that touches the tracks at this place? Even more ingenious, perhaps, is the way some tomato farmers tell their pickers what tomatoes are ripe for picking. The workers must pick only those tomatoes that are a certain shade of red, so this color is painted on one thumbnail.

Experimental work is constantly going on to determine both general and specific principles governing the selection and use of different media of communication. Most of the research applies to advertising and public relations. Management has still to learn more about its audience; but this should not be as difficult for administrators as for advertising and public relations men, since the audience in an organization stays relatively constant. One research technique which has been used is to measure supervisors' reading ability so that messages to them can be tailored to their competence.[4]

One of the rather general observations stemming from public relations research is that the written word is probably more effective when pinpointed to certain segments of the better-educated population, whereas the spoken word seems to be most promising in reaching a less educated audience or a cross-section of the population as a whole.[5] If one were issuing instructions to charwomen on how to sweep and mop the floors, he could assume that a mimeographed bulletin would be a poor choice, that oral instructions would be somewhat better, but that best of all would be demonstrations (audial-visual-tactile) or pictorial media (posters, motion pictures, cartoons, and the like) that do not depend on an understanding of words.

ORAL INSTRUCTIONS

A competent spoken order is much like a compressed interview, with both parties questioning and explaining, doubting and persuading, gesturing and inflecting, checking and re-checking, as they strive for the best possible understanding.[6] The efficiency of the spoken word is increased greatly by the accompanying gestures, facial expressions, tones, and other non-verbal communicative acts.

The recipient of an oral order is able to probe for exactness wherever the meaning is not entirely clear, provided he is not too unfamiliar with the subject matter. He may ask for a clarifying or confirming statement in writing, for a sketch or a chart, or for a demonstration of a manual operation. He is able to state his case, as long as the elements of give-and-take are preserved, if an order, as originally advanced, does not apply or cannot work out satisfactorily.

The order-giver has an opportunity for an immediate check-up and can see whether his order has produced understanding or confusion.[7] He can probably discern the recipient's attitude, whether it is one of acceptance or rejection, but the order-giver's attitude will also be apparent. It is difficult for an order-giver to get away with an oral order that is being issued only for the record or one that is manifestly inconsistent with previous orders or with the organization's known objectives. Similarly, it is difficult to camouflage the source of an order that is transmitted orally.

Oral media that provide for personal interchange and those that do not must be differentiated. Some of the impersonal oral media, such as public-address systems or large meetings, lack the advantages of spoken orders transmitted face to face.

The spoken order is flexible and readily adaptable to a variety of situations calling for different initial timing. Of course, the teletype and similar devices have made transmission of the printed word more flexible than when it depended entirely on letters. But inevitably emergencies arise that demand the issuance of oral orders, either by face-to-face contact or by telephone or other forms of voice transmission. Weeks or months later, when an order is out of date, there need be no delay in issuing an oral revision. It is a lot easier and quicker to change an oral order than to change Paragraph 217-b of Section III-A of a manual. Thus, an oral medium is highly suitable whenever it is believed that an instruction will be temporary.

The fact that the spoken word appeared first both in the history of man and in the conduct of management does not mean that it is a primitive medium. On the contrary, we can look for an increased application and refinement of oral media in the large and complex organizations of today and tomorrow.

WRITTEN INSTRUCTIONS

Written instructions are required when the action called for is complicated and vital and when it must be done in a precise and uniform way. Rare indeed is the supervisor who can recite the numberless details of a complex procedure without omitting or overemphasizing one or more items. Because of this, written instructions are used to confirm oral ones. The written word is not distortion-proof, but it suffers less from distortion over a period of time or in a lengthy channel than does its oral counterpart.

Written instructions are useful as reference sources regarding the organization and its workings. Employees from top to bottom, and in widely scattered locations, have available in permanent form a record of what has been done in the past and instructions anticipating problems that may come up only infrequently at some remote future date.[8] Of course, the instructions must be readily accessible to those who need them, and the technical features (indexing, coding, and the like) should facilitate actual use.

Written instructions are helpful for training, but this should not be a dominant consideration. An order is likely to suffer if it is written with too much of a training slant, and training is generally more successful if it has an educational rather than an order-giving bias.

The successful discharge of delegated authority depends greatly on a clear-cut and continuing understanding of the scope of that authority. When the nature of the delegation is defined in writing, subordinates can feel secure in their performance; and superiors, in the exercise of their control function, are better equipped to check on it.

Although oral instructions score high on acceptance, provided give-and-take is possible while they are being transmitted, written instructions also score high on acceptance because they seem authoritative. The spirit of authority is transmitted down the line more effectively with a written order than with an oral one. In our society written orders have come to carry a greater aura of formality than oral ones. It may be that subordinates believe there is less caprice in written orders because the order-giver cannot as easily avoid his responsibility if the order works out badly. "Will you put that in writing?" is a classic rejoinder to a dubious order in the armed services.

Subordinates may feel that they are protecting themselves from some real or imagined injustices by securing a written order. Most written orders apply to a number of positions, and they apply to all of them in the same way, giving the recipients some assurance of equality of treatment.

Written instructions suffer from at least three major drawbacks. First, there are some things that executives do not want everyone to know about;[9] for instance, certain policies and procedures in the field of personnel administration and actions in the sales field on discounts, rebates, and reciprocity. Second, it is frightfully difficult to provide for all the unanticipated, but not impossible, eventualities. To say in writing that the organization will pay salaries as good as or better than others in the community assumes that there will always be money enough to do so. The time may suddenly come when such a policy is impossible to fulfil.

Third, over a period of years written instructions may very well become a mass of red tape that protects some, frustrates others, and encourages among all an abject overdependence on the written word. There are frequent occasions in the dynamic course of business affairs when appropriate decisions cannot be made simply by flipping open a manual to a certain page. The fact that authority and responsibility are spelled out so clearly (which earlier we counted an asset) may instil a fear of overstepping; what were written as standards for minimum performance may become ceilings for maximum performance.

The challenge to preserve initiative in the face of these eventualities can be met, in part at least, if (1) there is a clear distinction between mandatory and discretionary instructions; (2) employees know that instructions are subject to continuous review and improvement; and (3) supervisors are authorized and encouraged to step in and take the action they think necessary whenever the written instructions are inadequate.

COMBINING ORAL AND WRITTEN MEDIA

Certain advantages are inherent in both oral and written orders and can be exploited according to the situation. There are promising opportunities for using both oral and written forms where one or the other has been employed alone heretofore. In a typical situation an order might originate as an oral policy statement in a directors' meeting. At the top-management level the statement is likely to be formalized in writing and then expanded to incorporate certain procedural details. This written statement of policy and procedure is probably suitable for large elements of the middle-management group, but others might want or need an oral exposition in one or more supervisory conference sessions. Finally, at the worker level, oral presentations alone might prove to be most effective.

A number of organizations have undertaken to use combinations of media where they had used only one before. One such organization is the California Department of Employment, which has a system of weekly written instructions for its branch offices. The branch managers meet with their subordinates at least weekly to present, explain, and discuss all new instructions. The managers must then report upward on any aspects of the instructions that appear to be unclear and unsatisfactory. This is far better than simply allowing written instructions to drift downward and outward. Completely unheralded, they are often equally unnoticed.

Much communication is already characterized by the use of several media. It is common practice to supplement written instructions with illustrations, such as flow charts and standard forms. A great deal has been done in the use of graphic techniques and oral presentations in the field of reporting. Educators and industrial training experts have much to offer on the use of visual aids to supplement the spoken word.

It is safe to say that two media, such as the oral and the written, will always be more effective than one, either by appealing to a wider audience or by getting a message across better within a limited audience. This assertion has been borne out experimentally by Thomas L. Dahle, of Michigan State University, who tested groups of students at Purdue University, a small group of employees in Lafayette, Indiana, and a larger group of employees at Spiegel's, Inc., in Chicago. In all three cases a combination of oral and written media proved to be more effective than any single medium. Interestingly, bulletin boards and the "grapevine" were the least effective among the media used in the experiments.[10]

Several years ago the Royal Bank of Canada suggested that communicators should ask themselves four simple questions before transmitting a message:

1. *What is it we wish to communicate?*
   (We must have it clear in our own minds.)
2. *To whom?*
   (It is childish to try to score a bull's-eye by aiming in the general direction of the target.)
3. *What is the best medium of communication?*
4. *How can we best utilize this medium for this audience?*[11]

This would make an excellent credo for everyone who is seriously concerned about his communications, regardless of his position in the organization.

Selected Readings

BOOKS AND MONOGRAPHS

FITZGERALD, STEPHEN E. *Communicating Ideas to the Public.* New York: Funk & Wagnalls Co., 1950. Chap. viii, "Some Experiments in Communications," and chap. ix, "Experiments with Media."

A summary of experimental findings on the effectiveness of different media in different situations.

PIGORS, PAUL and FAITH. *Understanding as a Condition for Success in Order-giving.* Cambridge, Mass.: Industrial Relations Associates, Inc., 1945. Pp. 26–27.

The pros and cons of oral and written instructions.

SEYBOLD, GENEVA. *Written Statements of Personnel Policy.* ("Studies in Personnel Policy," No. 79.) New York: National Industrial Conference Board, Inc., 1947.

Advantages and disadvantages of putting personnel policies in writing.

ARTICLES

COLBY, A. N., and TIFFEN, JOSEPH. "The Reading Ability of Industrial Supervisors," *Personnel,* Vol. 27 (September, 1950), pp. 156–59.

Report of an investigation, with a formula for estimating a person's reading ability from his age and years of schooling.

CORSON, JOHN J. "Weak Links in the Chain of Command," *Public Opinion Quarterly,* Vol. 9 (Fall, 1945), pp. 346–49.

Testing the effectiveness of various instructional media in a federal bureau.

DAHLE, THOMAS L. "Transmitting Information to Employees: A Study of Five Methods," *Personnel,* Vol. 31 (November, 1954), pp. 243–46.

Report of tests proving the superiority of the combined oral and written transmission of instructions.

HARRIS, W. S. "Selecting a Medium for Written Instructions," *Public Administration Review,* Vol. 2 (Autumn, 1942), pp. 324–28.

Choosing from among the three most common written media—the individual message, the circular, and the manual—on the basis of expected applicability, life-expectancy, and frequency of reference.

KLAPPER, JOSEPH T. "The Comparative Effects of the Various Media," pp. 91–105 in *The Process and Effects of Mass Communication,* ed. WILBUR SCHRAMM. Urbana: University of Illinois Press, 1955.

Summary of findings regarding the mass media as instruments of non-classroom teaching and of persuasion.

KROEGER, LOUIS J. "What Small Business Should Do about Manuals and Methods," *Systems and Procedures Quarterly,* Vol. 2 (March, 1952), pp. 14–17.

A strong argument for written instructions.

ROSENZWEIG, MARK R., and POSTMAN, LEO. "Frequency of Usage and the Perception of Words," *Science,* Vol. 127 (February 7, 1958), pp. 263–66.

How visual and auditory perception are affected by a word's frequency-rating and length.

VI / *Individual Messages and Circulars*

> It is not reasonable to suppose that the members of a large organization will regard co-ordination as of great importance, or indeed develop any marked respect for the wishes of those in authority, if the *form* in which those wishes and the consequent arrangements are expressed is not itself orderly, coherent, definite, timely, and easy of reference. And yet, in a large number of undertakings of all kinds, written instructions are neither uniform, clearly expressed, self-consistent, readily amendable, logically arranged, nor up-to-date.
>
> L. URWICK[1]

WRITTEN instructions are only a part, though an important part, of an organization's total system of administrative communication. Before World War II there had not been enough experience to justify a treatment of the written apart from all other instructional media. Since then, however, there has been a widespread and ever increasing interest in written items; and a number of the larger organizations have developed extensive systems which include many kinds of them.

Common features are often hard to find among the widely assorted written media, while the potential distinctions are clouded by the diversity of nomenclature; for example, manuals versus handbooks, circulars versus bulletins, and house organs versus employee publications. Our review of the written materials of a number of organizations suggests that five basic types are most often used for downward communication: the individual message, the circular or bulletin, the manual, the handbook, and the employee publication. The employee handbook may be regarded either as a separate type or simply as a special form of handbook. Not all these types are necessarily found, nor need they be, in every organization.

In the written instructional and informational materials of any large organization are a tremendous number and variety of details which are not discussed here, although they are of considerable interest to students and technicians. Furthermore, it is difficult, if not impossible, to develop, analyze, or even understand a given system without a fairly intimate knowledge of the particular organization, its personnel, its work, and its traditions. On these points an alert insider has a marked advantage over anyone working from the outside. Finally, there is an interrelationship among all the instructional and informational media in any one organization. The way a company uses individual messages is related to its way of using circulars, its handbooks are related to its manuals, and all forms of written communication are related to the non-written ones.

THE INDIVIDUAL MESSAGE

Letters, Office Memos, and Other Forms

Some organizations move a lot faster than others. Rapid communication comes to mind with the mere mention of transportation, utility, police, fire, or civil defense organizations. In any organization, if an urgent instruction must be issued in writing, individual messages such as letters, telegrams, teletypes, cablegrams, or office memos are the logical forms.

Some instructions that are not particularly urgent can also be transmittted effectively through individual messages. The smallest organizations, with only a handful of employees, seldom set down any instructions in writing, since they cannot see any need for elaborate or expensive systems of circulars or manuals. But files of individual messages are not expensive, and they provide an element of permanence that cannot be obtained through the use of oral media. Of course, in a large organization, with its manuals and circulars, individual messages would be regarded as the least permanent of the written media.

Uses and Limitations

Individual messages are useful when an order-giver wants to identify the recipient or recipients precisely. An individual message, as its name implies, is generally addressed to persons rather than to positions. Even when the addressee is a position, as in a message to the "Manager of the Cleveland Office" or to the "Commanding General of the Thirtieth Air Force," it is clear that one person in one position is being held responsible for the directed action. Such exact pinpointing of authority and responsibility is necessary from time to time, and the individual message meets the need well.

A personal letter or memo can convey the writer's personality more effectively than can any other written medium. There are frequent occasions when, although a written medium is required, a personal touch is either necessary or desirable.

Individual messages are, by definition, for limited distribution, and their cost is consistent with such usage. A study released by the Hoover Commission in 1955 cited these costs for a 175-word letter: when dictated to a stenographer, 70 cents to $2.45 each; when dictated to a machine, 60 cents to $2.25 each.[2] Considerable savings can be made by using form letters, guide letters, or circulars whenever there are approximately one hundred or more readers.

Whenever urgency compels the use of an individual message, the danger arises that the writer may overlook one or more previous instructions that are affected.[3] Rarely do individual messages carry a filing code, with the result that filing is not uniform. After a period of months or years it becomes a real problem to locate copies of individual messages. The filing limitation is very familiar to anyone who has had to search for individual messages in preparing a manual, in the event of a lawsuit involving old instructions, or in writing a history of the organization. Telegrams and teletypes suffer from two further limitations, to wit, their irregular size and their lack of the subtleties of punctuation and layout.

Reference has already been made to form letters and guide letters, the latter composed from collected standard para-

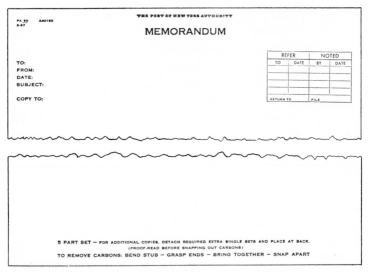

Fig. 3.—A memorandum form, as used in the Port of New York Authority

graphs which are put together for letters the same way whole walls are assembled for prefabricated houses. The distribution of individual messages can also be increased by using carbon copies and by routing copies to a number of readers. Such expanded usage has been provided for in the memorandum form illustrated in Figure 3. The snap-out form yields five copies, and the preprinted routing section eliminates clipping separate routing or "buck" slips to the circulating copies. In the example shown, provision is made for a filing record.

THE CIRCULAR OR BULLETIN

What Is a Circular?

The most widely used form of written instruction is designated here as the circular, or bulletin. There are many other designations for this same general form, among which the most popular are SPI (standard practice instruction), circular letter, regulation, CSP (company or corporation standard practice), procedure, standard procedure, and SOP (standard or standing operating procedure or practice). Still others that are encountered less frequently include the administrative or executive order, general or departmental order, memorandum, or notice.

When, as is often the case, a single organization uses two or more series of circulars, it may purposely choose a variety of designations. The Army Signal Corps, for example, uses general orders, special orders, letter orders, numbered memoranda, unnumbered memoranda, and several other circular series. The paramount twofold consideration is, first, that each series be reserved for a certain area (a particular activity, group of activities, department, or subject) and, second, that persons using the publication—as writers or readers—know what is covered under each heading. Only rarely do we find that organizations have issued definite statements describing the contents of each series.

Circulars are normally printed or mechanically duplicated, with the many copies going to the positions or units designated in the heading after the caption *To:, For:, Departments Affected:,* or *Concerns:.* Alternatively, the addressees may be set out in bold type at the beginning of each paragraph or group of paragraphs, or the audience may be determined routinely by a distribution schedule; or it may be everyone's responsibility to watch for all instructions concerning him. Circulars are dated or numbered, or both, and sometimes use both an issue date and an effective date. Customarily, but not always, they carry subject headings.

For speed of transmission, circulars fall between individual messages and manuals. For permanence, also, most circulars fall at or near the mid-point. Middle-level managers who are not authorized to change manual provisions are generally permitted to issue circulars, provided there are no conflicts with higher-level instructions.

Obviously, one of the main uses for the circular is as a semi-permanent medium pending the preparation or revision of a manual. Some organizations try to introduce all new instructions through circulars, allowing them to be tested in this form before incorporating them in a manual. Illustrated in Figure 4 is a United Air Lines bulletin issued to amend a section of the company's manual of regulations. It will be noted that recipients of the bulletin are told exactly where to file it.

Numbering, or Coding

Conventional systems of circulars are often referred to as serial circulars to make it clear that they are numbered in a single chronological sequence. The material in successive circulars is not necessarily related in any way; No. 1 may deal with purchasing, No. 2 with hiring, No. 3 with payroll deductions, No. 4 with manufacturing, etc. Different aspects of these subjects will no doubt appear in a number of circulars throughout the circular series.

The single numbering sequence may continue indefinitely or be started over again at an arbitrary number or at an arbitrary date. One practice is to start a new numbering sequence each year, and the year may be made a part of the numbering system (58-1, 58-2).

There is an elementary need for number control in order to insure that circulars appear in the proper sequence, and this task may be assigned to the chief of the appropriate steno-graphic pool or mimeograph room.

Quantity Control

As the number of circulars in effect at any one time increases, their usefulness decreases. It becomes more and more

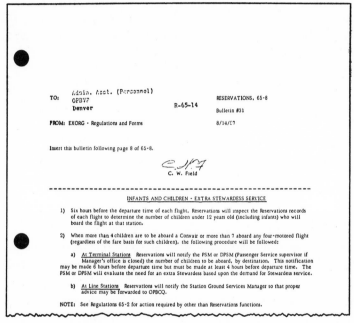

Fig. 4.—A bulletin amending a manual, as used by United Air Lines.

difficult for the user to find what he wants, and quantity control becomes important. If there are several series of circulars, some are likely to be active, while others are used only a few times a year. The system should be questioned when there are only a few circulars in a single series, just as when there are a very great number of circulars. (We have encountered separate series numbering well up in the thousands.)

Revision

There are many ways to revise circulars. One is to treat revisions simply as new issuances, using the next serial numbers. Circulars 1, 12, and 50 may all be initial instructions dealing with aspects of purchasing, while Circular 75 may revise provisions in one or several of them.

Another revision method calls for the re-use of the number that was assigned to the original issuance, with a serial letter added to it for each revision. Thus, Department Bulletin 69-L would represent the twelfth revision of Department Bulletin 69.

Either of these revision methods imposes a burden on the user, since he must check so many separate instructions on the same subject. In addition, gaps occur in the numbering sequence as some of the circulars become obsolete. It is far better to revise completely the original circular (technically this is a reissuance, as distinct from a revision) than to encumber it with a host of widely separated partial revisions.

Helping the User

Indexing.—The task of locating all the circulars touching on a given subject can be made less burdensome for a user if he has access to an up-to-date index. Preparation of an index requires supervision by someone well acquainted with both instructions and operations; only a person of this sort can produce a good cross-index and write in the jargon of the plant or office. If "expediters" are "stock-chasers," the index should give both references.[4]

The task of indexing can be simplified and made more error-proof by maintaining permanent panels of index entries, as is done, for example, in Remington Rand's "Flexoprint" process. Each entry is typed in a uniform style on a narrow card. The cards, arranged in proper order, are affixed to panels, and the resulting lists are photographed and reproduced as complete index pages. Changes are made by inserting and removing individual cards, as required, without retyping whole pages. Systems of this type are most often used for preparing manufacturers' catalogues and price and parts lists.

Periodic listings and reviews.—An annual or semiannual check list of circulars in effect will help keep files of circulars in order. Another aid is a monthly or quarterly list of revisions, additions, and cancellations. These lists can be disseminated through one or several media, including supervisory newsletters, to insure that everyone affected is advised. A good practice is to use Circular No. 1 (or its equivalent) to explain the nature and operation of the circular series and to use Circular No. 2 (or its equivalent) solely for the issuance of periodic listings.

What an organization does with periodic listings is related to its practices with respect to obsolescence and indexing. Circulars must be reviewed from time to time to make certain that no obsolete ones are still being used. Such reviews can be by-products of the listing process, or vice versa. A continuing indexing program makes periodic listing less important.

Record sheets for posting circulars.—The preprinted record sheet is another helpful device. Here users post circulars as they are received or canceled. This is the purpose of the "Record of Bulletins" form used by United Air Lines and shown in Figure 5. New record sheets are distributed whenever the ones in use are about to become full.

Distribution

Files of circulars can be kept up to date only if the initial distribution is made to a single controlled list of recipients and if the later distribution of revisions, cancellations, periodic indexes, and listings of circulars in effect follows the same list.

There must also be a rapid means for notifying the holders

whenever circular provisions are incorporated in a manual, a handbook, or another circular series. In our later discussion of manual revisions we commend the use of transmittal letters, which adequately notify those who have both the circulars and the manuals. Special provision must be made whenever the

UNITED
AIR LINES

RECORD OF BULLETINS

MANUAL TITLE OR NUMBER												LOCATION		
6C-141												PDXDS		
ASSIGNED TO (JOB TITLE) CASTRY COOK														

BLTN. NO.	INSERTION DATE	INSERT NEAR PAGE	BY	BLTN. NO.	INSERTION DATE	INSERT NEAR PAGE	BY	BLTN. NO.	INSERTION DATE	INSERT NEAR PAGE	BY	BLTN. NO.	INSERTION DATE	INSERT NEAR PAGE	BY
1	6/5/57	9	BB	/ /				/ /				/ /		
2	9/6/57	9	BB	/ /				/ /				/ /		
3	12/8/57	35	BB	/ /				/ /				/ /		
	/ /			/ /				/ /				/ /		
	/ /			/ /				/ /				/ /		

	/ /			/ /				/ /				/ /		
	/ /			/ /				/ /				/ /		
	/ /			/ /				/ /				/ /		
	/ /			/ /				/ /				/ /		

RETAIN THIS RECORD IN THE FRONT OF MANUAL OR CHAPTER
ON RECEIPT, INSERT BULLETIN IN MANUAL, ENTER BULLETIN NUMBER, DATE INSERTED, PAGE INSERTED NEAR, AND INITIALS
CROSS OUT ENTRY WHEN REMOVING BULLETINS

UFC 1594 PRINTED IN U.S.A.

Fig. 5.—A demonstration copy of a record sheet for posting bulletins, as used by United Air Lines.

distribution lists for the other media differ from the one for the circular series affected.

Circulars can be of real use, and can be really used, only if they are constantly controlled and if the users find them easy to use. In the absence of the control and facilitating devices that have been mentioned, or equivalent ones, circular series will assuredly become incomplete or obsolete, or both, and fall into disrepute and disuse.

Instructions for Completing Forms

Many procedural instructions are concerned primarily, or in large part, with the proper methods of using forms—order forms, shipping forms, application forms, and hundreds of others. Good practice dictates that early in every procedural instruction there be an explicit mention (perhaps a listing) of the forms involved in the procedure, as illustrated in Figure 6. Copies of the forms are generally included as part of the instruction, and some of the forms are partially filled out to demonstrate their use.

Users of any form need to be told when and how it should be filled out and what to do with it afterward. Most instructions on these matters can be incorporated in the forms themselves, reducing the amount of prose. Bare phrases such as "Applicant's Name," "Supervisor's Signature," and "Today's Date" are as clear as possible when placed right at the appropriate blanks on a form. Probably the only disadvantage is that a later change in the procedure will make the form obsolete along with the written instruction itself.

THE TRANSITION FROM CIRCULARS TO MANUALS

The evolution and growth of a typical organization can be traced through its development of different types of written instructional materials. The earliest written instructions in a young organization are simply individual messages assigning to a few people their initial areas of authority and presenting policy decisions required by problems when they first arise. As time goes on and the organization grows, steps are taken to extract from the files of individual messages those instructions that will be needed by a great number of people over a long period of time. The opportunity is also taken to capture practices that have grown up without benefit of written instructions. This is the period when conventional circulars of the se-

The New York Times
STANDARD PROCEDURE

SUBJECT	SALES		EFF DATE	4-1-57	SUBJ NO	8139
SUB HEAD	School and Camp Information Service		ISSUED	4-1-57	PAGE NO	1 of 12
					SUPPLEMENTS	

REVISES

APPROVED BY	AHB	HH	MG	CMC		CEO

OBJECTIVE
The objective of the School and Camp Information Service is to assist the School and Camp sales effort by furnishing advertisers with enrollment leads. To invite reader inquiries as to schools and camps which are Times advertisers. To answer each inquiry by sending to the inquirer the names of several schools or camps that most nearly meet his specifications as to location, cost, program, etc. To send the reader's name to the advertisers named. To get necessary descriptive data from each advertiser, record it, match inquiries against it, and give out advertiser names in such a way that each inquiry is answered with reasonable accuracy and each advertiser who meets a given set of reader specifications is named as often as others who do so. To set up a clerical system that performs the foregoing objectives as automatically as possible and with a minimum of specialized or individual attention.

SOURCE MATERIAL
Inquiries may be received personally, by mail, or by telephone. Most of these inquiries originate with individuals although some will come from associations, government organizations, other schools or camps, and various manufacturing, financial, and industrial concerns.

SCHEDULE
Answers to inquiries must be made within one work day after receipt except when volume exceeds a normal work load. Then answers will be made as quickly as possible until normal work load level is attained.

CROSS REF
None suggested.

FORMS
Applicable forms in this Standard Procedure are usually referred to only by form number. The form title and form number of applicable forms are listed below. A demonstration copy or reproduction of that form which shows an "x" may be found immediately following this page.

Form Title	Form No.	Form Title	Form No.
School Inquiry Record	8101 x	School and Camp Inquiry Record	8105 x
Camp Inquiry Record	8102 x	School and Camp Inquiry	8106 x
School Reference Card	8103 x	Telephone Tab School & Camp Inquiry	8107 x
Camp Reference Card	8104 x	School & Camp Inquiry Tabulation	8108 x

INDEX

DISTRIBUTION

9006—JAN 57   * POINT OF REVISION, ADDITION DELETION   ** COMPLETE REVISION

FIG. 6.—A procedural instruction with a listing of related forms, as used by the *New York Times*.

rial type make their appearance. But before too long the files of circulars begin to grow beyond usable proportions, and conflicts and omissions become increasingly frequent and burdensome.

At this date the organization has achieved enough stability to permit systematic arrangement of substantially all its instructions. These instructions, along with practices that have persistently eluded any write-up, can be classified in logical groups, and the classifications can be coded.

Classification and Coding

Classification is the process of subdividing and arranging all instructions in an orderly manner, such as by organization unit or by activity. Selling instructions are separated from manufacturing instructions, instructions for the foundry are separated from those for the machine shop, with further breakdowns as required. This book is classified into parts (e.g., downward, upward, and horizontal communication) and further classified into chapters. The parts, the chapters, and the pages are all coded numerically. The same techniques are evident in other books as well.

The straight sequence of numbers in serial circulars gives way to a two- or three-part code. The base portion of the code, identifying the major breakdown, may be a key word or letter, as in Purchasing-01 or P-01. If units or activities have already been coded for other purposes (such as cost accounting), these codes may be used again. Suffixes, identifying subsidiary items within each major breakdown, may be coded in numbers or letters, which may be either separated from the base portions by a dash or decimal point (10-02, 10.03) or run together (1002, 1003).

Shown in Figure 7 are several of the Tennessee Valley Authority's "administrative releases," which are regarded collectively as a manual. The base portion of the TVA coding sys-

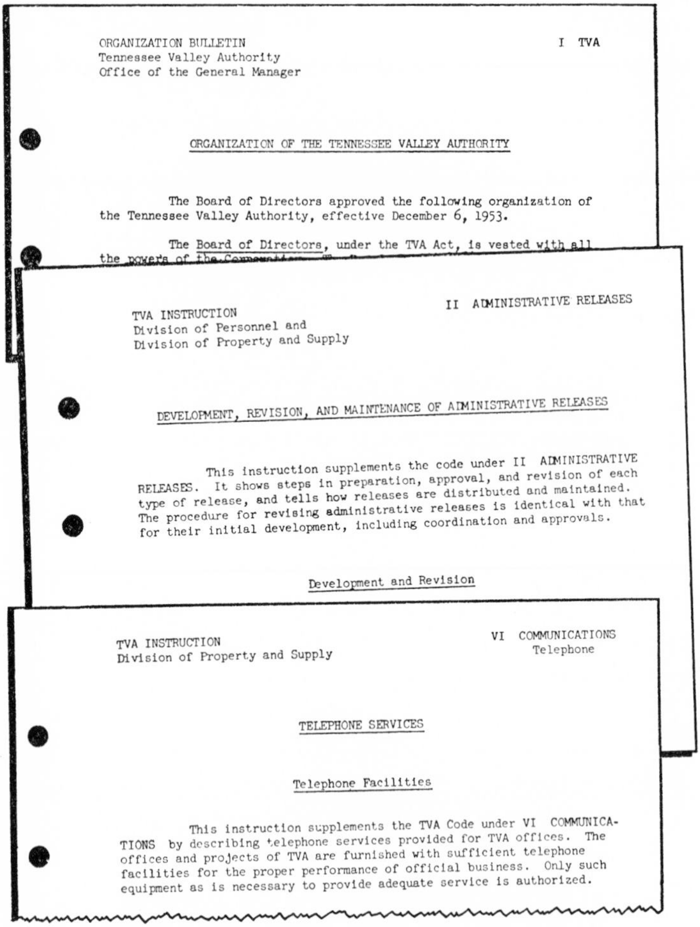

ORGANIZATION BULLETIN
Tennessee Valley Authority
Office of the General Manager

I TVA

ORGANIZATION OF THE TENNESSEE VALLEY AUTHORITY

The Board of Directors approved the following organization of the Tennessee Valley Authority, effective December 6, 1953.

The Board of Directors, under the TVA Act, is vested with all the powers of the Corporation.

TVA INSTRUCTION
Division of Personnel and
Division of Property and Supply

II ADMINISTRATIVE RELEASES

DEVELOPMENT, REVISION, AND MAINTENANCE OF ADMINISTRATIVE RELEASES

This instruction supplements the code under II ADMINISTRATIVE RELEASES. It shows steps in preparation, approval, and revision of each type of release, and tells how releases are distributed and maintained. The procedure for revising administrative releases is identical with that for their initial development, including coordination and approvals.

Development and Revision

TVA INSTRUCTION
Division of Property and Supply

VI COMMUNICATIONS
Telephone

TELEPHONE SERVICES

Telephone Facilities

This instruction supplements the TVA Code under VI COMMUNICATIONS by describing telephone services provided for TVA offices. The offices and projects of TVA are furnished with sufficient telephone facilities for the proper performance of official business. Only such equipment as is necessary to provide adequate service is authorized.

FIG. 7.—Examples of the guide-word coding system, as used by the Tennessee Valley Authority.

tem is a Roman numeral, from I through XII, referring to sections of the manual. (I is for "Organization," II for "Administration," and VI for "Office Services.") The system is unusual in its use of word suffixes, called "guide words," rather than numbers or letters. Searching and filing are done initially in accordance with the Roman-numeral headings, then alphabetically for the first and second "guide words." The user need not remember or look up a numerical code beyond the twelve-part classification; he merely looks alphabetically for the logical key word, just as he would search for a plumber or an appliance repair man in the classified pages of a telephone book. A cross-referenced index is available, if needed, at the beginning of the compilation. This system of word-coding would probably not serve so well if there were a large number of issuances within a single classification. And companies that may have occasion to use their instruction codes on accounting machines must have numerical codes.

The use of classified and coded circulars as permanent loose-leaf manuals is quite common. Adapting files of circulars as manuals depends entirely on the prior establishment of a classification system. Such adaptability is wholly unattainable with circulars of the serial type.

Selected Readings

BOOKS AND MONOGRAPHS

A Guide to the Writing of Business Letters. London: British Association for Commercial and Industrial Education, n.d.
Reprint of a training booklet prepared for Tube Investments, Ltd.

MENNING, J. H., and WILKINSON, C. W. *Writing Business Letters.* Rev. ed. Homewood, Ill.: Richard D. Irwin, Inc., 1959.
Many worthwhile suggestions.

SHURTER, ROBERT L. *Effective Letters in Business.* 2d ed. New York: McGraw-Hill Book Co., 1954. Chap. xii, "Writing the Memorandum."

Suggestions on the organization and form of memoranda.

ARTICLES

BERGSTROM, W. E. "Suggested Procedures for the Issuance and Control of Procedures," *Bulletin of the National Association of Cost Accountants,* Vol. 24 (December 1, 1942), pp. 384–89.

One company's practices, emphasizing the distinction between policy and procedure.

GRADY, JAMES F. "Training for Better Letter Writing," pp. 19–28 in *Getting Full Value from the Business Letter.* ("Office Management Series," No. 93.) New York: American Management Association, 1940.

A letter-appraisal chart.

HAGA, CLIFFORD I. "A Cookbook Approach to Procedures Writing," pp. 8–11 in *Papers of the Sixth Annual International Systems Meeting, Chicago* (1953). New York: Systems and Procedures Association of America, 1954.

Numerous suggestions for procedures writers, including one that all statements should be positive—using *dos,* not *don'ts.*

———. "Procedures for the Procedure Writer," pp. 155–67 in *Workshop for Management, Proceedings of the Eighth Annual International Systems Meeting, Detroit* (1955). Greenwich, Conn.: Management Publishing Corp., 1956.

Specific features of organization, layout, and style to increase the effectiveness of written procedures.

MATTHIES, LESLIE H. *The Playscript Procedure.* New York: Office Publications, Inc., 1961.

How to write procedure instructions using personal pronouns and short, snappy orders.

MILLER, RAY. "Evolution of a Wartime Procedure Manual," *Public Administration Review,* Vol. 6 (Summer, 1946), pp. 228–34.

The development of a complex system of instructions through the letter, circular, and manual stages.

ROGERS, R. C. "Written Policies and Standard Practice Instructions," *Personnel Journal,* Vol. 28 (November, 1949), pp. 206–14.

Comments on the preparation, distribution, and revision of written instructions.

ROLLAND, KERMIT. "Making Intra-office Communications Count," pp. 19–24 in *Planning and Controls for Office Efficiency.* ("Office Management Series," No. 130.) New York: American Management Association, 1952.

Report on one company's correspondence-improvement program.

"Writing Better Letters," *Royal Bank of Canada Monthly Letter* (Montreal), April, 1951.

Good writing described as an art to be practiced, not achieved by rules and devices, the best letters being those that express both the writer's personality and that of his company.

VII / *Manuals*

WHAT IS A MANUAL?

THE TERM "manual" is not particularly descriptive. How-to-do-it books on such subjects as gardening, home maintenance, and dancing are published as "manuals." If there were more space, we could offer here a manual on the preparation of manuals.

In management parlance it is customary to designate as a manual any compilation of written materials brought together between covers. More precisely, a manual is an integrated system of long-term instructions, brought together between covers, classified, coded, indexed, and otherwise prepared to maximize its reference value. The two forms of manuals are the loose-leaf, or revisable, and the bound, or non-revisable.

Other characteristics of most manuals are these:

1. *A high degree of authority.*—As organizations grow older and larger, we see a pattern of maturation in their written instructions, culminating in the manual form. The sense of finality, that "this is it," has a strongly authoritative connotation. Other written instructions in the same areas become subsidiary to and dependent on the manual.

2. *A highly formal presentation.*—A manual is formal, legalistic, and systematized in accordance with a detailed code that can be referred to by a manual user. The few illustrations to be found in manuals are themselves formal, concentrating on specifications, maps, flow charts, and other diagrams.

3. *Centralized preparation.*—Since a manual is the binding expression of policy or procedure, its preparation is carried on at an appropriately high level of management.[1] The processes

98

of clearance and review must be strictly enforced at the highest levels before a chief executive will affix his signature to a manual as an expression of top-organization thinking.

4. *A limited audience.*—Manuals have a limited and closely controlled distribution at the executive and middle-management levels and among professional and technical personnel. Manuals are rarely available to persons outside the immediate organization.

Much has been written recently on the technical aspects of manuals. The reader is referred particularly to the works of Ahern, Conarroe, Cooper, Drescher, and Sloat and Creaghead. These works, with others on the subject, are listed among the "Selected Readings" at the end of this chapter. Much of the material on circulars in the preceding chapter applies also to manuals. For, as was noted earlier, collections of classified and coded circulars are often regarded as manuals.

In recent years the tendency has been to use the term "handbook" interchangeably with "manual," but there are good bases for distinguishing between them. Handbooks are subsidiary to, and therefore less authoritative than, manuals. Handbooks are less formal, with fewer impersonal constructions ("It is the policy of this company to . . .") and more personal ones ("We want you to . . ."). The preparation of handbooks is not so highly centralized; and, since handbooks apply chiefly to subordinates, they are given a wider and less controlled distribution than are manuals.

Whether for the processes of initial preparation, revision, or development of devices for increasing usefulness, the majority of the techniques apply to manuals and handbooks alike. The unique features of handbooks are discussed in the next chapter. Here we will concentrate on a few major aspects of manual preparation and use, supplementing our remarks with actual illustrations from modern business and government practice.

There are many opportunities for ingenuity in the field of manuals and related media, because the field is still a new one. In some organizations, where the supervisors were thoroughly resistant to the use of conventional manuals, distribution of manuals has been done away with in favor of a telephone information service. The clerk at the phone is prepared to answer the supervisor's questions as spelled out in her up-to-date copies of the manuals.[2] All persons concerned with the preparation of any of the media should, from time to time, test different techniques within the relatively stable audience with which they work.

SETTING UP A MANUAL

A manual is potentially more usable than are files of individual messages or circulars, but usability and usefulness are not routine by-products of the manual form. Fairly often, manuals are hailed with great fanfare when they first appear and later fall into disuse. In other cases, manuals prove to be unsuitable for some of their anticipated uses and have to be supplemented with handbooks and other media.

Every manual should be written with effective order-giving in mind, and certain aspects of order-giving are highly pertinent.

Content

Is the manual to deal with policy or procedure, or both? Is the focus to be on substantive matters, which have to do with operations and products, or on institutional matters, dealing with administration and housekeeping? Organization is a major subject, and it can be presented separately or along with other institutional material. General information is not in character with our concept of a manual and fits better in other media, such as handbooks, house organs, and newsletters.

The manuals in use today are made up primarily of material dealing with policy, procedure, or organization, or with subclasses of these subjects.[3] The typical sales manual concentrates on substantive policy and procedure having to do with selling. The typical supervisors' manual focuses on institutional policy and procedure, with the greatest emphasis on personnel administration, plus material on organization structure and interdepartmental relationships.[4]

No one can say arbitrarily that only certain subjects may be included within the covers of a manual. A more practical goal would be to give each manual its own central focus—a basic theme and content. A limited amount of whatever other material is desirable, even though it does not conform to initial editorial policy, can then be added. The following quotation from Policy Bulletin PO-1 of the Cherry-Burrell Corporation illustrates how, from a practical standpoint, a manual may be extended beyond its central focus (in this case, policy):

> In the preparation of President's Policy Bulletins it will be the endeavor as far as possible to confine the bulletins to policy matters only. However, there will be instances in which dollar or other limits will need to be part of the policy. In so far as possible, procedures will be left out of Policy Bulletins, and implementing procedure bulletins, where necessary, will be issued separately, generally by the various Groups.

Any manual is typically rigid, but the degree of rigidity may vary. A top-level policy statement that the organization will comply with all laws on fair labor standards can be unequivocal. A mandatory procedure can also be stated in suitably mandatory fashion; but, whenever the exercise of discretion is needed, the manual issuer should make this fact clear. The introduction to the Los Angeles Probation Department's manual of policy and procedure cautions users of the manual that the words *shall*, *will*, or *must* indicate mandatory instructions, while *should* or *may* indicate practices that are desirable but not mandatory. Or the manual issuer can go further, as did the authors of International Harvester's Public Relations Manual, and break each subject down into its mandatory and discretionary aspects.

Audience

To which audience is the manual to apply: the entire organization, the headquarters or central office, field or branch offices, or certain units or positions? It is easy to see that supervisory manuals apply to all line supervisors, but accounting manuals, for example, must aim at designated units or positions doing accounting work in the business. When a single manual is made to apply to a great number of audiences, clarity and adequacy may suffer. The original decision about the audience will determine the initial distribution as well as the subsequent distribution of revisions and supplements.

Improper audience determination can have the effect of changing content. A top-policy statement on manufacturing has all the attributes of policy to officials and supervisors in the shops, but it is downgraded to the level of general information when it reaches salesmen. This interesting phenomenon can be used to advantage. An attractively prepared policy manual (such as *Aldens Principles* or the Green Giant Company's *Policy Book*) can have a secondary distribution at intermediate levels, where it serves as a handbook. The concept of the handbook, as discussed in the succeeding chapter, centers on getting information beyond the limited audiences for manuals.

As a general rule, a clear definition of content and audience will safeguard a manual from excessive detail, which is one of the chief causes of premature obsolescence.[5] Very helpful here is the concept of a line of demarcation on detail, as developed in chapter iv. If a top executive operates at his proper level, he will want any manual that he signs to concentrate on policy and perhaps a few major procedures addressed to his principal line and staff officials. These men, in turn, will be able to issue their own manuals, circulars, or handbooks, filling in both policy and procedure appropriate to their levels and their audiences.

Only rarely can a manual satisfy the wide variety of needs which an organization has for written instructions. A manual that is essentially order-giving in nature is not necessarily a good training medium, nor is a manual designed for high-level management likely to be a satisfactory directing medium at lower levels. The fact that every manual has only limited areas of applicability presents management with a threefold challenge: (1) to determine what the primary areas of applicability are and adhere to them, (2) to secure acceptance within the predetermined limits, and (3) to make judicious use of a manual, or portions of it, as originally written or as rewritten, among secondary audiences for informational or training purposes.

TECHNICAL FEATURES

Classification and Coding

One of the principal advantages of the manual form is its detailed system of classification and coding.

Determining the scope and applicability of a particular manual is the first step in classification. Classification then proceeds through one or several further breakdowns. The initial breakdown is most commonly by major subject, with subclassifications arranged in a variety of ways: by portions of major subjects, by organization units, by types of content material (e.g., policy or procedure), or in a way that best meets the users' requirements. (A salesman or field auditor carries his manual when on the road; the office files and bookshelves of references are not accessible to him.) The several intermediate breakdowns are referred to as parts, chapters, and sections, but not always in that order. There is a final mechanical breakdown into paragraphs, subparagraphs, items, and sentences, which may be numbered or lettered.

In our "Selected Readings" on manuals, and in manuals in use, one will find suggested topics for subject classifications. Figure 8 illustrates how a typical classification scheme works. The sample page is from a Sears, Roebuck personnel manual, Part I, which is set aside for "Employment," one phase of personnel administration. The next breakdown provides for dif-

PERSONNEL MANUAL   RETAIL
PART I - EMPLOYMENT

EMPLOYMENT RESOURCES

1001. GENERAL EMPLOYMENT POLICY

    a. Promotion from within the Organization

        It is Sears policy to promote people from within the organization whenever possible. Promotion from within creates high morale and eliminates the uncertainties of hiring people whose capabilities are unknown. In addition, it reduces training time necessary to prepare a person for his new position.

    b. Advance Planning

        It is the responsibility of the personnel department and the store manager to plan in advance adequate replacements for any job vacancies that might arise. When it is necessary to go outside the organization to fill a position, several suggested sources for recruiting are listed below.

1002. EMPLOYMENT RESOURCES (FULL-TIME)

        The following are sources of good applicants for full-time work:

    a. Applicants who were not hired at the time they applied because there were no jobs available. Such applications should be kept for 3 months.

    b. Former employes. See section on "Reinstatements," beginning at paragraph 1301.

    c. Persons recommended by present employes.

        For further information concerning these sources, refer to the "Selection Guide."

Fig. 8.—An example of classification and coding, as seen in a Sears, Roebuck & Co. manual.

ferent aspects of the employment process ("Employment Resources" in this case), with a further breakdown between policy and advisory procedure (paragraphs 1001 and 1002); and there is a final breakdown into lettered subparagraphs and sentences. The final sentence on this manual page gives a cross-reference to the "Selection Guide," a subsidiary handbook of procedural instructions on employment.

A sales manual of the Linde Company, a division of Union Carbide Corporation, is broken down into three major parts: products (coded P), process (coded PS and covering processes where the company's products may be used), and reference (coded RF). The first two parts deal with the work of selling, but the reference part is set aside for instructions to salesmen on institutional or administrative procedures. A page from the reference part (Fig. 9) illustrates how the material is broken down, first by subject ("General Letters"), then by activity ("Classification and Distribution" in this case), and, finally, in numbered and lettered paragraphs and subparagraphs.

There are a variety of coding methods to fix permanently the various classification patterns. Roman and Arabic numerals, decimals, capital and lower-case letters, and key words and abbreviations are all used. Some codes in use today are quite complex—probably too complex for the people who are supposed to use them. Our experience with numerical coding suggests two precautionary rules:

1. *The coding system should be as simple as possible.*—A two-digit base number (00–99; PS, RF) and a two-digit suffix (00–99) are adequate for most manual requirements, and less extensive manuals can get along with even simpler codes. As manuals attempt to cover more territory, their codes become more complex, which may signal the need to break down a single manual into two or more smaller ones. Codes which per-

sistently end with one or two zeroes are obviously more elaborate than they need to be.

2. *Coding systems throughout a single organization or large segments of it should be as consistent with one another as possible.*—Among the various series of written instructions, similar or related coding systems should be used to the greatest extent possible. The Cherry-Burrell Corporation authorizes its

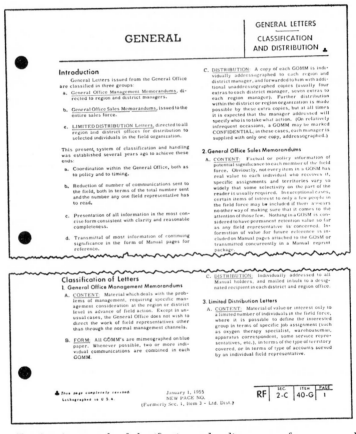

Fig. 9.— An example of classification and coding, a page from a manual of the Linde Company, a division of Union Carbide Corporation.

divisional managers to implement the President's Policy Bulletins with their own bulletins; but the latter must carry the same subject titles and numerical codes as the former. (Each division adds its assigned prefixing digit for identification.) The provision for parallel numbering will, of course, create gaps in the numbering of the respective publications, since there are bound to be unique provisions in each of them.

Pagination and Dating

Related to coding are the methods of pagination and dating. As in any other bound book, a bound manual has chapters and page numbers that are permanently fixed in a straight sequence, affording an elementary type of coding. In a loose-leaf manual, however, it is common practice to use separate sequences of page numbers within each chapter or section. Some manuals have no page numbers at all, depending instead on their codes. In lieu of conventional page numbers, the upper left and right corners of each page can carry the first and last code numbers for items appearing on that page, in the manner of a dictionary.

Regardless of the method of pagination, it is wise to begin each section on a new page. Such makeup reduces to a minimum the number of pages affected when revisions are made. There may be a resulting blank space on the final page of each section, which can increase the total number of pages, although this is usually not serious.

Initial dates appear on all individual messages and on most circulars (which may also carry effective dates), but there is good reason to omit initial dates from manuals. Dates can be a distinct liability, since after a period of several years, employees may be inclined to ignore the "old stuff," even if it is perfectly valid. The page from the Sears personnel manual (Fig. 8) is an initial issuance and bears no date. Some manual editors, however, insist on using initial dates in anticipation of the time when they will release a revision carrying both the initial and the later dates. An initial date is often prefixed by a phrase such as "First Issued."

Revisions are generally numbered and dated. The revised page may carry, with the date, a phrase such as "Second Revision" or "New Page" (Fig. 9).

Revision

The fact that manuals and other forms of written instructions become so easily obsolete often outweighs all their advantages. Bound manuals present an insurmountable revision problem that can be overcome only by publishing an entirely new edition. Loose-leaf manuals, on the other hand, are readily revisable, if the methods of classification, coding, and pagination have anticipated revision.

The frequency of revision depends on the nature of the other media available. If instructions must be issued in written form even though they are probably going to be temporary, it is wise to use an available circular series. Another temporary medium is a "recent developments" page added to an entire manual or to each chapter or section.[6] Handwritten corrections and paste-ins are poor techniques: the users may fail to make the corrections or make them inaccurately. If there are many write-ins or paste-ins, it is not long before the manual takes on a bedraggled appearance. No matter what revision devices are used, the manual editor must pick up the permanent items periodically for incorporation in the manual.

If a revision is important enough to be made at all, it can be made most successfully by incorporating it in a newly added page or in a new edition of the affected page. After several revisions of the same subject, it is advisable to eliminate the patchwork by preparing a thorough reissuance. Indeed, an entire manual will profit from reissuance periodically—particularly after periods of several years during which many changes have occurred. The expense of keeping a manual up to date is insignificant compared to the potential losses that can result from obsolete instructions, which are as bad as, or worse than, none at all.

Revision signals.—Several techniques have been developed to improve the revision process. The first one is to use some sort of signal to direct the reader's attention to the revised portion of the text. This is done in various ways: a vertical line in the margin running the length of the revision, asterisks, arrows, heavy black dots, underlining, or boldface type. Another technique is to preserve the previous version (for comparison or emphasis) by putting it in a footnote.

Transmittal letters.—A device often used is to send out revised pages under cover of transmittal letters, which may also be called either manual or revision letters. Those revisions being transmitted at one time are enumerated and summarized briefly, and filing and indexing instructions may also be furnished.

Transmittal letters have great value for announcing revisions and alerting people to them. Also, the revised pages themselves do not have to circulate, but can be filed promptly. In Figure 10 we show the type of transmittal letter used by United Air Lines, which has been made as simple as possible. Some companies spell out the nature of the transmitted changes in more detail.

Revision record sheets.—The holder of any manual must have assurance at all times that his manual is complete and that he is up to date on all revisions and deletions. Although we saw this same type of problem in connection with circulars, manual revisions are unique in that they require serial numbers separate from the numbers of the material they amend. The revisions are, in a sense, a special circular series, and they must be controlled chronologically regardless of the chapter or section where they apply. When a person receives a revision, he should be able to check whether he received the preceding ones.

A preprinted and prenumbered revision record sheet can be used to post all revisions. It may require only that the pertinent revision number be crossed out or that the person inserting the revision enter the date and his initials. Two types of

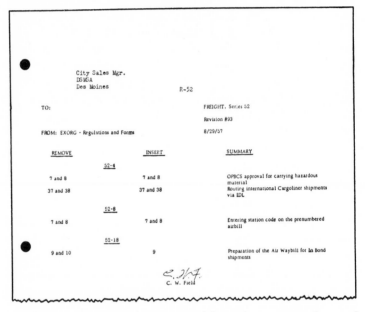

Fig. 10.—An example of a transmittal letter for a group of manual revisions, as used by United Air Lines.

record sheets calling for each of these procedures are illustrated in Figure 11.

Manual check lists.—A supplement to the revision record sheet is the manual check list, or check sheet. Here the user has a further reference to instructions in effect, including revisions, arranged by location in the manual rather than by revision number. If the user discovers that he is missing one or

REVISION RECORD

Revisions will be numbered in sequence as released. It is important that corresponding numbered revisions be checked off, as received, on the revision record below. Notify the State Department of Social Welfare if a revision number is skipped without receipt of a revised page bearing the corresponding number.

1	43	85	127	169	211	253	295	337	379	421	463
2	44	86	128	170	212	254	296	338	380	422	464
3	45	87	129	171	213	255	297	339	381	423	465
4	46	88	130	172	214	256	298	340	382	424	466
5	47	89	131	173	215	257	299	341	383	425	467
6	48	90	132	174	216	258	300	342	384	426	468
7	49	91	133	175	217	259	301	343	385	427	469
8	50	92	134	176	218	260	302	344	386	428	470
9	51	93	135	177	219	261	303	345	387	429	471
10	52	94	136	178	220	262	304	346	388	430	472
11	53	95	137	179	221	263	305	347	389	431	473
12	54	96	138	180	222	264	306	348	390	432	474
13	55	97	139	181	223	265	307	349	391	433	475
14	56	98	140	182	224	266	308	350	392	434	476
15	57	99	141	183	225	267	309	351	393	435	477
16	58	100	142	184	226	268	310	352	394	436	478
17	59	101	143	185	227	269	311	353	395	437	479

UNITED

RECORD OF REVISIONS

MANUAL TITLE OR NUMBER 60-14   LOCATION PDXDS

ASSIGNED TO (JOB TITLE) PASTRY COOK

REV. NO.	INSERTION DATE	BY	REV. NO.	INSERTION DATE	BY	REV. NO.	INSERTION DATE	BY	REV. NO.	INSERTION DATE	BY
1	6/28/57	BB		/ /			/ /			/ /	
2	8/9/57	BB		/ /			/ /			/ /	
3	9/13/57	BB		/ /			/ /			/ /	
4	9/27/57	BB		/ /			/ /			/ /	
5	10/20/57	BB		/ /			/ /			/ /	
6	11/18/57	BB		/ /			/ /			/ /	

Retain this record in the front of manual or chapter.
On receipt of revisions, insert revised pages in the manual, and enter revision number, date inserted, and initials.

UEF 1898 REV. 8-57 PRINTED IN U.S.A.

FIG. 11.—Examples of revision record sheets, from the California Department of Social Welfare (*above*) and United Air Lines (*below*).

several items, whether they are revisions or original issuances, he can use the check list as a preprinted order form (Fig. 12).

United Air Lines sends an up-to-date check sheet with about every tenth revision. There are always a few recipients who return their sheets requesting one or more pages.

Removing obsolete pages.—The removal of old material is just as important as the addition of new. Manual users who are zealous about adding new things are often reluctant to give up anything.

Union Oil Company of California, among a number of com-

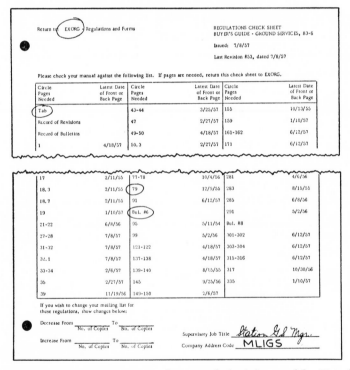

Fig. 12.—Demonstration copy of a manual check list, used by United Air Lines. The circled items are being ordered.

panies, now furnishes an envelope with each revision and requires every manual holder to return his obsolete pages to the manual editor. The retention of old material is justified only in those few manuals that are being maintained as archives for historical or possible legal purposes.

Tables of Contents and Indexes

Manuals provide tables of contents, indexes, or both. A table of contents is helpful in presenting the scope and arrangement of a manual, although alone it is not an adequate "searching" device. This limitation can be overcome in large part by providing subsidiary tables of contents for each part, chapter, or section. The greatest help will always come from an extensive and up-to-date index, especially one that offers all the synonyms possible.

The design of indexes affords one of the best opportunities for ingenuity in manual preparation. Several indexes can be provided: one arranged alphabetically for subject matter, another for form names, and possibly others for form numbers and equipment.[7] Manual indexes can be at the beginning, right after the table of contents, instead of at the end, as in conventional books. Another possibility is to print indexes on distinctively colored paper, as in the catalogues of the Chicago mail-order houses.

Divider pages.—The insertion of dividers between parts, chapters, and sections is a device that can make a manual considerably more usable. The most successful dividers are made of manila, or comparably heavy stock, with projecting tabs. A tab imprinted with either an identifying word caption or code number is better than none at all, while a tab imprinted with both will do even more to reduce the need to refer to the table of contents or index.

Layout and Typography

Layout and typography can contribute to a manual's attractiveness, legibility, and ultimate usefulness. The correct size will vary, but pocket-sized editions have little to commend them if they are not going to be carried in pockets. Most paper-work forms are letter size, and they can be portrayed most effectively in a manual that size or a bit larger.

The choice of paper stock and cover or binder will depend in part on the funds available, but again consideration should be given to the way in which the manual will be used. Will it be in a factory, an office, or a briefcase? Will it have hard use, and will the users have dirty hands? Do the covers or some of the pages need to be laminated in acetate sheets? (Machines now available make this a simple operation.)

Formerly one had to employ expensive printing processes to get any choice of type faces, but today variations are available to some extent with typewriters and mechanical duplicating processes. In the selection of type faces the published experimental findings on reading preferences and legibility can be utilized, or tests can be made in the plant or office where the manual is to be used.[8]

Space for notations.—Since there will always be a certain amount of local interpretation, organizations might do well to allow for it. In preparing manuals, space can be provided for supplementation by printing only one side of each sheet, leaving the reverse side blank for employees' notations. Such a technique makes it easier for management to find out just what local adaptation has been made.

TRAINING IN MANUAL USE

To many of its potential users a manual will be a strange and forbidding thing—especially to new employees, because of the variations from one organization to another. Manuals, and other written forms of administrative communication as well, are unique to business, government, and similar organizations. No educational curriculum now offers training in their use. And, surprisingly enough, this is rarely included in organizational training programs.

Managers, supervisors, and subordinate employees must be shown how to use the organization's manuals and other written materials. It is a waste of time and money to supersede a collection of circulars with a manual if the users are going to leaf through it page by page in hopes of finding the needed reference. The users should be encouraged to bring their manuals and circulars to staff meetings and to refer to them for answers to specific questions. It is part of an order-giver's responsibility to make certain that his subordinates are familiar with methods of classification, coding, revision, and tables of contents and indexes. It is equally important that the members of an organization understand the objectives of each system of written instructions and the relationship each bears to the organization's other forms of administrative communication.

Selected Readings

BOOKS AND MONOGRAPHS

COOPER, JOSEPH D. *How To Communicate Policy and Procedure.* New London, Conn.: National Foremen's Institute, 1956.
The technical features of revisable manuals.

DALE, ERNEST. *Planning and Developing the Company Organization Structure.* ("Research Reports," No. 20.) New York: American Management Association, 1952. Part II, chap. x, "Preparing the Organization Manual."
Content, arrangement, technical features, and costs. Bibliography.

HALL, GEORGE L. *The Management Guide.* San Francisco: Standard Oil Company of California, Department on Organization, 1948.
The most widely read and accepted treatment of organization manuals, based on experience in the Standard Oil Company of California.

NEUSCHEL, RICHARD F. *Streamlining Business Procedures.* New York: McGraw-Hill Book Co., 1950. Chap. xiii, "Developing and Maintaining Procedure Instruction Manuals."

How to arrange, index, distribute, and revise manuals and illustrate the accompanying paper-work forms.

PFIFFNER, JOHN M., and LANE, S. OWEN. *A Manual for Administrative Analysis.* Dubuque, Iowa: Wm. C. Brown Co., 1951. Chap. viii, "Development of Procedure Manuals."

A step-by-step account.

ROSS, H. JOHN. *How To Make a Procedure Manual.* Miami, Fla.: Office Research Institute, n.d.

ARTICLES

BORTZ, A. F. "The Organization and Evaluation of a Procedures Manual Program," pp. 13–24 in *Improving Office Reports, Manuals, and Records.* ("Office Management Series," No. 141.) New York: American Management Association, 1955.

The preparation of procedures manuals at Lord Manufacturing Company.

CONARROE, E. H. "Preparation and Use of Office Manuals," *Bulletin of the National Association of Cost Accountants,* Vol. 24 (June 1, 1943), pp. 1193–1206.

Comprehensive statement, based in part on an analysis of manuals and circulars used in fifty-two companies.

HULEN, JOHN W. "Manuals for Business," *Systems and Procedures Quarterly,* Vol. 5 (May, 1954), pp. 12–15, 22.

Organizing, printing, and revising manuals.

PARRISH, LAWRENCE L. "Organization Manuals Improve Communication," *Advanced Management,* Vol. 17 (September, 1952), pp. 22–25.

Advantages of manuals over charts for the communication of basic organizational data.

SLOAT, DONALD M., and CREAGHEAD, ROBERT M. "Foreman's Manual Answers All His Questions," *Factory Management and Maintenance,* Vol. 52 (October, 1944), pp. 101–4.

Incisive report on preparing an integrated manual of policies, procedures, organization, regulations, and paper work, derived from experience at Pratt & Whitney Aircraft.

VIII / *Handbooks and Employee Handbooks*

ALTHOUGH "handbook" and "manual" are terms that are often used interchangeably, we have suggested that the two are distinct. In comparison with manuals, handbooks are less authoritative, less formal, less rigidly controlled, and they apply at most levels. Personal pronouns appear frequently in the texts of handbooks; one seldom sees them in a manual. There are other features that will identify most handbooks. Conventional page numbering is the rule, and the coding, if any, is simple. There are more pocket-sized handbooks than larger manuals.

Most of the principles in chapter vii apply to handbooks as well as to manuals. Although the preparation of a handbook will differ from that of a manual, the handbook editor must also decide what to do about content, applicability, and such technical features as classification, coding, indexing, and methods of revision.

The most popular form is the employee handbook, which is discussed in the next section. It is the purpose here to show, in general, how the handbook differs from the manual, illustrating the unique functions of the handbook in administration—for training, for ready reference, and for the dissemination of general information.

Handbooks for Training

A handbook may be eminently suitable for training purposes where a manual is not. Suppose a company suddenly receives a defense contract requiring the immediate employment of dozens of personnel interviewers and clerks. There is no time for prolonged training programs, and the existing manuals of policy and procedure are too impersonal, too detailed, too big, and too strange to be useful for training purposes. The solution lies in the preparation of concise handbooks differing from the manuals in several important respects.

The specific questions to be answered in preparing training handbooks are: What instructions are most important for the new personnel? How briefly and clearly can this information be presented, and how can it be made to elicit interest and acceptance? What would be the most attractive and usable form and layout?

The most pressing subjects, with as little detail as possible, should dominate these handbooks. Brevity, clarity, and greater readability and interest value can be achieved by rethinking, rewriting, and adding illustrations. Since newcomers will be familiar with books but probably not with manuals (and there is no time for training in manual use), coding should be simplified or conventional page numbering should be used instead.

Although a manual can be prepared with an eye to training, it will in some ways be an imperfect training medium, and its order-giving function will suffer. Training can be done by means of a handbook without impairing the manual. The United States Bureau of the Census, which must employ thousands of temporary enumerators before each federal census, uses a handbook, portions of which are illustrated in Figure 13. The Bureau's handbook has been successful as a training medium where manuals would have fared poorly.

Handbooks for Ready Reference

The handbook is a ready reference source. For instance, an accounting department has developed a manual which, of course, is almost exclusively procedural. The accountants and a limited number of operating officials agree that it covers ev-

FIG. 13.—Extracts from a handbook used for training in the United States Bureau of the Census.

ery conceivable accounting problem and is excellent. But the majority of the operating people do not want or need such a manual. What they can use is a handy compilation covering the high points of the manual, with special attention to the questions that occur most frequently and references to the basic manual for details and for problems that come up only rarely.

In one organization the handbooks were so much more practical for day-to-day use that even higher-level supervisors began to use them instead of their manuals. This was an unfortunate development, since the manuals were considerably more authoritative and comprehensive. The remedy, of course, was to reissue the manuals in a more usable form.

Handbooks for General Information

According to the "horizon concept" (discussed in chapter iv) a person should receive information only if it applies directly to his position and his work. There is a real danger that such a practice would deny to employees a worthwhile knowledge of aspects of the organization beyond their immediate horizons.

Handbooks covering the work of an entire organization give middle-management people and others a means for developing beyond their restricted job horizons. An office supervisor, for example, could use the handbooks to learn something about the factory and the sales department without having to labor his way through the detailed factory and sales manuals—which probably would not be available to him anyway. In much the same manner, a foreman or a salesman could learn something about the office.

The limited knowledge of most managers, supervisors, and foremen about operations other than their own indicates a deficiency in communication *to them*. It is small wonder, then, that they prove to be poor communicators *to others*, as evidenced by their failure as conference leaders or by their inability to maintain a company-wide viewpoint when dealing with grievances. The handbook affords management a means of overcoming this kind of deficiency. All that is needed each time a manual is prepared for limited distribution is an equivalent handbook for wider distribution. The modest cost of such a program should be compared to the savings it would produce by developing supervisors who can see and think in terms of the organization as a whole.

There is little reason to believe that anyone can prepare a single manual or a single handbook that will serve a number of levels, units, activities, and objectives equally well. A manual *and* a handbook can do what neither can do alone.

EMPLOYEE HANDBOOKS

What Is an Employee Handbook?

There has been such widespread adoption of the employee handbook that it deserves separate treatment as a written instructional medium. It is an interesting commentary that, although employee handbooks are properly subsidiary to authoritative manuals, more companies have the former than the latter.[1] This cart-before-the-horse situation would indicate that many organizations have merely been copying each other's employee handbooks without taking time to set down in writing their own underlying policies and procedures.

Employee handbooks are the least formal and the most personal of the major forms of written instructions. They are authoritative only to the extent that they deal with the duties and privileges of individuals; that is to say, in laying down the rules of the game. The balance of their content is simply general information. Employee handbooks serve primarily to introduce the organization to the new employee. In addition they are used to refresh the old employee's knowledge about the organization and to influence anew his relationship with it.

Content

Ever since they first appeared, employee handbooks have emphasized the duties and privileges of the individual worker. The early efforts were literally rulebooks in which employees were given lists of dos and don'ts and oftentimes warned of the specific penalties for violations. In 1856, Carson Pirie Scott and Company issued this statement of rules:

Stores must be open from 6 A.M. to 9 P.M. the year around.

Stores must be swept; counters, bases, shelves and showcases dusted. Lamps trimmed, filled and chimneys cleaned; pens made; doors and windows opened; a pail of water, also a bucket of coal brought in before breakfast (if there is time to do so) and attend to customers who call.

Stores must not be opened on the Sabbath unless necessary, and then only a few minutes.

The employee who is in the habit of smoking Spanish cigars, being shaved at the barber's, going to dances and other places of amusement, will surely give his employer reason to be suspicious of his integrity and honesty.

Each employee must pay not less than $5 per year to the church and must attend Sunday school regularly.

Men are given one evening a week for courting and two if they go to a prayer meeting.

After 14 hours of work in the store, the leisure time should be spent mostly in reading.[2]

Rules—phrased much differently now than they were in 1856 —are still the principal features of employee handbooks, although there are said to be a few without a single rule.[3] The trend is away from rulebooks and toward what have been called "working partnership handbooks."[4] Employee handbooks of this new type include their share of rules of conduct and conditions of employment, but they emphasize non-directing information that promises to create among employees a greater sense of identification with, or belonging to, the organization. In the words of the British Institute of Personnel Management:

An employee handbook . . . can, and should, be one of the corner-stones of a progressive personnel policy. . . . An employee handbook should, therefore, serve almost as a "Bill of Rights," an acknowledgment that employment involves a voluntary agreement between free and honest parties. It should stand as a statement of good faith, setting out clearly the rights and obligations of each party, the measures of redress which exist for each, and the obligations of the individual towards his fellow workers.[5]

Employee handbooks, in short, are designed to strengthen the organization by enhancing the standing of each individual in it.

As a result of numerous studies and surveys, lists have been compiled of as many as several hundred specific items found in employee handbooks, and these may be seen in most of the books and monographs among the readings for this chapter. The following model is illustrative of current practice.

YOU *and* YOUR JOB *at* DOAKES STEEL

Welcome!

Here the chief executive addresses a message to the employees, or two messages—one for new employees and another for all employees.

About the Company . . .

A description of the company, its products, and their use.

Policies You Will Want To Know About . . .

Types of employment (salaried, hourly, permanent, temporary, probationary); policies governing advancement, layoff, and termination; vacation and other leaves; and collective bargaining.

The Rules of Your Job . . .

Hours of work, wages and taxes, and safety; relationships with supervisors and staff personnel officers; and rules on gambling, drinking, fighting, parking, checking in or out for others, and the use of company phones for personal business.

In Addition to Your Pay . . .

Employee benefits: social security, group insurance, pensions, hospitalization, and suggestion awards.

Services and Activities for You . . .

Recreation; cafeterias, canteens, and the company store; lost and found.

Studying Your Way Up ...

Training programs within the plant or office and outside educational programs in conjunction with public or private institutions.

Other Facts You May Wish To Know ...

Miscellaneous items not treated elsewhere, such as a history of the company, and the company and the community.

Brevity, simplicity, and the light touch characterize employee handbooks. Photographs and drawings abound, and many of the most stringent rules are presented as cartoons.[6] Frequently the recipient's name is lettered on the front cover, and inside the front cover may appear the name of his immediate supervisor. A related technique is to include a blank organization chart and in the proper boxes insert the names of the new employee, his superior, and others with whom he will be working.

Audience

Since employee handbooks are normally given to everyone at the lower levels, they apply to a larger audience than does any other instructional medium. Some organizations, however, issue different handbooks for different portions of the organization, such as the office and the factory, or for different classes of positions, such as the salaried and the hourly wage groups. Others use a core of common material for everyone, adding necessary special material appropriate to different units or positions.

The new-employee audience.—When an employee handbook is used in its primary application, that is, for new employees, it is a fitting adjunct to an orientation and indoctrination program.[7] The probationary period, according to the National Foremen's Institute, works both ways: "From the company's viewpoint, the new employee is on probation. From his point of view, however, it is the company that is on probation; he looks the company over to decide whether or not he wants to work there permanently."[8]

There is no guaranty that even the most skilful preparation and utilization will succeed with the new-employee audience. Too much depends on the reception given each employee by his new work group, including his superior. A beautiful publication, no matter how persuasive, will not withstand the social hurts that can be imposed by an unfriendly work group, while a warm welcome from one's co-workers and superior will probably outweigh the initial effects of a primitive publication—or of none at all.[9] Before using an employee handbook as an introductory device, management should make sure that the effectiveness of the handbook is not doomed in advance by the actions and expressions of the other employees, including superiors.

The all-employee audience.—Employee handbooks are generally distributed among all subordinate employees, which is a different audience from the new employees alone. This secondary application is justified on the basis that the handbook will refresh the knowledge of old employees about the organization and give them a continuing reference source to facts about it.

The objective of long-term usefulness is not combined too easily with the objective of initial use. The typical letter of welcome from the chief executive may actually be an affront to an employee who has been with the company for years. Also, the old-line employee probably knows all the simple rules and elementary facts about the organization and is more interested in details. But whenever employee handbooks are refined in favor of such details, the pages increase, the type becomes smaller, and the over-all appeal to the new employee suffers.

The practice of having two different opening letters indicates that some managements recognize the differences between the two audiences. This differentiation will no doubt proceed even further, so that ultimately the traditional employee handbook will be reserved for use among new employees, while another type emerges for general use.

Technical Features

Many of the technical aspects of preparing an employee handbook are the same as those encountered in preparing other handbooks and manuals. But because employee handbooks have grown up as something of a specialty, a number of articles and monographs have been written on this subject alone. Some of these are listed among the "Selected Readings" for this chapter.

The bound booklet has persisted in employee-handbook practice, although it has given way to revisable formats in the preparation of other handbooks and manuals. It is not surprising, therefore, that we find more obsolescence among employee handbooks than in any other medium. (In one instance the welcoming letter in use was from an official who had since been sent to prison.) If employee handbooks are to be kept in circulation, methods will have to be developed for revision; the alternative—frequent and complete reissuance—is too expensive.

Some of the bound booklets now provide pockets inside one or both covers for non-permanent items, such as the names of company and union officials, education and recreation calendars, transportation schedules, and copies of collective bargaining agreements. A few companies, including United Air Lines and the Port of New York Authority, are using attractive file folders, into which they insert appropriate and timely booklets and letters. Techniques of this sort overcome the obsolescence problem easily.

Modern management uses individual messages, circulars and bulletins, manuals, handbooks, and employee handbooks for downward communication, as well as bulletin boards, posters, signs, management and supervisory newsletters, payroll inserts, annual reports to employees, newspapers, magazines, and a host of other written media.

Each medium has its particular potentiality, and yet all must be interrelated. An individual message is a rapid way of dealing with a purely transitory matter or of meeting a contingency not covered in a manual or a circular; a circular or bulletin can be used to test a policy or procedure before it becomes part of a manual; and a manual can furnish the guide lines for everything subsidiary to it. A handbook can be used to reorient whatever is in a manual in ways more appropriate to different audience situations; a supervisory newsletter or an employee publication can be used to carry lists of circulars in effect and notices of revisions to manuals; and folders of letters and pamphlets can supplement, or substitute for, conventional employee handbooks.

Written instructions fit into the broader context of all instructions, including oral ones, and the giving of orders through any medium is affected by the types of training programs within an organization and the educational program outside. It makes quite a difference if the nearest suitable college extension courses are in the same community as the company or if they are fifty or one hundred miles away. Downward communication, of which order-giving is the most important aspect, does not exist apart from upward and horizontal communication. On the contrary, there is a continual feedback, with the communicatees' responses constantly affecting the communicator's immediate and subsequent actions. As we said earlier, an order-giver who says nothing is, in effect, telling his subordinates to continue what they have been doing. If all the information flowing to a superior kept him convinced that none of his subordinates could do better, there would be no need for any overt downward communication at all.

Selected Readings

BOOKS AND MONOGRAPHS

BAKER, HELEN. *Company-wide Understanding of Industrial Relations Policies*. Princeton: Princeton University, Industrial Relations Section, 1948. Chap. iv, "Methods of Keeping Employees Informed."
Content analysis of sixty-four employee handbooks.

MacDONALD, J. H. *Office Management*. 3d ed. New York: Prentice-Hall, Inc., 1947. Chap. xvi, "The Office Manual."
Preparation, distribution, and revision of various kinds of manuals and handbooks.

NELSON, LENORE P. *Employee Handbook Printing Practices*. (University of Minnesota, Industrial Relations Center, Research and Technical Report 3.) Dubuque, Iowa: Wm. C. Brown Co., 1950.
Research findings on readers' preferences among, and the comparative legibility of, different type faces.

NEWCOMB, ROBERT, and SAMMONS, MARG. *Speak Up, Management!* New York: Funk & Wagnalls Co., 1951. Chap. iii, "The Employee Handbook."
A contents check list; also, recommendations on indexing, editing, and distribution and the measurement of employee reaction.

POWELL, LEONA, and SCHILD, HERBERT W. *How To Prepare and Publish an Employee Manual*. 3d ed. New York: American Management Association, 1947. Illustrated.
Employee handbook practices in 113 companies, step-by-step accounts of the preparation of two employee handbooks, and a discussion of production methods and costs.

Preparing an Employee Handbook. London: Institute of Personnel Management, 1947.
A new approach to employee handbooks, getting away from the conventional rulebook, with recommendations regarding preparation.

SEYBOLD, GENEVA. *Company Rules—Aids to Teamwork*. ("Studies in Personnel Policy," No. 95.) New York: National Industrial Conference Board, Inc., 1948.
Includes twenty pages of rules presented in cartoon form.

SPRIEGEL, WILLIAM R., and LANHAM, E. *A Survey of Bank and De-*

partment Store Employee Handbooks. ("Personnel Study," No. 4.) Austin: University of Texas, Bureau of Business Research, 1952.

Detailed report on 76 banks and 117 department stores. Bibliography.

ARTICLES

BRODY, WILLIAM. "You and a Handbook for Your Employees," *Public Personnel Review,* Vol. 10 (October, 1949), pp. 216–21.

Objectives, contents, preparation, production, and distribution of employee handbooks.

FARR, JAMES N. "Readability and Interest Value in an Employee Handbook," *Journal of Applied Psychology,* Vol. 34 (February, 1950), pp. 16–21.

A before-and-after study on the refashioning of an employee handbook to increase its ratings on Flesch's readability and human-interest scales.

LAWSHE, C. H.; HOLMES, W. H. E., JR.; and TURMAIL, G. M. "An Analysis of Employee Handbooks," *Personnel,* Vol. 27 (May, 1951), pp. 487–95.

Eighty-four employee handbooks analyzed in terms of contents, readability, and human interest.

SCHMIDT, FRED G. "Introducing the New Employee: How To Convey the Right 'First Impression,' " *Personnel,* Vol. 29 (July, 1952), pp. 62–66. (Reprinted in M. JOSEPH DOOHER [ed.], *Effective Communication on the Job* [New York: American Management Association, 1956], pp. 80–84.)

Nine suggestions for making the new employee's introduction more successful.

IX / Employee Publications

By AUDREY E. HEUSSER

THE HOUSE ORGAN, as the industrial or house publication was originally called, received its first big boost during World War I. In a period when new employees were hired in such droves that no one remembered their names or what they needed to be told, the plant periodical eased many a fast-growing defense industry through a difficult phase in its development. Many such publications were largely experimental. They had no definite purpose, but since cost was not a major consideration, any idea likely to bridge the gap between an overworked management and an inexperienced work force seemed worth trying. Some of these publications were personal projects of company officials only beginning to explore the field of human relations in industry. Almost all carried news about what employees were doing as well as what management thought they ought to be doing. Employees liked them for the former; management liked them for the latter.

Then came the black frost of the Great Depression with industry measuring every expense in the cold light of its dwindling revenue; and the house organ withered fast.

World War II brought many of the orientation problems of the earlier conflict. House publications sprang up again like mushrooms, almost over night. It might have been expected that they would have the same short life as those of twenty-five years earlier, and some of them did. What made the difference was the long memory of editors who had weathered the depression and were anxious to prevent a recurrence of that earlier experience.

Now grown to professional stature, they began a concerted effort to improve the skills of the neophytes in the field. They organized industrial editors into associations and study groups, they persuaded colleges to introduce courses in business journalism, they gave generously of their time and skills to improve the professional level of the field. Over and over again they warned that the publication sponsored by an industry becomes a part of that industry's operating expense and must expect the same close scrutiny as the cost of washing windows or training an apprentice. Many editors whose publications had grown happily under a cost-plus government contract could not believe this. After the war, suddenly caught in the squeeze of a competitive economy, they found their budgets cut and cut again until, in a great many cases, the publications were discontinued altogether. By contrast, the publications that were geared to their company's business prospered. Gradually, editors began to see that their role was one of maintaining an important line of communication.

One would be badly misled to believe that all industrial editors now operate on the principle that their publications must be justified as a cost of doing business. A significant minority still considers their purpose to be entirely intangible. Yet a study made in 1956 among a small but outstanding group of company publications showed that, although half of them had no specific budget, practically all had accurate figures concerning their costs.[1]

More than six thousand employee publications now circulate among two hundred and fifty million readers at an annual cost of three hundred million dollars.[2] Delman M. K. Smith of Opinion Research Corporation has estimated that 77 per cent of the companies with over five million dollars in assets have employee publications. It can be assumed that in these companies employee publications are regarded as effective methods of communication—effective in the sense that the publication contributes something to the efficiency of the operation.

WHAT IS AN EMPLOYEE PUBLICATION?

The term "house organ" in its broadest sense refers to almost any wholly or partially subsidized periodical sponsored by a corporation, association, organization, or institution and addressed to a specific audience rather than the general public. It covers employee publications of all kinds, those sponsored by such widely divergent groups as newspapers, state highway departments, and farmers' co-operatives. It also covers publications prepared by churches, chambers of commerce, and even by hospital patients or prison inmates. A common distinction between a trade publication and a house organ is that the former can usually qualify for a second-class mailing privilege since it is available for general distribution, has paid subscriptions, and paid advertising.

"Industrial publication" has a narrower meaning and is the description usually applied to publications that represent management communication. Two types are in common use: the company publication, produced by a paid staff alone, and the employee publication, in which the paid staff is supplemented by a corps of volunteer reporters and/or writers from the audience group.

To refine the subject, the International Council of Industrial Editors recognize two audience groups to which the so-called "internal" industrial publication, of either the company or employee type, may be addressed—employees in a single community and employees in multi-plant or more-than-one-community operation. They list as "external" those publications addressed to customers, dealers, or trade associates.

The International Council further divides the field by format —magazines (with covers, stapled), newspapers (news on the first page, unstapled), news-magazines (some combination of the two), and newsletters. Internal publications are also separated according to their primary purpose—those concerned entirely with news and features and those frankly devoted to employee education and persuasion.[3]

TO WHOM AND WHY?

In choosing an industrial publication for a specific enterprise, the sponsoring management needs to answer two questions: (1) To whom will the publication be addressed? (2) What is the purpose in publishing? Until these two questions have been answered, all debate on such things as responsibility, editing, method of distribution, and format remains academic.

Audience

To whom will the publication be addressed? For the purposes of this chapter, we will assume that the answer is going to be "primarily employees," but what follows applies equally if the answer is the employee's family, customers, stockholders, and/or community civic leaders. Although there will almost always be secondary audiences, it has to be decided which group will receive first consideration. Usually it is a mistake to have a primary audience so diversified that one publication could not reasonably be of common interest.

Even if the audience is limited to employees, it is sometimes difficult (especially in a large organization) to shape the publication so that it is equally interesting to all of them. For this reason, once the primary audience is established, it will be necessary to secure a clear idea of what sort of people comprise this group—the number of years of schooling, the various age groups, the number of dependents, the number of foreign-born, the percentage of women, and so on. Employee files and personnel statistics are good sources of information, as are supervisors and volunteer reporters.

Purpose

Having decided upon the audience, the next question is "Why?" Purposes are not hard to find. Some of the most common include:

1. To acquaint employees with conditions of employment; to show the company as a good place to work.

2. To create a family feeling among employees; to help them become familiar with their place in the organization; to show them the advantages of long company service.

3. To promote the reduction of accidents and waste, and to increase productivity.

4. To answer employee questions and to provide advance information about plans and policies.

5. To make plain to employees, their families, and the community that the company is a good corporate citizen and an asset to the locality.

The answer to the purpose question should be specific and should be something that justifies the use of company funds. Every effort should be made to get it into a form and language that will provide a constant, easy reminder to editors and managers alike.

Many times we forget the importance of a clearly established purpose in the first flush of enthusiasm for the new publication. Even today, with more and more new publications starting, something like 10 per cent of them suspend operations every year and nearly 15 per cent change editors. It is better not to start publishing at all than to begin for no better reason than that it is the popular thing to do.

LAUNCHING THE EMPLOYEE PUBLICATION

Once it has been thoroughly established that there is a clearly defined audience to which an employee publication could be addressed and that such a publication could conceivably improve some condition representing a cost of doing business, the organization is ready for the next step.

Responsibility

Who will be responsible for the publication? Shall it be the advertising, the public relations, or the industrial relations department? Shall it be some combination of these groups, or shall it be a separate organization? Answers to the questions of audience and purpose should make this decision easy.

Advertising.—Originally most employee publications were prepared by the advertising department, even when they were addressed to production workers. This is still the logical place to put the responsibility for a publication addressed to customers or to an employee group that is highly sales-conscious. Such publications need to be attractively packaged, and their stories should show the same attention to display that characterizes advertising copy.

Public and/or community relations.—In the first part of World War II, public relations departments were instrumental in the establishment of many new employee publications, some of which remain outstanding in the field. The public-relations approach has decided advantages for publications addressed to the community and civic leaders, stockholders, and employees' families. Skilfully written copy that humanizes the corporation and high quality mechanical production, particularly in magazine format, characterize the typical publication from this department.

Industrial relations.—Gradually during World War II and increasingly ever since, industrial relations and personnel departments have undertaken the supervision of publications for employees. They now have charge of 40 per cent of all industrial publications.[4] The industrial relations approach is advantageous where the audience is the rank-and-file employee. This is the same audience dealt with in grievance proceedings, in collective bargaining, and in the orientation and indoctrination of new employees. As a rule these publications are less expensive and more informal.

It is possible to set up a separate department to manage the employee publication, and in large organizations this is frequently done. However, in such cases the head of the department usually reports to the person in charge of one of the staff divisions mentioned above.

Occasionally a combination of representatives from the advertising, public relations, and industrial relations departments are brought together as a team for the purpose of launching a new publication. This same group may also serve as an editorial advisory board after the publication has started. However, such a team should not be an excuse for failing to assign full responsibility in one particular place. There will be need from time to time to hold some one individual accountable for reaching the audience and fulfilling the purpose.

Who Will Edit?

Somewhere between the time the decision is made to have a publication and the time the money is provided for it, a further decision will have to be made as to who will edit it. Regardless which department has final responsibility, editing the employee publication is no longer something that can be safely left to the amateur.

This type of editing is now a clearly defined profession, and even though some 80 per cent of the editors have duties besides producing the employee publication, these duties are in closely allied fields. The trend is toward more full-time editors, more mature editors, and more editors with one or more full-time assistants.[5]

Industrial editing calls for a special knowledge of graphic arts skills plus a broad knowledge of the subject of administrative communication. Usually the industrial editor must have more first-hand knowledge of printing processes, typography, and photography than would be generally required in the advertising or public relations fields. In a small company he may have to be a Jack-of-all-trades, even doing his own photography and layout. In a large company, where he can hire most of the specific skills, he must still have experience enough to know whether he is getting his money's worth.

What comprises a competent background for the job of editing an employee publication? Let us pinpoint the answer by specifying that this is an editor who will spend all his time on the publication or on related jobs.

First of all he should have a broad classical education. Today, this almost certainly means a college degree, even though 18 per cent of those now editing major publications are getting along without one. Second, there must be training in news-gathering, interviewing, and writing. Seventy-one per cent of the editors presently in the field are believed to have had experience in newspaper work, publicity, or some other form of paid writing.[6] Third, there must be training in layout and design—not necessarily actual experience, although this is helpful.

Whether it is better to follow a liberal arts college education with graduate work in journalism or to attend a journalism school and follow up with actual daily newspaper experience is an open question. A liberal arts education gives the broad background so important in understanding a diversified employee audience; journalism school provides the theory of editing and basic training in the mechanics of production. Actual newspaper work rubs the sharp edges off the theoretical training and makes working under the pressure of deadlines and emergencies easier. Schools of journalism turn out fast writers, while newspaper experience adds skill in news-gathering; but without a liberal arts background, the writing may be dull and the news pedestrian.

What Should It Cost?

A rule of thumb sometimes heard among editors is that production costs should never exceed the price of a pack of cigarettes. This rule is out of date now. One survey in 1956 showed that the average cost of nine hundred leading publications, exclusive of salaries, was forty-eight cents per copy.[7]

Two things govern the cost of mechanical production: the amount of material that goes into the publication and the number of press impressions. The amount of material will dictate the amount of type to be set and (in the case of letterpress) the number of engravings. The use of color, the number of forms (multiples of four or eight pages), and the number of copies all have a bearing on the number of press impressions.

Although a magazine, page for page, generally costs more than a newspaper of exactly the same size, this extra cost lies almost entirely in the cost of paper and of engraving. All other costs are about the same. In 1958, a newspaper of four pages for five thousand employees could be produced for about nine cents a copy. If only five hundred copies were printed, the cost would rise to sixty cents a copy; and if fifty thousand copies were printed, the cost would drop to less than three cents a copy.

But, on the other hand, the cost of the newspaper for five thousand employees mounts proportionately when the number of pages is increased and soon reaches the point where the magazine of fewer pages would be less expensive.

The other significant cost is the staff requirement. One rule of thumb has been that a third of the total cost of the publication may be spent on salaries. The rule breaks down where extensive research and news-gathering are required to prepare the material. Probably the best practice is to hire a competent editor at the most favorable salary possible and tell him how large a budget the publication can justify on the basis of its primary purpose. He can then recommend the best format and frequency of publication. If he has a budget for a three-cent-a-copy newsletter, he should be able to produce a good one. If he has a budget for a dollar-a-copy magazine, he should be able to carry out a purpose broad enough to justify the expense.

WHAT KIND AND HOW OFTEN?

In 1956, a survey showed that 63 per cent of the house publications were magazines and that the proportion of newspapers—roughly 26 per cent—had not changed much in five years. Among nine hundred publications studied recently by the International Council of Industrial Editors, more frequent publication and a greater number of pages were the two significant trends noted.[8]

Magazine format is desirable for presenting both historical material and documentation by the case method. If, for instance, the purpose is to reduce the turnover rate and one of the arguments is the company's generous fringe benefit program, it might be highly effective to illustrate these benefits by citing individual instances of how they worked to the employees' advantage. A magazine, including its front cover, feature story, and more elaborate artwork, would offer decided advantages for this purpose.

A newspaper format has much to offer when timing is important. A newspaper is good for reporting day-to-day developments, such as progress in negotiating a new union contract. It is also effective for straight reporting where that alone will suffice to present the company story.

Newspapers have one disadvantage. All of us have been conditioned through the commercial press to expect news in a newspaper. When management is unwilling or unable to pass along the cold facts while they are still news, this format should be avoided. Omission of any significant development is so conspicuous in a newspaper that readers are quite likely to question the authenticity of everything else that is published.

Frequency of publication may range from daily to quarterly. Newspapers are usually weekly or biweekly. Magazines are usually monthly or bimonthly. The purpose of publishing should be the deciding factor in setting a publication schedule.

EFFECTIVENESS

There is still a great deal to be learned about the whole subject of reader response. This is no less true in relation to the readers we find in employee groups.

Employee Acceptance

It is a mistake to think of employees as a captive audience for informational material not essential to their work. They may read or refuse to read, believe or refuse to believe. In fact, so successful are employees in disguising their true feelings toward any management message that, without careful checking, audience acceptance of the employee publication is difficult to measure.

Employees seem to measure what they read in the employee publication by the respect they have for the source of the information and its consistency with their personal experience. This is true throughout administrative communication.

Two Messages

It has to be remembered that the employee publication always carries two messages. First, there is the information which it presents. Second, there is the impression created by the publication as a whole, which may be that the reader can believe the information or that he should not give it much credence.

When the reader finds himself in the position where the information says one thing but his total impression of the publication is quite the opposite, he is only momentarily confused. After that he merely ignores the information and assumes that the facts, if he had them, would be in line with his total impression.

The publication may say "People are our greatest asset," but the front cover shows the new five million dollar building without an employee in sight. Or, it may say "We are all one family," but the material handler is shown in dirty dungarees and the general manager in a custom-tailored suit. In such instances, the effort is not just wasted; actual harm has been done. To the extent that the employee noted the material at all, he has been convinced, first of all, that management and the editor put buildings ahead of people and managers ahead of production workers, and, further, that these things are done while management pretends an employee interest it does not actually feel.

Having once decided that the employee publication will be one of its methods of communication, a company should be prepared to give this medium the funds, attention, management support, and sincerity of purpose necessary to make it pay its way. Otherwise, it would be far better never to start, for the choice is not between good communication and no communication but between communication that influences a desired course of action and communication that makes the employee suspicious of what management says.

THE BASIC ELEMENTS

The four basic elements that go into every house publication are the material, the writing, the presentation, and the distribution. They are the means by which the primary purpose of the publication is implemented. They call for the professional skill and experience which the qualified industrial editor supplies.

The Material

Selection of material is always carried out with one question uppermost: Does it promote the primary purpose? Along with the information are involved the things which help to create a favorable climate in which the information can be most effective.

Once chosen, the subject has to be researched far beyond the dictates of space limitations. Arguments in favor of the suggestion system mean little to the employee, but the names and actual awards will carry conviction. Generalized editorials on safety shoes may cover the writer's ignorance, but they are dull reading. A photograph of the individual employee whose foot was saved by his safety shoes is a clear picture.

The item that says "The company is planting two trees in front of the office" is defective for several reasons. Aside from the fact that people, not companies, plant trees, the sentence gives no indication of what kind of trees or what office. Further research would have disclosed facts concerning the trees that would have solved these problems. If they were sixty-foot sugar maples, the moving itself would be an engineering feat. If they had to be planted alongside the company's water main, there is an interesting contradiction in the fact that they are watered by sprinklers even though the main passes within a few feet of their roots. To assure that copy will be read, the editor needs a native curiosity about everything he hears and an acquired ability to think the way his readers do.

The interests of the audience govern whether to print or omit such things as personal items and organizational changes. Do the personal items show that the people who work for the organization are good people to work with? Do the organizational changes show that this is a good place to work, that the company rewards long service and promotes from within, that its executives are people qualified to be leaders? These are some of the questions, and by no means all of them, that the editor has to answer in deciding the character of the material to be published.

The Writing

Nicholas Samstag, promotion director of *Time*, has said that "the first duty of every editor is to get his publication read." In the employee publication this may be taken to mean that the writing must be as interesting, objective, and pleasing to the audience as the trained writer can make it. Someone must pause long enough to start reading. The editor counts his publication well on its way to success when the employee who only intended to look finds himself halfway through the first paragraph before he knows it.

There is a good deal of work to be done in the area of writing and presentation if the employee publication is to compete for the employee-reader with the popular newsstand magazines.

Presentation

No matter how thoroughly an article has been researched or how effectively it has been written, it is so much waste paper if it is not presented in such a way that it invites reading. The employee publication, arriving in the employee's home along with *Life* and other commercial magazines, competes with them and with television for the employee's leisure time. Format, layout, and design all play their part, for the publication must carry a message to those who read and to the many who only look. Take the utility company's publication that carries on its front cover the picture of the grimy but smiling lineman, complete with steel helmet, safety belt, and safety gloves. The lineman-employee looking at the picture identifies himself with the man on the cover and with the company and gets a mental picture of the well-dressed lineman (the cheerful, healthy lineman he likes to think he is), and such a lineman wears safety equipment.

Distribution

The effectiveness of the employee publication depends to a large extent upon its reaching the maximum audience under the most favorable conditions. This brings up the choice between in-plant and mail distribution.

In-plant distribution is ordinarily about 80 per cent effective. Attractive packaging will increase this percentage. So will substantial size and material of interest to wives and families. Magazines seem to make out better than newspapers with in-plant distribution. It is estimated that only about 20 per cent of the leading employee publications are distributed this way.[9] Dividends from in-plant distribution include more enthusiastic employee participation and greater employee discussion of subject matter, fair test of publication acceptance, and no mailing costs.

In spite of these dividends, mailing is preferred by most companies, and over 15 per cent use first-class mail. Publications sent to the home usually have a larger family audience. A mailed publication reaches 80 per cent of the employee audience outright, and another 10 per cent get the information second hand through wives or other members of the family who read the publication and relay what it says.[10] Newspapers of four pages, being easily wrinkled or damaged by rain and brief enough for reading in full on the job, probably need to be mailed to the home if they are to get there regularly. Other advantages of home mailing include the avoidance of plant housekeeping problems, the maintenance of correct home addresses of employees, a general assurance of some family reading, and, if attractively packaged, a better-than-average chance of reading a second time.

Testing Reader Response

However successful by other standards, the publication should be tested from time to time for reader response. Free offers, with or without coupons, are quite effective if they involve some item that has wide audience appeal. Spot checks, such as picking one department each month and talking to every tenth person in it about the current issue, are revealing but time-consuming.

Questionnaires are usually disappointing unless very skilfully handled. (See chapter xiv on employee opinion polling.) If included in the issue and mailed home, considerable promotion and explanation is necessary. Post card questionnaires are particularly unsatisfactory. Offering an inducement for returning the questionnaire will increase the response substantially.

Whatever method is used, the results of any broad readership survey should be reported in the publication.

Employee publications, and handbooks as well, need to be woven into the broad fabric of administrative communication. This is partly a task for editors, but they need the facts and opinions which only their superiors can give them.

Employee publications and handbooks are subsidiary to an organization's central body of policies and procedures, as set forth in manuals, circulars, organization charts, and job descriptions. If editors are to interpret this material effectively, they must be able to obtain it from authoritative sources. An editor is to management what an engineer is to science. Neither the editor nor the engineer can create sound interpretations and applications without proof to back them up.

Selected Readings

BOOKS AND MONOGRAPHS

ARGYRIS, CHRIS. *The Present State of Research in Human Relations in Industry.* New Haven: Yale University, Labor and Management Center, 1954.

Outline of human relations research in thirteen universities and elsewhere.

BENTLEY, GARTH. *Editing the Company Publication.* New York: Harper & Bros., 1953.

BIKLEN, PAUL F., and BRETH, ROBERT D. *The Successful Employee Publication.* New York: McGraw-Hill Book Co., 1945.

This, and the book above, include step-by-step instructions for employee publication editors.

HOVLAND, C. I.; JANIS, IRVING L.; and KELLEY, HAROLD H. *Communication and Persuasion.* New Haven: Yale University Press, 1953.

Interim report on the Yale Communication Research Program.

More Business through House Organs. Boston: S. D. Warren Co., 1955.

Information on mechanical production problems.

Printers' Ink Directory of House Organs. New York: Printers' Ink Publishing Co., 1958.

List of house publications classified by location, name, and company. Frequently revised.

WHYTE, WILLIAM H., JR., and the EDITORS OF "FORTUNE." *Is Anybody Listening?* New York: Simon & Schuster, Inc., 1952.

The early chapters discuss how and why U.S. business "fumbles" when it talks with human beings.

ARTICLES

ALLISON, THEODORE. "Employee Publications: There's Room for Improvement!" *Personnel,* Vol. 31 (July, 1954), pp. 56–59.

A criticism of employee publications that are pretty to look at but lack vitality and impact.

BACHRACH, HENRY B. "Company Editors Today Proud of Profit Showing," *Personnel Journal,* Vol. 34 (March, 1956), pp. 368–71.

Report of cases in which employee publications contribute to company profits.

HAAS, GEORGE E., and ZAGAT, HERMINE. "Trade Union Journals vs. Company Magazines," *Personnel,* Vol. 34 (May–June, 1958), pp. 59–65.

Comparative content analysis of company and union publications.

HALLEY, WILLIAM C. "Lost Chords on the House Organ," *Public Relations Journal,* Vol. 12 (July, 1956), pp. 13–14.

Examples of stories which produced tangible results in solving plant and operational problems.

HEUSSER, AUDREY E. "Editing for Employees Who Read Hardly Anything," *Personnel Journal,* Vol. 32 (April, 1954), pp. 423–27.

Problems peculiar to the audience of reluctant readers.

————. "Open Letter to a Novice House Organ Editor," *Personnel Journal,* Vol. 34 (September, 1955), pp. 131–36.

Relative importance in the employee publication of messages that really influence the readers.

"How To Play the House Organ," *Fortune,* Vol. 46 (October, 1952), pp. 144–47, 182 ff. (Reprinted in PERRIN STRYKER [ed.], *A Guide to Modern Management Methods* [New York: McGraw-Hill Book Co., 1954], pp. 145–61.)

Statistics and comments on the expanding field of company publications.

LYMAN, ROGER T. "Of, for and *by* Employees," *Personnel,* Vol. 28 (January, 1952), pp. 319–21.

An employee periodical published by the employees themselves.

SCHOLZ, WILLIAM. "How To Make Employee Publications Pay Off," *Personnel,* Vol. 32 (March, 1956), pp. 449–57.

Needed improvements: reader rewards, less mental effort, more evidence of validation.

VICKER, RAY. "Company Magazines," *Wall Street Journal,* March 24, 1955, pp. 1, 8.

Ways in which employee publications perk production, boost sales, shave costs, and reduce plant accidents.

PART III / *Communication Upward*
                                   and Inward

In order to maintain control and make decisions, executives need to know what is going on in their organization. As a general rule, necessary information does not flow upward and inward in the most useful fashion, either because of defects in the techniques used, lack of understanding regarding their use, or because of social and psychological barriers to communication. There are various methods for getting information to flow upward and inward efficiently, and the principal ones are treated here.

X / Communication and Control

> The essence of control is action which adjusts operations to predetermined standards, and its basis is information in the hands of managers.
>
> DOUGLAS S. SHERWIN[1]

IN THE initial pages of this book, the communication process was described in terms of the transfer of information from source to destination, from communicator to communicatee. We referred there to the two-way aspect of communication and mentioned the element of response or feedback.

In this chapter, and in the succeeding chapters of this part of the book, the emphasis will be on response and feedback. For administrative communication is something more than transferring information from source to destination; it is also a process of feeding information back to the original source in a never ending cycle.

CONTROL AND EQUILIBRIUM

A clue to the subtle nature of communication and control in human pursuits is seen in the need to use models to describe the process. Interestingly, the models have in large part reflected what their inventors viewed as aspects of human behavior. Thus the giant computer is an "electronic brain," and data is stored in its "memory."

Figure 14 is a diagram by Kenneth Boulding which to the biologist is a model of the process of homeostasis, that is, the mechanism whereby an organism seeks to maintain an equilibrium in relation to its environment. To the physicist this is a model of feedback, a concept developed by Wiener, Shannon, and Weaver in connection with their study of cybernetics.

Cybernetics, from the Greek word meaning "steersman," has been defined by Wiener as communication and control.

In looking at this diagram one can think of the "datum" as the temperature in the dining room, and the "receptor of information" as the thermostat on the wall which has been preset to seventy degrees. If the temperature in the room falls below seventy, the thermostatic mechanism "tells" the furnace

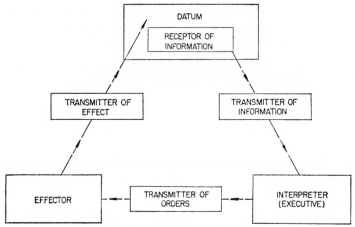

FIG. 14.—The homeostatic mechanism. (From Kenneth E. Boulding, *The Organizational Revolution,* Harper & Bros., 1952. Reproduced by permission.)

control switch (the "interpreter" or "executive" in the diagram) to turn on the furnace. The furnace (the "effector" in the diagram) goes into operation and, through the pipes or ducts, sends additional heat into the room (the feedback), changing the body of datum to match that requested by the receptor of information. The thermostatic mechanism now "notifies" the furnace control switch to turn off the furnace, and that condition continues until the heat again falls below seventy degrees.[2]

The thermostat is perhaps the most familiar example of

what have come to be known as process control mechanisms, which today are installed in an increasing number of processing industries—pipelines, refineries, chemical and pharmaceutical plants, and even steel mills.

It is easy to see how this model applies to communication. An executive has certain standards (e.g., standards of performance or inventory balances), like the seventy-degree setting on a thermostat. When the conditions within the organization markedly deviate from those standards, an action cycle is initiated through the vehicle of communication. The deviations are signaled to the executive, perhaps by dots or lines on a chart or a graph. The executive then orders the appropriate effector elements of the organization to take the necessary remedial actions. These actions are intended to affect the body of datum in a manner which will bring conditions back into line with the standards.

This same analogy has been drawn by Sherwin:

A process control mechanism thus acts to adjust operations to predetermined standards and does so on the basis of information it receives. In a parallel way, information reaching a manager gives him the opportunity for corrective action and is his basis for control. He cannot exercise control without such information. And he cannot do a complete job of managing without controlling.[3]

The value of this model is that it dramatizes the element of response or feedback in a closed system. Producing and service organizations are very largely, but not exclusively, closed systems. In mass communications (advertising or commercial motion pictures, for example) the element of response is often delayed, sometimes absent, and generally elusive. An advertiser measures his response in terms of sales, but he cannot always be sure to which advertisement the public has responded. In the field of administrative communication the element of response or feedback is generally rapid and tangible, and never absent. Just as a buyer's response is likely to be non-verbal, so may be the response of a member of an organization. The way in which work is performed is a response just as is the rendering of a report about it.

CONTROL AND REAPPRAISAL

Administration in general, and administrative communication in particular, have already been affected by the theories of homeostasis and cybernetics. (The reader is referred to the "Selected Readings" for the articles by Karl W. Deutsch.) The cyclical nature of the administrative process has also been evolving quite independently in administrative theory. Indeed, Urwick has called it "perhaps the most arresting single fact about modern ideas of management." He was referring specifically to Fayol's original conception of the various aspects of administration operating in a cycle. Fayol's cycle started with forecasting, then went on to planning, organizing, co-ordinating, commanding, and controlling. Thence to forecasting again; for, as Urwick put it, "much of the material thrown up by a modern system of control is as valuable for looking forward as for looking at the past."[4]

In 1956, Chancellor Litchfield carried the Fayol-Urwick suggestion forward by an important step. Litchfield's cycle starts with decision-making, then moves in turn through programming, communicating, controlling, and reappraising. The term "control" is reserved for the activities of standard-setting and enforcement. The "looking-forward" aspect of control is provided for by the activity of "reappraising," i.e., reconsidering basic decisions. These are the decisions, of course, which led to the programs that are being controlled.[5] Thus, an organization can be performing satisfactorily to meet its program objectives, but are the programs themselves still aimed properly at meeting the needs at this later time? One is reminded of a helmsman keeping a ship on a straight course—but not in the right direction.

Contemporaneously with Litchfield's work, Sherwin developed a similar two-part analysis of the control process, diagrammed in Figure 15. Control is defined as "action directed toward bringing operations into conformity with predetermined standards; it is exercised by managers; and its basis is information in their hands after-the-fact." Sherwin's process of "aiming

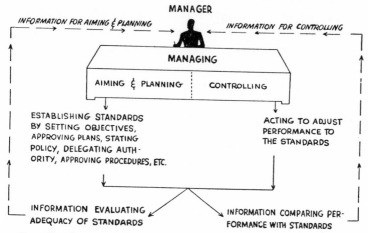

Fig. 15.—The meaning of control. (From Douglas E. Sherwin, *Dun's Review and Modern Industry*. Reproduced by permission of the author.)

and planning" is like reappraising. It differs from control (which could conceivably bring operations into conformity with obsolete standards for obsolete programs) in that it results in new decisions leading to new programs with new standards.[6]

CONTROL AND DECENTRALIZATION

Since World War II there has been a marked trend toward decentralization. This trend has involved not only geographical decentralization but managerial decentralization as well. The latter may or may not be geographical; it is equated so completely with delegation that the words "decentralization" and "delegation" have come to be used synonymously.[7]

Decentralization has some practical and some theoretical advantages. It has been indorsed for the way it places decision-making authority nearer the locus of operations. As a corollary, it has been favored for the way in which it frees managers from close supervision, thereby encouraging their exercise of initiative and broadening their view of administration, both processes contributing to the development of candidates for promotion in the top areas of general management. Another benefit sometimes mentioned is the increased identification with and participation in local civic and community activities.

Profound theoretical reasons lead us to want and seek more decentralization. Peter Drucker, Marshall Dimock, David Lilienthal, and Bertrand Russell are among the thoughtful observers who have spoken out in favor of it. They have said that decentralization is so vital for the preservation of our free society—for the protection of the individual from the dangers of bigness—that we dare not foresake it or even compromise it.

No doubt many organizations have chosen decentralization not as a way of life but as a way out of a morass of red tape and communication failures. Decentralization was viewed by these organizations as a way of solving a few big problems by converting them into a greater number of small ones. But the small problems have not stayed small and decentralization has been anything but a universal success. The missing link has been communication and control.

Managerial decentralization requires, above all else, an effective system of communication and control. Superiors must not only be willing to delegate but must possess the administrative machinery to make delegation work. Willingness is largely psychological, reflecting past experiences of the potential delegator. Perhaps just one error by a subordinate years before has foreclosed any subsequent attempts at delegation. The executive who will delegate (or decentralize) must select his subordinates wisely, insure their identification with the organization's objectives, and stop supervising and start controlling.

The function of control involves, as has been indicated, standard-setting and enforcement. Standards in the present context are of two general kinds. First, there are the traditional comparative measures of performance, of which the most popular are the following: historical standards (last year, last month), interdepartmental standards, intercompany standards, engineered standards (e.g., a machine gun will fire so many rounds per minute, giving us a measure of military capability), and goals and forecasts. Besides these, managers control adherence to a group of elements making up what Sherwin has called "the framework of management." Included are objectives, plans, policies, procedures, job descriptions, organization charts, and so forth.[8]

Both kinds of standards must exist and be known, for adherence to them and performance in accordance with them measure successful delegation and decentralization. The establishment of such standards and their enforcement are difficult and complex activities. They depend, as in the enunciation of policies and procedures, primarily on downward communication; and in the preparation and analysis of performance and control reports, they depend primarily on upward communication.

The Prospect of Recentralization

We are witnessing today the rapid introduction of large-scale and medium-scale computers. These computers are central to the operation of elaborate data-processing systems which can and do process massive volumes of data at fantastic speeds. They promise a way out of the paper-work morasses that sometimes forced decentralization. Thus decisions can again be made centrally and with sufficient speed to satisfy operating needs.

Some companies, having centralized their data processing,

have been able to inaugurate a policy of managerial recentralization. The question which we can only ask here is whether this signals a trend. One prominent observer, editor of the management department of *Business Week,* was voicing not only his own opinion when he wrote, "Centralization of decisions, therefore, once again becomes possible. It isn't likely that top management, with such a tool, will forego the chance to centralize merely to satisfy an outmoded philosophy of decentralization that no longer meets the needs of the company."[9] Other observers believe that the centralization of data processing will not be so far-reaching in its effect. The degree to which smaller data-processing equipment is introduced will no doubt affect the total picture. The final choice between centralization and decentralization remains a matter of policy, not a problem for a computer.

For many years to many people the word "control" has had an unpleasant, restrictive connotation. One of the dilemmas of administration has been to secure the benefits of control without having people resent being controlled.

We need to foster the concept of control as a positive, liberating element. Sir Geoffrey Vickers has made a strong case for "control and initiative," pointing out that only a justified confidence in a system of controls gives an executive liberty to exercise initiative. A novice skater, according to Vickers, is so busy controlling that he cannot innovate; the professional has such a perfect set of controls, and obeys them so much more closely, that he do what he pleases and can even execute maneuvers that shift his center of balance most violently.[10]

At the other end of the managerial spectrum are the man and woman who are being controlled. They should perceive, according to Sherwin,

that as their authority is broadened, their superiors must place increased reliance on control as a means of safeguarding their own accountability. But at the same time, supervision of their activities by

superiors becomes less close. . . . As the real nature of control becomes better understood, managers will come to recognize that their
being subject to it in increasing measure is as sure a sign as any of
their progress in the organization and in the fulfillment of their position.[11]

Selected Readings

BOOKS AND MONOGRAPHS

BOULDING, KENNETH E. *The Organizational Revolution.* New York:
Harper & Bros., 1952. Preface, "Internal Determinants of Behavior."

The basic pattern of control mechanisms.

DIMOCK, MARSHALL E. *Free Enterprise and the Administrative State.*
University, Ala.: University of Alabama Press, 1951. Chap. iii,
"The Limits of Decentralization."

Discusses decentralization as one means of counteracting the bad
effects of overbigness.

RUSSELL, BERTRAND. *Authority and the Individual.* London: George
Allen & Unwin, Ltd., 1949.

Condemns the stultification of personality development in large organizations with their elaborate controls over subordinates.

URWICK, L. *The Elements of Administration.* New York and London:
Harper & Bros., 1943. Chap. vii, "Control."

The concept of control in modern administration.

WIENER, NORBERT. *Cybernetics: Control and Communication in the
Animal and the Machine.* New York: John Wiley & Sons, 1948.

———. *The Human Use of Human Beings: Cybernetics and Society.*
Garden City: Doubleday & Company, 1954.

ARTICLES

BRECH, E. F. L. "The Balance between Centralization and Decentralization in Managerial Control," *British Management Review,* Vol.
12 (July, 1954), pp. 187–98.

How successful decentralization depends on communication and
control.

DEUTSCH, KARL W. "Communication Theory and Social Science,"

American Journal of Orthopsychiatry, Vol. 22 (July, 1952), pp. 469–83.

Analysis of all organized activity according to the cybernetics model.

DEUTSCH, KARL W. "On Communication Models in the Social Sciences," *Public Opinion Quarterly,* Vol. 16 (Fall, 1952), pp. 356–80.

The communications approach to the study of organizations.

FOLLETT, MARY PARKER. "The Process of Control," chap. viii in *Papers on the Science of Administration,* ed. LUTHER GULICK and L. URWICK. New York: Institute of Public Administration, 1937.

Emphasizes the constantly changing relationship between the controllers and the controlled.

LITCHFIELD, EDWARD H. "Notes on a General Theory of Administration," *Administrative Science Quarterly,* Vol. I (June, 1956), pp. 3–29.

The administrative process as a cycle—decision-making, programming, communicating, controlling, reappraising.

PFIFFNER, JOHN M. "The 'Third Dimension' of Organization," *Personnel,* Vol. 28 (March, 1952), pp. 391–99.

The structural, procedural, and psychological aspects of decentralization and delegation.

SHERWIN, DOUGLAS S. "The Meaning of Control," *Dun's Review and Modern Industry,* Vol. 67 (January, 1956), pp. 45–46, 83–84.

The constructive nature of control.

VICKERS, SIR GEOFFREY. "Initiative and Control," *The Listener* [of the B.B.C.], Vol. 55 (January 19, 1956), pp. 93–94.

Control is prerequisite to stability, which is prerequisite to the exercise of initiative.

XI / *Administrative Reporting*

LENT UPSON once commented that "the idea of operating reports was doubtless thought up by the first paleolithic administrator who sent somebody to do something over a hill where he couldn't be watched."[1] One of Socrates' legends was about the shepherd Gyges at a meeting where the shepherds had gathered "to send their monthly report about the flocks to the king." How far this legend antedated Socrates, himself an Athenian of the fifth century B.C., we do not know.

Reporting is crucially important in the United States, where the President's only authority to control the heads of the executive departments—short of dismissal—is in the reporting clause of the Constitution. ("He may require the opinion, in writing, of the principal officer in each of the executive departments, upon any subject relating to the duties of their respective offices.") George Washington had been in office less than six weeks when he had to use this authority to get from his cabinet officers a "general idea of the affairs of the United States."[2] "To whom does he report?" is now a routine question asked in every management audit or classification and salary survey.

THE NEED FOR REPORTS

Experience has shown that orders and instructions—like laws—are not complied with automatically or uniformly. But even in the event of absolute compliance, the results may not be those that were expected. Failure may be traceable to the basic decision, to the instructions that were given, to some unforeseeable human frailty, or to changed circumstances which force reappraisal of the decision and the program based upon

161

it. Only as the executive receives information from below can he weigh results, make new decisions, issue new instructions, and take whatever other action he sees fit. But specialization has limited the executive's horizon, as it has all others, so that he has no ready access to information circulating at lower levels.

Reporting is mentioned in all the lists of central control devices, of which there have been many in recent years. Reports are used to measure performance and to control costs, to serve the needs for both long-term planning and current scheduling of work, to check conformance with organizational policy and procedure, to transmit information of special interest or importance, and to facilitate the co-ordination of widely separated operations. Reports are also used to establish written records of events that may have future reference value for anything from the substantiation of a patent to a dismissal.

At lower levels it is not so often necessary, from the standpoint of productive efficiency alone, to have systematic information about the work of other segments of the organization. But at each higher level information from and about other departments becomes more and more helpful. Efficiency at the top depends to a great extent on the quantity and quality of information flowing from the remote corners of an organization to a glass-topped desk in a spacious office.[3]

TYPES OF REPORTS

Administrative reporting lies within the limits of administrative communication. That is to say, systems of administrative reporting are established and maintained by a formal organization and are intended primarily for use within that organization. Instructions sometimes overflow the organizational boundaries to apply outside; the same is often true with administrative reports. But one can differentiate between a controller's report to top management and top management's report to the Securities and Exchange Commission. The former is an administrative report, whereas the latter is not.

Reports may be oral, written, or recorded; or a combination of media may be used. The reporting processes are essentially the same in all media; and the presentation in the succeeding paragraphs is based primarily on the written report, which is the most popular form. Through the written report an item of business is made a matter of record and is thereby useful to a number of persons at one time, or to one or more persons referring to it at different times.

Performance, Planning, and Information Reports

Classified by purpose, reports fall into three groups. In the first group are performance and control reports. Reports in this category measure performance against established standards and answer the colloquial question: "How are we doing?" A differentiation is sometimes made between (a) the performance or activity report covering one's own unit, plant, or department, and (b) the parallel report rendered by a staff control unit, such as the internal auditor or the budget director.

There are both long-term and current planning reports. The former typically addresses itself to the period five or ten years into the future. These reports are concerned with identifying anticipated problems, presenting alternative ways of meeting them, and recommending current and future actions in support of one or another alternative. A popular short-term planning report is the one prepared annually in support of budget requests. Here we find statements of the past year's progress toward long-term objectives and projections of accomplishments in the same or in other areas during the year ahead.

Conceivably all the information needed by the executive heads of an organization could be furnished in the performance and planning reports. But some information is not translated readily or at all into concrete terms of performance or planning. It is difficult to say whether this is inherent in the nature of the material or is a defect in the basic reporting system. An information report typically contains news items and ideas incidental to the reporter's area of activity. The reporter assumes that the information may be useful, but he does not presume to know exactly how or where. For this reason, information reports are generally given wider circulation than are other reports.

Regular and Special Reports

Reports are either regular (periodic or recurring) or special (non-recurring). Regular reports may cover periods of varying length, from annual, semiannual, and quarterly down through monthly, weekly, and daily. The monthly report is the one most widely used, and the weekly report is the one used less than any other type, including even the daily report. Annual, semiannual, and quarterly reports fall in between in their usage.[4]

Special, non-recurring, or "when occurring" reports cover events rather than periods of time. The results of an employee opinion poll or of an advertising campaign would be likely subjects of special reports. When a project is assigned to someone, he may be required to submit reports on its status at indeterminate dates, such as at the beginning, at the halfway mark, and at the conclusion. The intervals between these reports would be governed not only by the calendar but by the rate at which the funds are spent or by the reporter's judgment of events.

Statistical, Financial, and Narrative Reports

All administrative reporting is of three basic types—statistical, financial, and narrative. Under statistical fall those reports of transactions cast in quantitative terms other than money. Illustrative of this group are reports of units of work done or items produced, which might include personnel transactions, volume of traffic or correspondence, or number of complaints, returns, and adjustments. Many activities that take place do not appear in financial reports, and yet they can be reported statistically.

Other reports are cast in financial terms: increases, decreases, and balances in cash, investments, accounts receivable and payable, and inventories; income and expense; budget accounts and profits or losses. Analysts and cost accountants can combine statistical and financial data to develop a wide range of cost data: historical costs, standard costs, class costs, and variances. These are the data that are so useful for budgeting and budgetary control.

Narrative reporting is used not only for information reports but also to supplement and interpret statistical and financial reports. Advisory reporting, which goes beyond interpretation, is largely narrative in form. Supplementary narrative comments, according to a Controllers Institute survey, are used in 21 per cent of all the financial reports covered.[5]

PROBLEMS IN ADMINISTRATIVE REPORTING

The guiding principles advanced in chapter iii apply to reporting just as they did to order-giving. Obviously reports should be clear, consistent, adequate, and interesting. It is not so obvious that the order-giver is just as responsible for receiving, accepting, and responding to reports as he is for giving orders. One of the major things that people need to be told is how to report.

Certain problems are particularly bothersome in reporting. Some of the problems, such as timing and distribution, are largely procedural. Others, such as distortion or overemphasis on reporting at the expense of the job, derive from human factors. At many points the procedural and social problems overlap, and permeating all of them is the question of how the use of formal channels affects reports.

Consolidating and Interpreting Reports

The formal reporting process begins when the first record is made. It may be just a notation of production—merit rating forms reviewed or employee handbooks printed and distributed. At the other extreme, the initial record may be of an extensive counseling interview or of the investigation of a request for a wage increase for thousands of employees.

The original data are assembled and consolidated for groups of workers, for particular categories of information, and for specified periods of time. Further consolidations occur as the reports proceed up the line, and the original data become less and less identifiable. The more levels there are, the more the digestion and interpretation. "Between the sheer volume of detail to be selected from and the successive stages of selection at each level, the man at the top, the Big Boss, ends up with only a vague and highly generalized picture of what is going on."[6]

Although a steady stream of reports should flow to every executive, there is a danger that they will drown him. A good picture of an executive about to drown in reports, along with other communications, is seen in the following comment by a management consulting firm describing the office of the president of a large and sprawling organization:

> During the first several months of 1948, there was a monthly average of about 1,500 individual letters, reports, forms and other written materials—approximately 60 each working day—requiring his personal attention. . . . During this same period there existed a continuous backlog of 200 to 500 matters awaiting decision, in addition to a normal backlog of 15 to 20 outgoing telephone calls and 50 to 70 scheduled office interviews.

In a situation such as the one described above, the recipient consciously or unconsciously applies his own system of priorities; he will examine only a few of his reports thoroughly, give most of the others a hurried reading, and barely glance at some as he pushes them aside.

It is clear that the multitude of reports must be consolidated and interpreted—a quantitative and qualitative filtering task for which the hierarchical organization is potentially well adapted. Unfortunately, as reports move upward, distortion creeps in, and the distortion may be so subtle that even the person who is alert to the danger may not recognize it either in the reports he receives or in those he transmits. There is a constant and commendable effort to make reports brief and interesting so that they may compete successfully for the superior's limited time and attention. But, in the process, too many reports become biased in favor of those things most likely to attract attention and favor.

The person transmitting a report must discern the fine line that separates information for information's sake and information needed for control and planning. One guide for reporters lists these four essential types of information:

1. Completion of assignments
2. Progress on long-term or continuing projects
3. Deviations from approved plans
4. Anticipated problems.[7]

Another formula that has been offered is that "each member of an organization needs to report to his superior officer a little more than enough to meet the needs of that officer, so that both the subordinate and the superior may be certain that the superior knows about and has access to everything essential to his judgment."[8] This assumes that the superior will familiarize his subordinates with the nature of his responsibilities. Otherwise the reports coming to him will be limited by the reporters' positional blindness.

The executive has often been called a "generalist" to distinguish him from the specialists below. He is in fact a specialist also—a specialist in dealing with abstractions of all sorts rather than with the raw material of the organization's work. It is in this role that he leans heavily on reports which, when they get to him, are so largely abstractions. The success of the organization depends to a great extent on the ability of the executive to interpret these abstractions, to visualize the facts behind a bar on a graph or a line on a chart so that he can act. The underlying situation may involve questions of organizational structure, policy, or procedure that he alone, at the top of the hierarchy, can fully comprehend and do something about.

Timing and Distribution

Reports exist primarily to help an executive exercise control (an immediate matter), also to improve the quality of his planning (often current but not, usually, immediate), and finally to give him a variety of incidental or long-term information. If a report is long delayed in its preparation or transmission, it ceases to be a control medium; if it is delayed too long, it becomes a historical document.

One need not look beyond the reporting system itself for causes of delay. Channels are clogged with a multiplicity of reports: some are new, others vestigial, some overlap others, many are simply copies of reports written for someone else. If formal reporting is to be consistent with concepts of formal organization, each activity (or major aspect thereof) should be the subject of a single report, and each report should be aimed at a well-chosen target—the person or persons responsible for taking action. Information copies, if there are any, should be so labeled, or summaries should be furnished.

There is justifiable confusion as to the proper routing of reports in complex organizations that have secondary formal channels. Typical is the organization that has, in addition to its central line structure, staff or technical specialists in the central office and in its field offices. Should reports flow directly from one personnel officer to another, or should they be made to flow through command channels? If, in fact, the staff specialists are free to work together outside the line, it would be impractical to delay reports simply to make them conform arbitrarily to one set of channels. It is probably wiser to establish parallel reporting channels, one for command and the other for staff, marking each copy of the report accordingly. This practice is already prevalent in many large organizations, including the military.

Corrective measures.—Timing and distribution can be improved greatly by means of comprehensive report schedules indicating the activity being reported on, the title, number, and nature of each report, the dates for submission, the distribution, and the action to be taken by each designated recipient.[9] By just such a systematic approach, one corporation was able to reduce the number of its reports from 78 to 30 and the number of copies from 546 to 74.[10]

Another approach is to provide for a continuing review of the reporting requirements to make certain that coverage is adequate but not excessive. The Dime Savings Bank of Brooklyn has a statements committee that performs a periodic audit of all recurrent reports and statements, and it is usually able to eliminate some or to curtail the distribution of others. The committee is made up of officers and department heads serving on a rotating basis. Two or three men are changed at a time so that new people are always getting the benefits of the committee's work but the committee has enough experienced men to accomplish its objectives. There is hardly a better way to broaden executive horizons than through a study of an organization's system of administrative reports.

A case has been made against reports-improvement programs which accept as a starting point the reports already in existence. The suggested alternative is to make a fresh analysis of the information needs of the executives. Neuschel has developed a program which requires, first, isolating the four to six critical factors on which success of the enterprise depends; second, breaking down each factor into its important and measurable components; and, third, establishing yardsticks to measure performance of each of these components. The application of this approach in one company resulted in a reduction of recurring reports from 560 to 140 and the number of copies from 2,800 to 460. In this instance, the number of reports received by the president was reduced from 83 to 18.[11]

Reductions in the number of reports and in the number of copies should have a favorable effect on the speed of reporting. A number of techniques can be used specifically to speed up accounting reports in non-financial organizations. Amounts can be rounded off to the nearest dollar; reports can be handwritten and photocopied rather than typed; figures for the previous month and year can be filled in well before the closing date; all mathematical work can be assumed correct—and checked later; and some closing entries, such as overhead items and office payroll, can be prepared ahead of time.[12]

One difficulty for which there is no ready remedy is that external agencies often require extensive and unco-ordinated reports that depend, in turn, on internal administrative reports. Businessmen and local government officials alike complain (not always justifiably) of the reporting requirements imposed on them by federal and state agencies.

Distortion

Although the consolidating and interpreting processes can produce information that varies in its correctness, in practice we find a degree of distortion far greater than any produced by the effects of channels alone.

There is no assurance that all report-worthy items will be reported. For a given reporter, an incident may be without significance; or, if he has no stenographic or clerical assistance, he may find it too difficult to prepare a report. Rarely does an organization train a person in the reasons for and methods of reporting before moving him into a position requiring such knowledge. And because he does not know how to prepare reports, how or why they are used, or whether they are used at all, he has little incentive to bother.

The circumstance most likely to insure that an item will be reported is the belief that the superior already knows or will hear of it through some other source. Few things can be more painful than having the boss find out something about your department from someone else; and the boss will be embarrassed as well. Many administrative practices have been devised to provide secondary channels that will serve the twofold purpose of securing unreported information and impressing on supervisors the fact that they withhold information at their peril. None of these devices comes to grips with the underlying causes of non-reporting; so long as there are social and psychological obstacles to the free flow of information, there is no limit to the number of secondary channels that would have to be employed.

One psychological obstacle is fear of authority—fear of being fired, of not being promoted, of being disciplined, of displeasing a superior. Neither unionization nor civil service completely removes this barrier to free communication.[13] The subordinate must often choose between reporting what may be interpreted as a failure and taking a chance on keeping the information under cover indefinitely.

Other distortions, not unrelated to the feeling of fear, are stimulated by the need to make a good showing and the desire to report those things that the superior wants to hear. The *good* showing is easily confused with the *big* showing, causing the reporter to transmit lengthy accounts of all the minutiae of his accomplishments. Events that may be interpreted as failures, if reported at all, are skilfully understated and sandwiched between successes. Through experience the subordinate learns how much to report, what interests the boss most, how far one can safely go in confessing his own failures and in pointing out the boss's mistakes, and how co-workers at the same level report. In some memoirs on the beginning of the end of Hitler's Russian campaign, there is this account: "From the earliest days of the Russian campaign, Hitler, Keitel and Jodl were being deceived by the generals commanding the front-line troops. They reported what they thought Hitler would like to hear, not what in fact was happening."[14]

Distortion is a cumulative process, starting at the bottom and growing as it ascends the hierarchy, because those at the top foster it through a multitude of expressions and actions. As reports move upward, the implications of distortion become increasingly serious; at the top, distorted reports can corrupt the entire organizational effort. A former official in the American occupation of Japan has told about his experiences in reporting on successful Russian propaganda efforts in the Japanese press. "In theory," said this former official, "our reports would be passed along to higher authority and finally would become part of the material to be read by occupation and Pentagon officials. But anything that analyzed what the Russians were doing seldom saw the light of day." There was no special reason, this man concluded, other than the "Pollyanna attitude" of American propaganda officers who "wanted to show how well they were doing."[15]

As work groups become more closely knit over the years, there is an increasing tendency for members to "cover up" for each other. Wherever there are large numbers of white-collar workers we find the practice of checking in and out for others. These actions, and others like them, do not appear in the attendance report that is signed by the office manager and sent up through channels as an authentic document. One industrial engineer believed that his long-term relationships with the line operators justified his "covering up" for them in the report of a breakdown that was clearly their fault. Presumably that would cause the operating personnel to have a better opinion of the staff engineers and be more co-operative.[16] Knowledge that such misrepresentations are being made could eventually undercut any system of administrative reporting; only ignorance of such practices permits the entire system to maintain its seeming integrity.

Specialization in Writing and Reading Reports

In recent years there has been an ever widening acceptance of the staff principle, with a steady growth in the number and size of staff units. We find today that executives at the apex of each hierarchy and subhierarchy have staffs of one or many specialists, who are set apart from operations with the idea of being of service to the line organization. Writing and reading reports are among the first tasks to be pulled out of the line and assigned to report specialists in staff positions.

The implications of separating reporting from line operations may be serious. The person preparing a report may not know who reads it, or vice versa, or the true identity of both may be hidden or lost. From the standpoint of pure positional communication, this may not be important; but, as long as we continue to acknowledge the contributions made by individuals in the full expression of their personalities, the impersonalization of reporting can be harmful. How zealously will a person apply himself to the task of reporting to an anonymous recipient who may not even read his report? The comment of one personnel officer is indicative: "I pulled a boner in one of my reports," he said, "but at least I found out that the boss reads them."

The report specialist is a power to be reckoned with. He determines—often without any review of his action—whether information will go up the line in its original form or in a condensed version or not go up at all. Several years ago the Hoover Commission recommended that there be a staff secretary in the White House to report to the President on work in progress throughout the executive branch. The Commission described the staff secretary's position as one without authority; but the way in which information is given to or withheld from the President reflects the exercise of important power.

When Queen Elizabeth visited America in 1957 the Mink Breeders Association sent her a mink coat—with very long sleeves. When the Queen first wore the coat, the sleeves almost covered her hands. The sleeves were meant to be turned back in cuffs, but nobody could get in touch with the Queen to tell her so. The news had to filter through press secretaries, under-secretaries and a lady-in-waiting before the Queen found out how her coat ought to look.[17]

A line official has only so much time for all his work, including communicating, and he must therefore choose between reading reports himself or assigning the task to a staff member in his office. In his wartime position as chief of the Recruitment and Manning Office of the War Shipping Administration, Marshall Dimock chose the former procedure, but he hypothesizes that for another person in his position—one who was a slow reader, a fiend for detail, or one who was always anxious to take immediate action on reports—the results could be disastrous.[18] Before delegating the reporting function, it would be wise to determine whether the time load could be reduced through better reports.

Overemphasis on Reports

There is danger that at some point reports may become as important as, or even more important than, the job itself. Sometimes this results from an overemphasis being placed on the reports by those who prescribe them and, therefore, by those who prepare them. In other cases, the reports become so enmeshed with operations that neither can be revised without upsetting the other.

Individuals and work groups consider reports in terms of how they may affect the status quo. Production and cost reports, particularly, tend to become prescriptions for expected performance. When an employee knows what sort of results are looked for in reports, he can adjust his work accordingly, stabilizing his production at or near the standards. Through experience employees learn that a report of standard production raises no questions but that a report of higher production is a signal for the management engineers to come to see how it was done and for co-workers in similar posts to suspect the high producer.

The way a report can become a paramount consideration is described by Gardner and Whyte in their account of a know-it-all foreman who gave highly detailed instructions for the operation of certain machinery in order to attain the production he wanted. The operators knew from experience that the equipment could produce the required output, but only if they used their own method and not the one the foreman had ordered. They did this but put down the chart readings that the foreman would regard as being correct—not the ones they had actually observed. In this way, the reporting requirements were met, as were the production requirements, but the reports bore no direct relation to the actual work being reported.[19]

A supervisor confronted with a cost report needs to know the expected standard, but he soon finds out what others are reporting for similar operations. There is the case of the machine-shop superintendent who, when told that his reported labor costs were too high in relation to production, laid off enough inspectors to bring the ratio down. Some months later, when the rejects from customers skyrocketed, management found out about his ingenious method for bringing operations into line for a better report. In postwar Britain, during a period when the efficiency of public hospital administration was being measured according to costs per occupied bed, some hospital superintendents reportedly kept the beds occupied for as many days as possible, thereby distributing overhead as thinly as they could, even if it meant for some patients a few extra days of convalescence.[20]

Reports and operations may become so interwoven that they are mutually insusceptible of change. Organizations do not normally start out as large, highly segmented structures; most of the leviathans we see today began as small units. Suppose that at an early stage of its development an organization institutes a simple report—for example, a vendor's name-and-address card file with a figure for the amounts paid each month —as a by-product of the disbursing operation. The reports are first used in the preparation of lists of bidders for the purchasing department. Later they are used to prepare a report required by the tax authorities; still later, to furnish a check list for the inspectors who must verify compliance with fair labor standards. These lists and tabulations have soon become the source material for other reports. At this stage everything hinges on the little report that first appeared as a by-product; it has become vital and untouchable, as has the operation which produces it. Any scheme for a new disbursing system, no matter how meritorious it may be, is likely to be rejected unless the new system preserves the many secondary reports.

These many difficulties should not be allowed to divert our attention from the necessity for adequate administrative reporting. The lines of authority and accountability running between the boss and the worker, and between the central office and the field, are the supporting members of the formal structure. If they are inoperative, the structure loses its cohesiveness and becomes merely an assortment of unrelated parts. The issuance of instructions and the transmission of reports together vitalize the formal channels.

If reporting is to have maximum value, it is incumbent on the executive, as an order-giver, to tell his subordinates what kinds of reports he wants and to stimulate and facilitate the upward flow by responding to his reporters. Instructing and reporting are parts of one continuous process, and any other communicative processes used should be related to this central core.

Efforts to improve administrative communication can proceed in two directions. One is to abandon the basic channels and seek out a variety of substitute channels. This is a common occurrence, as evidenced by such devices as suggestion systems and employee opinion polls. These devices may indeed be useful for certain purposes. But efforts to improve administrative communication should be concentrated on the central processes of communication—instructing and reporting— through formal channels, thereby strengthening, rather than weakening, the formal channels themselves.

Selected Readings

BOOKS AND MONOGRAPHS

ANDERSON, CHESTER REED; SAUNDERS, ALTA GWINN; and WEEKS, FRANCIS WILLIAM. *Business Reports.* 3d ed. New York: McGraw-Hill Book Co., 1957.
Detailed text on the preparation and writing of reports. Bibliography.

BARISH, NORMAN N. *Systems Analysis for Effective Administration.* New York: Funk & Wagnalls Company in association with Modern Industry Magazine, 1951. Chap. xi, "Writing Systems Reports and Procedures."
Model arrangement and content of a systems report.

COPELAND, MELVIN T. *The Executive at Work.* Cambridge: Harvard University Press, 1951. Chap. iv, "Keeping Informed."
Numerous examples of breakdowns resulting from defects in both upward and horizontal communication.

GARDNER, BURLEIGH B., and MOORE, DAVID G. *Human Relations in Industry.* 3d ed. Chicago: Richard D. Irwin, Inc., 1955. Chap. v, "Authority System and Chain of Command."

Distortion resulting from the nature of subordinate-superior relationships, from lengthy channels, and from the consolidation of information.

HECKERT, J. BROOKS, and WILLSON, JAMES D. *Controllership.* New York: Ronald Press, 1952. Chap. xxi, "Internal Managerial Reports."

Describes and illustrates the control and informational reports likely to be prepared by every controller. Succeeding chapters deal with reports to employees, the public, government agencies, and stock exchanges.

RIDLEY, CLARENCE E., and SIMON, HERBERT A. *Monthly Administrative Reports for Cities.* Chicago: International City Managers' Association, 1943.

Standard formats for statistical and financial reports for municipal departments.

ARTICLES

BRUNNER, CHARLES I. "Reporting as a Technique To Compel Performance," pp. 161–70 in *Organizing for Effective Systems Planning and Control.* ("Special Report," No. 12.) New York: American Management Association, 1956.

Description of Cleveland Electric Illuminating Company's three-phase reporting system: long-range planning reports, annual budget planning reports, performance analysis reports.

CALLABY, FRANKLIN A. "Accounting for Human Nature: Management Accounting in Action," *British Management Review,* Vol. 14 (January, 1956), pp. 50–61.

The need for some sprightly advertising writing in accounting reports.

CARLSON, ERNEST A. "Techniques for Effective Reporting to Management," *N.A.C.A. Bulletin,* Vol. 33 (February, 1952), pp. 679–94.

Advances a series of principles and discusses some common problems.

GARDNER, BURLEIGH B., and WHYTE, WILLIAM F. "The Man in the Middle: Position and Problems of the Foreman," *Applied Anthropology* (special issue), Vol. 4 (Spring, 1945) (the entire issue was devoted to this article).

The foreman's complex relationships with management and with his subordinates, with considerable attention to the effects on administrative reporting.

JAMES, C. C. "Principles of Organization and Operation," *Advanced Management,* Vol. 10 (April–June, 1945), pp. 42–52.

Controlling the number, timing, and distribution of reports through detailed schedules.

JULIAN, FLORENCE. "Streamlined Reports," *American Journal of Nursing,* Vol. 55 (February, 1955), pp. 178–79.

Using recordings for shift-reports.

LANG, DANIEL R. "Training Executives in the Preparation of Special Assignment Reports," pp. 221–31 in *Better Business Communications: The Third Business Communications Conference, Wayne University, School of Business Administration, 1951.* Detroit: Wayne University Press, 1952.

Outlining a program of (1) direct instruction, (2) the study of books on reporting (which are listed), and (3) detailed criticism of actual reports by superiors receiving them.

LATHAM, EARL G. "The Technique of Administrative Reporting," *Public Administration Review,* Vol. 3 (Spring, 1943), pp. 106–18.

Historical reporting, based on experience in a government department.

MCLEAN, JOHN G. "Better Reports for Better Controls," *Harvard Business Review,* Vol. 35 (May–June, 1957), pp. 95–104.

Two improvements: identify critical factors, and group material for ease of interpretation.

NEUSCHEL, RICHARD F. "Strengthening and Simplifying the Structure of Management Reports," pp. 3–12 in *Improving Office Reports, Manuals and Records.* ("Office Management Series," No. 141.) New York: American Management Association, 1955.

The first requirements: isolate the key elements of performance and establish yardsticks for measuring them.

PLANTY, EARL, and MACHAVER, WILLIAM. "Upward Communications: A Project in Executive Development," *Personnel,* Vol. 28 (January, 1952), pp. 304–18. (Reprinted in M. JOSEPH DOOHER [ed.], *Effective Communication on the Job* [New York: American Management Association, 1956], pp. 141–57.)

The need for, and methods of, upward communication.

SMITH, PAUL L. "The Operations Letter as the Controller's Medium of Expression," *The Controller,* Vol. 21 (November, 1953), pp. 505–8, 536 ff.

A model monthly interpretive letter.

WEROLIN, A. E. "Effective Controls for Top Management," *Advanced Management,* Vol. 12 (September, 1947), pp. 120–28.

Recommendations for selecting the right types of reports, preparing them carefully and promptly, distributing them only to those who need them, and providing comparisons against previous periods or budgetary standards.

XII / Communicating Suggestions
and Complaints

THE LOGIC of efficiency governing the conduct of an organization is not normally the concern of the subordinate employee; he is hired to furnish a day's work, as measured by hours of attendance, units of production, or both. The offering of ideas, opinions, suggestions, and complaints is rarely mentioned in job descriptions.

Although suggestions, complaints, and even attitudes might be transmitted upward through formal channels, there are many obstacles to such communication. Recognition of these obstacles has led to the development of devices that depend on substitute or parallel channels. The most popular of these is the conventional suggestion system. Recently conventional suggestion systems have been modified and improved, and employee suggestions have become important by-products of systems of employee participation in management.

Present-day suggestion systems have roots in both industry and government. One of the earliest programs was that of Alexander Hamilton, who, while Secretary of the Treasury under Washington, requested his officers at United States ports "to carefully note and from time to time communicate whatever might serve to discover the merits or defects of the revenue system and to point out the means of improving it."[1] To Scottish shipbuilder William Denny goes credit for installing, in 1880, the first suggestion box for employees.[2] Ten years later a suggestion system patterned on Denny's was started in this country at the Yale and Towne Lock Company. In 1894, the National Cash Register Company installed a similar system and soon afterward followed others: at Eastman Kodak, Bausch & Lomb, Westinghouse Electric, Western Electric, and the United Shoe Machinery Corporation.[3] The War Department's arsenals and the Navy Department's shore establishments were in the vanguard of governmental organizations that adopted formal suggestion systems, with legislation authorizing cash awards dating back to 1912 for the War Department and to 1918 for the Navy.[4]

It was not until World War II that suggestion systems came to be numbered in the thousands. Under the sponsorship of the War Production Board's Labor-Management Division, suggestion systems were established along with conference training programs as devices for increasing defense production. In 1942, with representation of only twenty-eight companies, the National Association of Suggestion Systems was established. By 1955 membership in the Association, whose Chicago headquarters serves as a national clearing-house for suggestion-system information, had grown to more than seven hundred. There are an estimated four thousand formal suggestion systems in operation today, and an estimated nine million dollars is awarded annually.[5] Although conventional suggestion systems are significant on the industrial scene, for the past five years they have not shown a growth trend.

WHAT IS A SUGGESTION SYSTEM?

Every suggestion system incorporates, in more or less detailed fashion, five elements: (1) a basic policy statement establishing the system; (2) a designated organizational unit to operate the system; (3) a body of operating procedures; (4) an award program; and (5) a program of employee information.

The Basic Policy Statement

The governing board of a corporation or of a governmental jurisdiction must provide the basic authority for any suggestion system, especially if it offers direct or indirect monetary awards. The basic statement may be specific, permissive, or merely implicit in the act of budgeting funds for the program.

It is necessary to determine at the outset which supervisory and staff positions, if any, are eligible to participate. On the premise that supervisors, systems men, industrial engineers, and people in similar staff positions are being paid in part for developing new ideas, they are generally excluded from participation. Sometimes they are permitted to participate but are ineligible for direct awards. At the General Motors Corporation, skilled and semiskilled employees, such as inspectors, group leaders, and maintenance men are eligible "provided their suggestions are outside the scope of their regular job assignments." In the very large firms, one will generally find separate management proposal plans.

A Unit To Operate the System

The basic policy statement establishing the system usually designates the form of organization for processing suggestions. Most common are committees of supervisory and staff personnel appointed by management, and in large organizations there may be a hierarchy of such committees. Each committee is generally provided with a secretary or administrator on a full-time or part-time basis. Some large organizations have full-time suggestion units or departments, which may be either separate or part of the personnel, industrial engineering, or systems departments.

Operating Procedures

The designated organizational unit is responsible for developing detailed procedures for receipt and acknowledgment; coding and classification; recording, filing, and suspending; investigation and follow-up; recommending and determining final disposition; and for periodic reporting on individual suggestions and on the entire system. Many a firm has learned too late how complicated and time-consuming these procedures can become.

There is usually a prescribed manner for submitting suggestions. The basic pattern has been to provide printed and numbered suggestion blanks at various locations throughout the shops and offices and at these locations to furnish suggestion boxes (not unlike mailboxes) for the completed blanks. A typical suggestion blank is shown in Figure 16.

Some organizations have given up printed forms entirely, and others have eliminated suggestion boxes, permitting em-

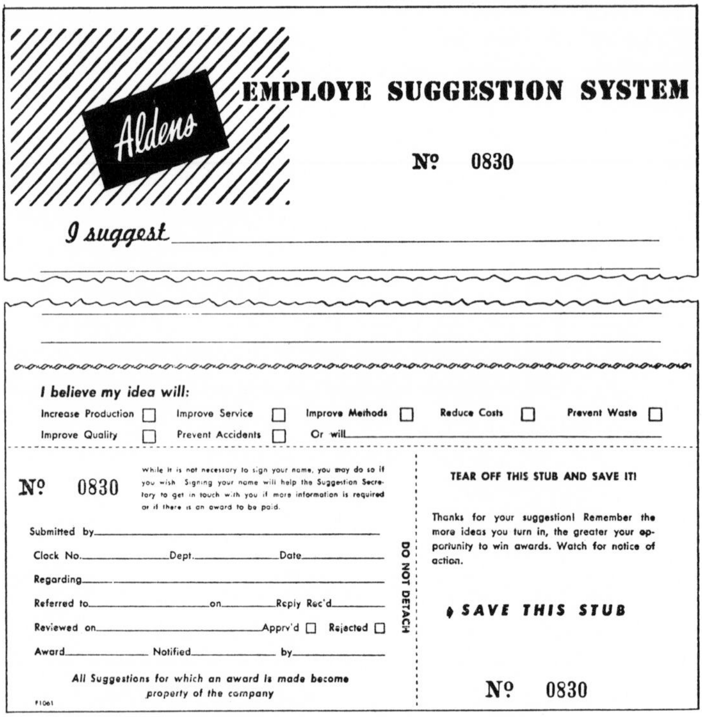

FIG. 16.—A typical suggestion blank, from Aldens, Inc.

ployees to transmit their suggestions to a designated office however they may choose—by mail, in person, or through supervisory channels. Sometimes the suggestion must be written out in duplicate, with one copy going directly to the suggestion unit and the other routed through channels.

The Award Program

The lump-sum cash award is the hallmark of conventional suggestion systems. Letters of commendation, certificates of merit, and medals and other insignia are also popular. As part of its Centennial Program, Swift and Company supplemented its cash awards with shares of company stock. The California Department of Employment and the Southern California Gas Company offer no tangible awards, monetary or otherwise, and no doubt other organizations do the same.

Among cash-award systems the most common practice is to pay an award equal to 10 per cent of the first year's saving, either gross or net (for instance, some of the cost of putting the suggestion into effect, such as the cost of new tools, may be deducted from the gross saving). General Motors and Ford pay awards equal to one-sixth of the first year's saving, and a few organizations, including the Pitney-Bowes Company and Rand McNally and Company pay as much as 50 per cent.[6] Some companies pay the income tax levied on the awards, but generally the tax is deducted and withheld. The foregoing remarks apply to suggestions for tangible or measurable improvements. Amounts awarded for intangible benefits, such as improved working conditions, are necessarily discretionary.

Provision is almost always made for minimum and maximum awards, usually five or ten dollars at the bottom and one or several thousand dollars at the top. The aggregate amounts of some award programs are quite staggering. General Motors Corporation pays out more than two million dollars a year.

This is about one quarter of the total paid throughout the entire country.

Information for Employees

Organizations use various media to stimulate suggestions and to help the less-educated employees formulate and write up their ideas. Posters and other forms of announcements are posted on bulletin boards or above suggestion boxes. A chapter or section in the employee handbook is likely to be devoted to the subject, and the employee publication is often used to carry feature articles on newsworthy suggestions and awards. A number of organizations distribute to employees monthly or semimonthly reports on suggestion activities.

PROBLEMS IN THE ADMINISTRATION
OF SUGGESTION SYSTEMS

The frequently reported successes of suggestion systems and their widespread growth tend to obscure some critical problems. Not so well publicized are the suspensions and failures, even though 90 per cent of the suggestion systems initiated in this country have gone out of existence.[7]

Complaints

Only a fine line distinguishes suggestions from complaints, and the difference is often in the way they are communicated. If employee Abbott says, "It isn't safe for a man to work on a machine like this," his remark would no doubt be regarded as a complaint. When employee Bruce, commenting on the same situation, says, "A protective guard, such as the one being used at the XYZ Company, would make this a safe operation," his words would be looked upon as a suggestion. Both men believe that the machine is not safe and that a safety guard should be provided, but, for any number of reasons, they express themselves differently. Abbott's complaint would not qualify as a suggestion in organizations that insist that all suggestions be "constructive," yet to exclude complaints is bound to constrict the carrying power of suggestion systems. At the Southern California Gas Company, where complaints have been welcomed along with suggestions, the complaints in 1949 exceeded the suggestions by a ratio of six to one. In an unpublished study of a new suggestion system, Raymond Villers found that the men who submitted suggestions were the same ones who had been submitting grievances.

Suppose that Abbott feels a closer allegiance to his union steward than to the remote "management" that sponsors the suggestion system. In such a case, the unsafe machine and the missing protective guard constitute a grievance that is communicated upward not through the suggestion system but through the established grievance procedure. Indeed, a grievance may be defined simply as a complaint that is transmitted through the union.

Thus the administrative communication systems of two overlapping organizations are brought into competition with one another. There appears to be little doubt that unionization tends to reduce the upward flow of ideas through conventional suggestion systems, some of which already prescribe that "matters subject to established grievance procedures shall not be submitted." The large national unions have refrained to date from taking a public stand on suggestion systems, while some locals have prohibited their members from submitting suggestions and others have indorsed the systems. In the competition for allegiance and power between two overlapping formal organizations, information is an element of power. The question of whose channels of communication shall be used is an important one.

Superior-Subordinate Relationships

Suggestion systems have traditionally ignored the two basic social relationships in which an employee at work is involved:

worker-and-supervisor and worker-and-worker. If suggestions were transmitted through the formal hierarchical channels promptly and without distortion, and if the design of a formal organization gave each employee a wide rather than a narrow horizon, suggestion systems would not be necessary.

In their early years, suggestion systems were, above all else, means for bypassing hostile or inadequate supervisors. Too often a supervisor was competing with his subordinates for an executive's favor, either taking credit for their suggestions or discouraging any that might place him in a bad light. A retired employee of the General Electric Company has recounted an experience early in the century when, during his foreman's absence, he developed several devices for markedly improving a punch-press operation used in several departments. His foreman and the superintendent had themselves tried unsuccessfully to make such devices and had informed the plant manager that they were not practical.

> To make a long story short, I had several of the devices installed and working satisfactorily when the old foreman returned and I found myself really in hot water. He scolded me on several occasions and finally . . . he told me that I was through at the end of the week. Meanwhile, the foreman of the Punch Press Department had told the manager about the devices and he had expressed the desire to see them in operation and meet the man who had made them. Accordingly, I was called in and the manager told me that he liked what I had made and asked me if I could make any more such improvements. I told him that I thought so but didn't have much time because I was getting through the end of the week. He then sent for my foreman who became quite flustered and said that I had misunderstood, and it was all a mistake! That was the one and only time I was fired from the General Electric Company, but it served to demonstrate to me the need for some means by which employees could get a hearing for their ideas.
>
> Later on . . . I suggested . . . that we set up a suggestion system. . . . In 1906 such a system was established at the General Electric Company in Schenectady.[8]

A similar situation was encountered in the course of a recent management survey, when a clerk took the opportunity to confide to us a new and purportedly speedier way to carry out an impending readjustment of work loads. Later the office supervisor happened to complain about the lack of facilities for processing suggestions. We told him that one of his employees had a suggestion for speeding up the periodic readjustments of

"*Peebles, we've found the proposals you've been dropping into the suggestion box not only stimulating but provocative—so much so, in fact, that we'd feel guilty confining a man of your alertness and ingenuity within the limits of your present position. Effective the first of the month, therefore, we're releasing you from our employ.*"

Reproduced by permission.
Copr. 1950 by The New Yorker Magazine, Inc.

work loads and that perhaps he ought to discuss it with the employee. The supervisor immediately took on a defensive manner, asserting that he knew in advance that the idea was worthless and that he would not even talk to the man about it!

Employee-Group Relationships

Suggestion systems also ignore the relationships existing within groups of workers. Members of a group, through the exercise of social pressures and sanctions, can effectively en-

force the group will.[9] An employee group may look with dis-
favor on any suggestion that will eliminate a job, necessitate a
speed-up, increase production without increasing wages, or
strengthen the position of an unpopular superior. Or individuals, without regard to group pressures, may withhold suggestions on the basis that they would be foolish to aggrandize the
present boss when they themselves may have an opportunity
to use the ideas when they become bosses. A cohesive group is
probably most opposed to suggestions that would disturb the
group's structural equilibrium, whether by physical division,
relocation of all or some of the members, or the introduction
of new people who are generally assumed to be unacceptable.

In some organizations where suggestion systems had been
unsuccessful, it was believed that publicity to award winners
engendered among other employees pressure against the win-
ner. As a result, anonymous suggestion blanks were introduced.
Winning numbers, instead of names, are posted, and winners
present their numbered stubs to collect awards. One company
not only posts anonymous numbers but also avoids any publicity regarding the size of awards.

But anonymous systems are not the solution, for it has been
observed that anonymity is seldom preserved and that the factor of anonymity alone does not increase suggestions. Thus a
growing number of companies now permit or even require
employees to sign their names, and, wherever the signature has
been made optional, it has not been long before most suggestions are signed.[10] Communication between an anonymous
suggestion unit and Suggestion Number 1234 is not an entirely
gratifying human relationship.

The imposition of employee-group sanctions appears to be a
highly selective process, well understood among the employees
themselves and related, no doubt, to the precise nature of the
suggestions and the prevailing attitudes at the time. Thus there
is a preponderance of minor suggestions and a high percent-

age of suggestions that apply *outside* the areas of primary-group relationships. A mail clerk, for example, may suggest a new arrangement for parking cars in the parking lot but never mention his ideas for revising the mailing procedures. In one hospital system, the dietitians and clerks submitted many suggestions about nursing but none about their own work.

A successful supervisor is likely to be a staunch member of his employees' social group. He identifies himself with their aspirations and frustrations as much as with the aspirations and frustrations of the management group of which he is also a member.

Supervisors are rarely eligible for awards. And many appraisal schemes use as one measure of performance the number of suggestions submitted by a man's subordinates. Thus a supervisor can distribute some of the potential bounty by having his ideas submitted as suggestions by subordinates. At the same time, he can improve his performance rating. In one case, a supervisor whose requisition for a new mimeograph machine was denied by the budget office had the mimeograph operator submit a suggestion calling for the new machine. The supporting data were the same in both cases, but the suggestion succeeded where the requisition had failed. (The operator was happy to divide the windfall with her ingenious boss.)

Investigating Suggestions

The introduction of a direct channel for suggestions, bypassing the supervisory hierarchy, is not based solely on supervisory hostility or ineptitude. Each supervisor has been assigned a job that presumably requires his full time and attention, with little opportunity for the contemplation of possible changes in work methods.

It is very difficult to investigate expeditiously any proposal that would change an organization's policies or procedures. To maintain a satisfactory atmosphere for communication, not only the investigation but the award process as well should be completed in a period of not more than several weeks. But only rarely can a suggestion of any importance be processed that quickly. A model West Coast organization follows a rigorous time schedule but still expects to take forty-five to sixty days for most investigations and an even longer time when necessary. A protracted period of investigation appears to the employee as managerial indecision; employee interest and enthusiasm may give way to doubt, suspicion, and resentment. To the suggester the potential benefits may seem obvious; he usually does not understand the organization-wide implications and the possible conflicts with plans already under way.

The immediate supervisor has neither the time nor the scope of knowledge to conduct a prompt and comprehensive investigation of any but minor suggestions. Groups of supervisors gathered into suggestion committees are better equipped with broader collective knowledge; but a suggestion may lie untouched for weeks until it comes before the suggestion committee, and more weeks may elapse before the committee acts. Full-time investigators, such as industrial engineers or systems men, are the most efficient. But few organizations can afford to have them give much time to investigating suggestions.

Awards

One of the major—and troublesome—aspects of a conventional suggestion system is the making of awards, particularly cash awards. In an environment dominated by the logic of efficiency, where "equal pay for equal work" is the creed, a money-saving suggestion is something extra and (assuming it is wanted) calls for extra compensation.

In reviewing employee handbooks and other promotional material, one is impressed by the frequent references to the maximum award—the mythical pot of gold. The largest award in history was the twenty-eight thousand dollars paid in 1948 to a Cleveland Graphite Bronze machinist. (He left the company soon afterward.) Since that notable award, according to the National Association of Suggestion Systems, there have been three ten-thousand-dollar awards and one of fifteen thousand dollars. But certainly most awards are quite modest. In 1957 General Electric reported that its average award during the preceding year was about twenty-five dollars, and at the same time General Motors and the United States Government reported average awards of approximately fifty-six and thirty dollars, respectively.[11] The preponderant number of small awards results in part from the practice, in a few companies, of giving at least the minimum to almost anyone who submits a suggestion rather than cause any hard feelings.

There has been some concern regarding the equity of the various award formulas, which already range from 10 to 50 per cent. One does not need to pass judgment on the formulas, however, since the problem arises if an employee only *believes* that the award is unfair. He worked hard and long at the suggestion, he knows others have received higher awards, his suggestion is better, but his award is less! According to one executive, an employee is likely to say, "Yes, they gave me $100 for that suggestion, but after all the company got $900. No wonder they like to see us submit suggestions."[12] Furthermore, each award is subject to comparison by prior award winners who may belatedly conclude that they were treated unfairly. For every friend that an organization may make through a monetary award, there is a good chance of making one or several enemies.

Since awards constitute additional compensation, unions can be expected to try to bring them within the scope of collective bargaining. Management, however, may react as it did in a large aircraft corporation several years ago, when, confronted by such a union demand in the course of its contract negotiations, it terminated the suggestion system immediately.

SUGGESTIONS AND COMPLAINTS THROUGH
SUPERVISORY AND EMPLOYEE PARTICIPATION

One cannot disregard the apparent productivity of suggestion systems as upward channels of communication. Employees have countless ideas for worthwhile improvements; and even systems offering no immediate monetary awards are quite successful. These successes indicate also that every organization has its share of deficiencies and either that these deficiencies are not presently known to management or that management has not been able to overcome them.

Yet the long-term outlook for conventional suggestion systems is not too promising. The bypassing of supervisors and a dependence on intragroup competition rather than on cooperation, no matter how expedient they may be, can hardly produce the atmosphere of mutual trust without which satisfactory communication is impossible. Thus the variations that have already appeared in the systems of some companies and the radically different methods that have been introduced in others are highly significant.

Supervisory Participation

Many organizations, having used conventional suggestion systems bypassing supervisory channels, are now making efforts to enlist supervisory support. One approach is to underwrite supervisory support for suggestions. Some companies make awards periodically to the foreman whose department has turned in the greatest number of acceptable suggestions during the preceding period.

Other means are also being used to overcome supervisory hostility and, at the same time, to secure the benefit of supervisory thinking. Several companies have instituted the practice of sending a copy of each suggestion to the foreman concerned. Both the B. F. Goodrich Company and Northrop Aircraft, Inc., require foremen to investigate suggestions coming from their subordinates, but final determination of acceptability and the amount of award are reserved to the central suggestion units. The Goodrich Company has an unusual system of accepting and rewarding for solutions to problems that foremen have assigned to particular workers.

Since 1949, the Western Electric Company has been sending the suggestion department's initial report of investigation to the appropriate supervisor, who is required to confer with the individual who submitted it. If either the employee or the supervisor is dissatisfied with the investigation, the company authorizes the return of the suggestion for reinvestigation. A contingent advantage of this procedure is that it gives the supervisor a good opportunity to interview the employee about his work and anything else he wants to talk about. Several General Electric plants and Esso Research and Engineering Company have revised their suggestion systems in similar fashion to strengthen the role of the immediate supervisor.

In 1955, ten companies reported in a survey that they had discontinued their suggestion systems primarily because they took too much time of key people.[13] Another large corporation recently dropped its suggestion system, announcing at the same time, "Suggestions are still welcome, but hereafter they must come through regular channels." This typifies a rather general change in the thinking about the role of supervisory personnel in the communication of suggestions and complaints. Fifty years ago, when conventional suggestion systems originated, line supervisors and foremen had very little status with their superiors. Today, however, supervisors at all levels are looked on as key members of the managerial structure, and organizations are spending large sums to improve the quality of supervision. It follows that, as a general rule, suggestions and complaints should be made to flow *through* the supervisory personnel, not around them.

The continuing development and expansion of the field of

work simplification are having a marked effect on conventional suggestion systems. In line with the slogan, "Work smarter—not harder," the basic analytical methods used by systems men and industrial engineers are being taught to supervisors. They, in turn, are instructing their employees in the elements of flow charting, work measurement, and related techniques. The Maytag Company, a leader in this field, processes work simplification proposals through the suggestion-system machinery, culminating in monetary awards.[14] This is a pattern which several other organizations, including the Standard Register Company, are following.

Employee Participation

Out of the labor-management committees of World War II, and without monetary awards, came suggestions that saved an estimated two hundred million man-hours of labor per year—equivalent to a full year's work for about eighty thousand men. This striking success points to the potential value of employee suggestions elicited through joint management-employee endeavors.

The Illinois Central Railroad was perhaps the first company —in peace as well as in war—to depart from the tradition of exclusive management representation on suggestion committees. There, union and management representatives share the places on the general and local suggestion committees. In the years since this change was instituted, the Illinois Central's suggestion system has been far more productive than it had been before, in terms of both suggestions submitted and suggestions adopted.[15] At the Pacific Mutual Life Insurance Company, the investigation and awards subcommittee is made up of nine non-supervisory employees who serve on a rotating basis. This group's recommendations are subject to approval by the company's suggestion plan guidance committee.

Employee participation in an even broader sense is a subject of current interest to professional management groups and to the general public. We find a growing number of companies and unions again introducing labor-management committees, although in a number of different forms. The most popular adaptations today are based on the Scanlon Plan (after Joseph N. Scanlon of M.I.T.), under which employees at all levels join with their superiors in the formulation of new policies and procedures. Participation is intensive, and no subjects pertaining to the operation of the business are barred. Although subordinates take part in formulating decisions, top management does not give up its authority, or avoid its responsibility, for final decision-making and order-giving.[16]

Organizations using the Scanlon Plan pay bonuses for increased production on a proportionate basis to all members of the group concerned, always including some levels of supervision and sometimes including all management people just short of the top.[17] All members of the participating unit are closely related to the rewarded effort—more so than in the case of conventional profit-sharing schemes, as pointed out here by George P. Shultz:

Generally speaking, incentives such as profit-sharing are too broad. The measure should be related more closely to the productivity of the participating group. Only on the basis of the group's efforts should it be rewarded—not on the basis of fortuitous price changes or inventory speculations. . . . A bonus is paid when, with a given payroll, the group produces more than the "norm" production value. This method does not, of course, give an exact and scientific measure of productivity. *There is no such measure.* It does give, however, a rule of thumb that is roughly accurate and is easily understandable.

Members of the participating group know what went into the original calculation, and so, if basic conditions change, they will agree to revise the norm. For example, changes can be made in the event of revisions of product prices, basic wage rates, or major machine installations. Experience with such rough measurements and with changes for good and proper reasons has been uniformly successful. Thus the "formula" works, not because it is precise and invulnerable but because the parties approach the problem of sharing the gains with understanding, good faith, and mutual trust.[18]

There have been some highly successful experiences with the Scanlon Plan. Suggestions have arisen where none arose before, and previous changes that management had not been able to introduce have now been accepted. Competition between superiors and subordinates has been markedly reduced, and the sanctions which employees often impose against suggesters appear to have been eliminated. The problem of determining equitable awards solves itself when the bonuses are determined jointly by labor and management, giving everyone the necessary *belief* that awards are fair.

SUGGESTION CAMPAIGNS

An interesting new development is the suggestion campaign, modeled after the sales campaign. A short campaign can elicit a spirit that the permanent programs are seldom able to maintain. And, interestingly, the campaigns have reportedly stimulated employees to submit suggestions through the established suggestion systems. Campaigns can be run during slack periods, reducing the burden on the investigating staff. Conceivably they could be administered without any permanent staff.

In 1954, the Corning Glass Works conducted a five-month new-product contest among its thirteen thousand employees, who submitted almost twenty-eight thousand suggestions. Many of the suggestions were so valuable that the company has refused to publicize them. (One novel suggestion was for a glass doghouse, which would be easy to clean and give the dog more sunshine. In addition, the dog would not have to leave his house on rainy days to check for intruders—it could just look through the glass wall.)[19] First and second prizes in the Corning campaign were vacation trips, or the equivalents in cash. Also awarded were radios, television sets, cameras, and similar merchandise. By giving merchandise prizes rather than cash awards based on monetary savings, a company avoids the difficult problem of computing satisfying awards and speeds up the award process as well.

Other successful suggestion campaigns have been conducted by the Elmira plant of the Remington Rand Division of Sperry Rand Corporation and the New Zealand Government Post Office. In both organizations, the campaigns conformed to the procedures and award schedules of the existing suggestion systems. Over a six-year period the Remington Rand Suggestion Day campaign has become an annual event. The *Minneapolis Star and Tribune,* in the conduct of a "Wipe Out Waste" campaign in 1954, supplemented its established award schedule with two vacation prizes and weekly merchandise drawings among employees who had qualified by submitting accepted suggestions.

As long as there is no marked change in the environment of most formal organizations, conventional suggestion systems will have some utility as devices for upward communication. Their high mortality rate, however, is eloquent testimony to the difficulties in administering them successfully. Suggestion systems will yield few, if any, major suggestions; on the contrary, there will be a predominance of minor ones, of which only a modest percentage may be expected to be useful.

By changing the environment and emphasizing co-operation instead of competition, many obstacles to upward communication will be removed, and suggestions and complaints will flow much more freely. We may find, in an ideal situation, that two communication systems are joined together, for certain functions, instead of being in competition with each other.

Selected Readings

BOOKS AND MONOGRAPHS

DALE, ERNEST. *Greater Productivity through Labor-Management Cooperation* ("Research Reports," No. 14.) New York: American Management Association, 1949.

Survey of various programs for labor-management co-operation, including an evaluation of suggestion systems. Bibliography.

DAVIS, KEITH. *Human Relations in Business.* New York: McGraw-Hill Book Co., 1957. Chap. 16, "Development of Participation."

Discusses five participative plans: consultative supervision, democratic supervision, production committees, suggestion programs, and multiple management.

LESIEUR, FREDERICK G. (ed.). *The Scanlon Plan: A Frontier in Labor-Management Cooperation.* New York: John Wiley & Sons, Inc., 1958.

Major study by a student of the originator of the Scanlon Plan.

SEINWERTH, HERMAN W. *Getting Results from Suggestion Plans.* New York: McGraw-Hill Book Co., 1948.

The operation of conventional suggestion systems.

STRAUSS, GEORGE, and SAYLES, LEONARD R. *The Local Union: Its Place in the Industrial Plant.* New York: Harper & Bros., 1953. Chap. iii, "The Grievance Procedure in Action," and chap. iv, "The Decline of the Steward."

Insight into the union's processes for communicating grievances and the decreasing importance of the steward.

Suggestion Schemes. London: Industrial Welfare Society, 1950.

Review of British practice.

WHYTE, WILLIAM F. *Money and Motivation.* New York: Harper & Bros., 1955. Chap. xiv, "The Scanlon Plan."

The Scanlon Plan compared to conventional suggestion plans.

WHYTE, WILLIAM H., JR., and the EDITORS OF "FORTUNE." *Is Anybody Listening?* New York: Simon & Schuster, Inc., 1952. Pp. 136–44.

Questions the validity and direction of existing programs for employee participation.

ARTICLES

DAVENPORT, RUSSELL W. "Enterprise for Everyman," *Fortune,* Vol. 41 (January, 1950), pp. 55–59, 152 ff. (Reprinted in WILLIAM M. Fox [ed.], *Readings in Personnel Management from FORTUNE* [New York: Henry Holt and Co., 1957].)

Laudatory report on the Scanlon Plan.

HENEMAN, HERBERT G., JR., "Suggestion Systems—Symptoms of Failure?" *Personnel Journal,* Vol. 29 (March, 1951), pp. 378–80.

Advocates better managerial planning and more fundamental research in human relations instead of reliance on suggestion systems.

HORTON, JOHN E. "Methods Simplification and the Suggestion System," *Office Economist,* Vol. 33 (July–August, 1951), pp. 4–5, 12–13.

Relating the training of employees in work simplification techniques to an increase in the productivity of suggestion systems.

KRULEE, GILBERT K. "The Scanlon Plan: Co-operation through Participation," *Journal of Business of the University of Chicago,* Vol. 28 (April, 1955), pp. 100–113.

Describes the parallel increase of productive efficiency and employee satisfaction.

SAWCHUK, HENRY A. "The New Federal Incentive Awards Program," *Public Administration Review,* Vol. 15 (Winter, 1955), pp. 43–45.

The anticipated merits of the Government Employees' Incentive Awards Act of 1955.

XIII / *Interviewing*

INTERVIEWING fits into our portrayal of upward communication as prerequisite to downward communication. A superior cannot act wisely without good and sufficient information from below on which to base his action. Interviewing produces facts plus a wealth of other information that would not flow upward routinely—attitudes and opinions, suggestions and complaints, rumors, beliefs, feelings, needs, hopes, frustrations, and motivations.

A person skilled in interviewing techniques and endowed with a good interviewing personality can help a respondent become more articulate than he would be unaided. Since some types of interviewing are highly specialized, many people tend to regard all interviewers as specialists. But interviewing methods are being applied by some people all the time, and as Professor Roethlisberger has pointed out, the "skillful application has gone under a number of different names: good breeding, manners, tact, diplomacy, courtesy, personality, charm, wisdom and understanding."[1]

There is a tendency among writers and speakers to disparage communication techniques, while favoring face-to-face contacts. Some of these contacts are no doubt purely social and purposeless, but most of the purposeful ones qualify as interviews. As observed in the chapter on oral and written instructions, the transmission of an oral order may be regarded as a compressed or telescoped interview. Most interviews, of course, are something more than "contacts," since the interviewee actually drops his work to speak with the interviewer.[2]

THE STATUS OF INTERVIEWING TODAY

There are many established interviewing processes in administration. Some of them are:

Preliminary and final, or placement, interviews—conducted by personnel officers and superiors in recruiting and hiring.

Induction and instructional interviews—conducted by training officers, counselors, and superiors for new and transferred employees.[3]

Follow-up interviews—conducted by personnel officers or counselors both with newly placed employees and their superiors several weeks or months after initial placement, transfer, or promotion.

Transfer and promotion interviews—conducted by personnel officers and superiors in advance of transfer or promotion with applicants and designees, including those who are being turned down.

Complaint and disciplinary interviews—conducted by superiors.

Job analysis and personnel audit interviews—conducted by personnel officers, outside consultants, and superiors. Job analyses seek only to describe positions, as reported in part by the incumbents, while personnel audits are also concerned with the qualifications of the incumbents.

Evaluation interviews—conducted by superiors in connection with periodic rating programs.[4]

Separation, or exit, interviews—conducted by superiors, personnel officers, and counselors to ascertain the true reasons for an employee's leaving, to get opinions and suggestions that might be helpful to the organization, and (in some cases) to reduce turnover by encouraging the employee to stay in his job or to accept a transfer.

Postexit interviews—conducted by staff specialists or outside consultants with former employees several months after separation to validate and supplement exit-interview findings, and, in the case of retired employees, to check on their adjustment.[5]

Polling interviews—conducted by staff specialists or outside consultants principally to find out facts about employees, their knowledge of their work and other matters, and their opinions.*

Counseling interviews—conducted by counselors, and sometimes by superiors, to help employees with their personal problems, whether or not directly related to their work.

Lest one be too impressed by the many interviewing opportunities, it should be noted that interviewing is not widely accepted as a method of getting information. Enthusiasm for the method was great in 1927–32, when more than twenty-one thousand employees were interviewed at the Hawthorne Works of the Western Electric Company for their opinions about supervisory practices. The findings in that case were used to develop supervisory training material, although this aspect of the program has been overshadowed by some collateral findings that were of great importance in industrial sociology.[6] Counseling interviewing, one by-product of the Hawthorne experiment, has elicited great interest, but only a few companies have instituted such programs. Two companies that deserve mention are the Caterpillar Tractor Company, which, in 1945, instituted a mental health program as part of its medical service at Peoria, and the Prudential Life Insurance Company, which, in 1948, instituted a mental hygiene service at Newark.[7]

Today, as in the past, interviews are used primarily in connection with initial employment, where the emphasis conventionally is as much on giving information as on getting it. Exit and polling interviews have had the greatest acceptance as information-getters, and probably next come evaluation inter-

* See also chap. xiv, "Employee Opinion Polls."

views.[8] Induction and instructional interviews, follow-up interviews, postexit interviews, and interviews incident to transfers, promotions, complaints, and discipline are potentially fertile sources for information that might not otherwise be revealed.

Non-directive Interviewing and Counseling

The results of the Hawthorne interviews far exceeded the original plans. The interviewers learned much more about the company than they had anticipated they would, and they discovered that the interviews had the additional effect of improving the adjustments of employees and supervisors to the work environment.[9] The interviewers had knowingly pioneered with a non-directive interviewing technique as opposed to the traditional question-and-answer type of interview and, as if by chance, became the pioneers in the field of employee counseling. The counselor's sole object has been "to lead the employee to a clear understanding of her problem such that she herself comes to realize what action to take and then assumes responsibility for taking it."[10]

The most significant characteristic of the non-directive interview is that the interviewee talks and asks questions about things that he is interested in and not necessarily about what the interviewer thinks should be discussed. As a result, the interviewer stands a better chance of learning what the interviewee actually believes rather than what he thinks the interviewer wants to know. In so far as possible the non-directive interviewer avoids asking questions or even answering them. He strives for a free narrative response and shies away from any cross-examination.

At the same time that non-directive interviewing was being developed at Western Electric, almost identical techniques were being developed by Carl Rogers in the field of clinical psychology.[11] The impact of these developments has been tremendous, and the reported successes with non-directive techniques have even led to their use to some extent in employment interviewing.[12] A skilled employment interviewer may invite an interviewee to ask anything he wants to know, and, listening to the questions, can find out what the applicant is interested in. He will also, no doubt, obtain clues to what other applicants will be interested in.[13] In modern business, much interviewing is neither purely directive nor purely non-directive but rather a combination of the two methods—the so-called patterned interview. This is the case with Sears, Roebuck's counseling and opinion-polling interviews.[14] And even at the Hawthorne Works, according to a recent report, the purely non-directive approach has not been preserved in the conduct of counseling interviews. The assumption underlying the purely non-directive counseling interview is that the client has a problem and probably knows that it exists, even though he may not know exactly what it is. When, as frequently happens at Hawthorne, these conditions do not prevail, the counselor—in order to avoid embarrassment—is forced to take the initiative and carry the burden of the conversation.[15]

Thus the original purpose of interviewing as an upward channel of sometimes rather limited information has given way, under the impact of non-directive counseling, to diagnostic techniques, with the interviewer probing more deeply and getting considerably more intimate knowledge about the employee than heretofore. The securing of better and more accurate information is a logical communication objective for an employing organization, while the objective of counseling is to help employees make a better adjustment to their work.

There are signs today that some of the other organizations to which employees belong, notably their unions, are objecting to intensive interviewing programs on the basis that the type of information being elicited often belongs within the union's system of administrative communication. Western Electric sincerely disavows any anti-union motives, while it concedes that counseling "serves to modify excessive demands" and "dissipates many complaints and grievances before they develop into serious disturbances." A union paper has poked fun at the deep interview as an unfair labor practice, advocating that "the NLRB . . . award the worker concerned a back-frustration up until the time he was talked out of his grievance by a company-employed industrial psychologist."[16] Here again, as in the case of suggestions bordering on complaints and grievances, we find two overlapping systems of administrative communication in competition for control of the same information. Although there is evidence that counseling is not expanding, the only counseling programs that we know have been dropped under union pressure are those of the southern California aircraft industries.[17]

INTERVIEWING TECHNIQUES

Establishing and Maintaining Rapport

Professional interviewers are the first to proclaim the importance of rapport, which, though an intangible thing, describes the psychological atmosphere of the interviewer-interviewee relationship. When rapport is good, there is an atmosphere of friendliness and trust, with both parties mutually interested in the same thing and co-operating on it.[18]

For the staff interviewer or counselor the building of good rapport starts in the first interview—indeed, with the first greeting. Rapport then tends to improve or worsen as time goes on, though one may expect some seesawing along the way. When a line superior interviews a subordinate, rapport is less exclusively a matter of interview behavior—it extends beyond the interviewing relationship to the continuing relationship in the shop or office.

The physical setting contributes to rapport, as is seen in the psychoanalyst's use of a couch to make his client comfortable and at ease. Although interviewing facilities in business are not this elaborate, the interviewer does well to offer the interviewee comfort and privacy, to protect the interview from interruptions, and to maintain an atmosphere of leisure. The Hawthorne Works interviewers used a lunchroom—although there are now interviewing rooms throughout the plant—and others have successfully used alcoves and corridors away from traffic. Supervisors should be able to use their offices, provided they have allowed some of the luster of authority to rub off—possibly by having used the offices for conversations, interviews, and conferences in the past. The feeling expressed in "I've got to go to the boss's office" is akin to that of the youngster going to the principal's office. The successful line interviewer elicits a different reaction among his subordinates, who say, "I'm going to have a talk with the boss," with no mention of the office.

Occasionally we encounter an overemphasis and overdependence on the element of rapport, a suggestion that the greater the rapport, the better the interview. The objective, however, should not be a maximum rapport but something short of that, which Herbert Hyman labels "optimum rapport." With maximum rapport, bordering on intimacy, "the respondent may prefer not to hurt the interviewer's feelings, or may be eager to defer to the interviewer's opinion."[19] An interviewer who allows people to become dependent on him or to submit blindly to his leadership is pre-empting for himself and for the organization an intolerable and unwholesome burden. Moreover, communicative efficiency may be as low in such a relationship as it is when rapport is poor.

Listening

Interviewing has had its greatest impact on managerial thinking by emphasizing the importance of listening. The interviewers at the Hawthorne Works listened and found out many things that top management had never known. In the years that have followed, management—with and without professional interviewing help—has been trying to do a better job of listening.

One of the interviewer's special talents is his ability to listen. An interviewer does not say, "I know exactly what's bothering you. I had your job once, and I know what a headache it is." Were he to behave thus, he would become, in effect, the interviewee, who, by one definition, is the person in an interview who does the major part of the talking. Instead, the interviewer listens, listens, and listens. He listens for what the interviewee says, for what he does not say, and for what he apparently cannot say—at least without help—since he is probably not even aware of it himself.[20] A skilled interviewer knows the imperfections and limitations of bare words and strives constantly to perceive other meanings—meanings that might more truly reflect what the speaker intends to say. While the interviewer listens, he watches for telltale gestures and facial expressions in the interviewee, zealously avoiding those same non-verbal communicative acts himself.[21]

From non-directive interviewing the idea has developed that the interviewee should be responsible for clarification, since he alone knows best exactly what he means. For this reason, the interviewer avoids many of the opportunities offered him to comment on what he has heard, replying only with a noncommittal "Yes," "I see," or "Umhum." He may occasionally repeat, and possibly rephrase to some degree, what the interviewee has just said, with an implicit question mark added ("You think your foreman doesn't like girls who wear slacks and that he doesn't like you because you wear slacks"). This reflecting technique is often stimulus enough to elicit further clarification or additional information.

On the theory that the most direct way to get an answer is to ask a question, interviewers do ask questions; directive interviewing is defined as the question-and-answer method. Even when he intends to conduct a non-directive interview, an interviewer will sometimes find that he is not getting the information he needs and will be forced to ask questions. All questioning must be cautiously neutral, of course, lest the questions carry the seeds of their own answers. In interviewing, as in conference-leading, questions can be highly directive, and this is readily perceived by many people. All of us are well conditioned to give socially acceptable answers to questions about our vices and virtues, our politics and ambitions, our likes and dislikes.

The way in which an interviewer emphasizes one or another aspect of listening depends on his objectives and interests, the time available, the nature of the subject matter and the respondent. The listening may be motivated by a sincere desire to secure the respondent's opinions, which emphasizes the administrative communication aspect, or it may be a device for helping someone "let off steam," which emphasizes the therapeutic aspect. In this latter connection, we might note the instruction that the Egyptian Vizier Ptah-hotep gave to his son—sometime between 2700 and 2200 B.C.: "If thou art one to whom petition is made, be calm as thou listenest to what the petitioner has to say. Do not rebuff him before he has swept out his body or before he has said that for which he came. The petitioner likes attention to his words better than the fulfilling of that for which he came. . . . It is not necessary that everything about which he has petitioned should come to pass, but a good hearing is soothing to the heart."[22]

If, as in the census, interviewing is being used as an economical way to get objective information (the number of children and bathrooms in a household), direct questioning is indicated. If time is limited, unguided interviewing is inadvisable, for there is hardly a better way to shatter rapport than to watch the clock.[23] Moreover, it is needlessly time-consuming to probe extensively and circuitously when a respondent is entirely co-operative or when the scope of managerial involvement is neither deep nor needs to be.[24] The skilled interviewer draws on all his listening talents and techniques as required by the nature of his assignment and by the immediate circumstances.

Recording and Reporting

Interviewing is essentially an oral communicative process. Yet its effectiveness depends largely on written records and reports. Interviewers must make note of what they hear, then interpret and record it, and generally report on it. The interviewer himself finds the written record of one interview a help in preparing for the next one, and, at a later date, items that once seemed to be of no importance may prove to be significant.[25]

The notes taken during some interviews (in employment and polling, for example) may be simply fill-ins on a form or questionnaire, which can be used with minimum distraction. But note-taking at any time may arouse suspicion and inhibit response. A skilled interviewer is alert to the effects of taking notes and adopts the method seemingly indicated in each situation. In some cases it is prudent to take no notes or only the barest fragmentary ones, completing the record immediately after the interview; in other cases an interviewee will respond freely only if he can see the notes, either while they are being taken or afterward. Tape recording is a promising innovation. It avoids any loss of interviewing material and frees the interviewer to concentrate on the most subtle expressions of nonverbal communication. But if the interviewee dislikes being "taped," rapport will suffer and his responses will assuredly be altered.[26]

In his recording and reporting the interviewer must be careful to separate fact from inference and to move cautiously from the specific to the general. An interviewee may list ten different employments during the last ten years as a firsthand account of verifiable happenings. Although this type of employment history may suggest that the interviewee is some sort of problem employee, such an interpretation should be clearly labeled as an inference and not a fact.

There can be no complete reporting of information or sources in either counseling or opinion-polling interviews, since, in both cases, the relationship with the respondent is one of professional confidence. Some executives feel that an interviewer who has information useful to the organization is being disloyal when he withholds it, forgetting perhaps that every interviewer is subject to attack from another quarter—that of his respondents. "Being neutral," asserts the director of Industrial Mental Health of the Menninger Foundation, "means absolute confidentiality."[27]

Aside from the polls, individual interviewing programs do not incorporate systematic sampling procedures. As a result, the interviewer ends up with an assortment of individualized findings, and few, if any, practical generalizations. Yet any strong pressure from top management for less talk and more action may force interviewers to hazard generalizations and violate confidences in a manner inconsistent with the ethics of good interviewing practice. Any interviewer who must balance his confidential interviewing relationships against top management's reporting requirements eventually finds himself in an acutely difficult and unhappy situation. This is no doubt one reason why interviewing has not spread more rapidly in the years since the Hawthorne experiment.[28]

In order to safeguard the integrity of interviewing, it may be wise to curtail reporting requirements. One way to do this is to have line officials conduct their own interviews and utilize the findings themselves. With a little effort communication skills can be taught to almost every intelligent supervisor; directive and patterned interviewing are not exceptions. Western Electric's counselors, using the more difficult non-directive technique, are not required to have any formal preparation prior to their in-service training.[29] One of the skills that should be taught is the ability to recognize difficult cases so that they can be referred to specialists.[30] All the communication skills, including those of interviewing, appear to be elements of leadership, and the degree to which they are mastered is a useful measure of supervisory competence.

INTERVIEWING AND UPWARD COMMUNICATION

Successful communication depends to a great extent on the ability of a communicator to perceive how he is understood or why he is misunderstood. By tradition and by virtue of his role as order-giver, the superior is thought of primarily as a communicator, and the subordinate as a communicatee. In an interviewing situation the roles are reversed, with the interviewer, who in fact is a superior or is identified with him, taking the role of communicatee. This reversal of traditional roles is not an easy thing.

Interviewing Bias

Frequently the principal asset of an outside consultant (assuming he is skilful and reputable) is his acceptability to the members of the organization as a communicatee. The fact that he has no position in the organization may make it easier for employees to deal with him on an equal basis.

On the part of the interviewee.—For anyone within the hierarchy the ideally neutral role is more difficult to attain. Try as he may, a superior cannot divest himself completely of his mantle of authority. To most subordinates he will always be the boss, or represent the boss, and it behooves them to say what he likes to hear and to do what he wants them to do. It may be to their interest, also, to withhold certain information lest it be used against them or against others in the same work or social group.

Even in exit interviews, when the interviewees are presumably released from their intragroup ties, they have reason for being less than frank—particularly if they are skilled workers with limited opportunities for specialized employment. An actuary, for example, who leaves one insurance company will no doubt seek his next position with another insurance company in the area. The new employer may check with the previous employer only to learn that "Jones was a disgruntled fellow who complained about his superior and his salary." If Jones is at all sophisticated, he will depart with good grace, uttering no complaints in an exit interview. Jones may also want to leave the door open for his return to the first company at some later date, and there is a good chance that he knows that one of the questions on most exit-interviewing records is, "Would you recommend this man for re-employment?"

These examples of invalid responses are simply illustrative and fall far short of explaining all inaccurate responses in interviews. Certainly the presence of an interviewer is not the only reason why interviewees respond inaccurately, since they often fail similarly in completing self-administered questionnaires.[31] In America, and probably elsewhere, children learn not to tattle on their playmates, and this training may very well affect their behavior as adult respondents.

On the part of the interviewer.—In addition to the bias injected by the respondent himself, there is the further possibility of bias in the interviewer. A person in the role of interviewer can never wholly insulate himself from his total personality, his likes and dislikes, his group identifications, job requirements, and predispositions.

Tests have shown that even skilled interviewers will introduce subjective biases into their observations and records. A classic example is Stuart Rice's analysis of interviews with two thousand indigents at New York's Municipal Lodging House. One of the interviewers, who was a Prohibitionist, found that 62 per cent of the respondents owed their downfall to liquor and 7 per cent to business conditions. But an interviewer who was a Socialist found that only 22 per cent owed their downfall to liquor, while 39 per cent had been afflicted primarily by adverse business conditions.[32]

Since line superiors succeed or fail on the basis of production records and not interviewing records, it is not surprising that they should carry over into their periodic evaluations, and into the interviews that accompany them, their impressions of subordinates as producers. Confronted with a rating scale to fill out, a superior, influenced by a halo effect, is prone to give the high-producing employee a high rating on all factors and not just on those directly related to production.[33] The fact that interviewers can be unduly affected either by particular traits or by general impressions has widespread implications for employment interviewing and more or less directly pervades all interpersonal relationships.

On the part of top management.—There may be another bias to contend with; one that, strictly speaking, is beyond the scope of the interviewing process. Because interviewers, particularly counselors, must constantly assert their professional neutrality, some executives are bound to regard them as being "pro-employee." (This is probably an accurate appraisal in some cases, since counselors are highly interested in employees' personal problems that, in the eyes of many officials, are not germane to operations.) These superiors tend to discount their interviewers' work and thereby introduce a further bias.[34]

Interviewing bias, whether stemming from the respondent, the interviewer, or a superior official, is to some extent, inevitable. This should be expected, since bias is a function of judgment, and individual judgments have way of varying—in medical diagnoses, in metallurgical analyses, and in financial audits. One of the efforts being made to eliminate interviewing bias calls for the use of self-administered questionnaires. These, of course, can cover only part of the field traditionally covered by individual interviews, and they still fall short of eliminating all sources of bias. There is great promise that bias can be reduced through better selection and training of interviewers and superiors and through further study of the phenomenon of bias by scientists interested in its control and elimination.

Using Interviews in Combination with Other Methods

Interviewing processes frequently require information other than that elicited in the interview itself. One of the advantages of the individual interview over the anonymous opinion poll is the availability of factual personnel data, such as age and length of employment, which can be drawn from the personnel records. It is sometimes necessary, incidental to an interview, to get information on the respondent's physical condition, his mental health, his home life, and his suitability for his job.[35] A single interviewer may be able to follow through on several of these aspects, as when he administers an aptitude test or talks with a previous employer, but frequently he will have to combine his interviewing findings with the findings of others and arrive at an answer only after considering all the data.

Significant work has been done on the indirect measurement of attitudes, needs, and motivations, either alone or in conjunction with interviews and polls. Some companies study their attendance records to identify those employees who have been absent frequently or for an extended period and interview them to ascertain the true causes. Absence is not the only indirect measure of dissatisfaction or disinterest, which may be manifested also by tardiness, terminations, the nature and frequency of accidents, transfers, the prevalence and character of complaints and grievances, and decreased productivity.[36]

When these crude measures are refined and manipulated statistically for a particular plant or office, the results may furnish a good insight into the workings of the organization and indicate the need for specific managerial action. In one case the index of productivity has been intercorrelated with the indexes of efficiency affecting customers, efficiency not affecting customers, and several other factors to provide an "objective morale index." On the basis of the morale-index scores, individual interviews and polls are used for further validation and diagnosis.[37] A statistical analysis of turnover among new employees was the basis on which the Harwood Manufacturing Company revised its training program several years ago. The high turnover among trainees who were just short of reaching the established production standard suggested that they needed the satisfaction of accomplishment that could come from achieving intermediate standards along the way.[38] These are unusually good examples of indirect measurements by skilled and cautious researchers, who would themselves disclaim any general application of their findings.

The difficulty, of course, with any scheme for indirect measurement of attitudes, needs, motivations, and other highly personal elements of human behavior lies in finding those indirect factors to which they are directly related—not just once but again and again under varying circumstances. This difficulty has been underscored by those observers who have pointed to the hard-driving worker, who is a good producer but does not know why he works, is not interested in the organization, and is not particularly satisfied with his work.[39] This sort of fellow may well be an exception, and we can no doubt develop suggestive leads through various indirect measurements. But, fortunately, it is not likely in a free society that we will ever have indirect measures that are infallible guages of human behavior.

A recent development is the group interview, which combines the interviewing process with the small group discussion, or conference process. The cross-talk that takes place may stimulate and refine responses, overcome some of the restraints present in an individual interview (although introducing some new ones), and give insight into the individual's behavior in a group situation.[40]

The desire of executives to secure more and truer information from their subordinates has led to the use of interviews in combination with polling techniques. Interviews are used to identify problems of current interest to employees and to get a better grasp of the cultural milieu—including language—as aids in designing opinion-polling questionnaires.

Just the reverse of this is the use of a group poll (as discussed in the next chapter)—with its anonymity, speed of coverage, and economy—to locate areas of employee interest and concern and then to follow up with individual interviews to locate underlying causes. As James Worthy has put it: polls will tell you *where*, but you need interviews to find out *why*.[41]

Selected Readings

BOOKS AND MONOGRAPHS

BINGHAM, WALTER V., and MOORE, BRUCE V. *How To Interview*. 4th rev. ed. New York: Harper & Bros., 1959.

Widely used text, covering interviewing in administration and in various professional applications, such as social casework, mental hygiene, and journalism. Selected readings accompany each chapter.

BURNHAM, PAUL S., and PALMER, STUART H. (comps.). *Counseling in Personnel Work—1945–1949*. Chicago: Public Administration Service, 1951.

Counseling in Industry. Cleveland: Cleveland Public Library, Business Information Bureau, 1951.

Two annotated bibliographies.

GARDNER, BURLEIGH B., and MOORE, DAVID G. *Human Relations in Industry*, 3d ed. Chicago: Richard D. Irwin, Inc., 1955. Chap. xviii, "Personnel Counseling."

The counselor's dilemma in his relations with employees and with top management.

MAIER, NORMAN R. F. *Principles of Human Relations*. New York: John Wiley & Sons, Inc., 1952. Chap. xii, "The Supervisor's Dealings with Individuals."

Concise discussion of interviewing as a supervisory function.

PFIFFNER, JOHN M. *The Supervision of Personnel: Human Relations in the Management of Men.* New York: Prentice-Hall, Inc., 1951. Part V, "Clinical Approaches to Troubled People."

A strong argument for assigning traditionally staff-administered personnel activities, including counseling, to line supervisors. Chapter bibliographies.

ROETHLISBERGER, F. J., and DICKSON, WILLIAM J. *Management and the Worker.* Cambridge: Harvard University Press, 1939. Chap. xiii, "The Interviewing Method."

Original statement of the rules for non-directive interviewing established in the Hawthorne experiment.

WEINLAND, JAMES D., and GROSS, MARGARET V. *Personnel Interviewing.* New York: Ronald Press Co., 1952.

Quite detailed text on the various interviewing processes in administration.

ARTICLES

BUCHER, RUE; FRITZ, CHARLES E.; and QUARANTELLI, E. L. "Tape Recorded Interviews in Social Research," *American Sociological Review,* Vol. 21 (June, 1956), pp. 359–64. (For a slightly condensed version, see *Public Opinion Quarterly,* Vol. 20 [Summer, 1956], pp. 427–39.)

Advantages, effects, some applications, and the cost of tape recording.

HYMAN, HERBERT. "Interviewing as a Scientific Procedure," pp. 203–16 in *The Policy Sciences,* ed. DANIEL LERNER and HAROLD D. LASSWELL. Stanford, Calif.: Stanford University Press, 1951.

Comprehensive statement on the current status of interviewing methods. Asserts that interviewing is the most promising avenue to subjective information despite existing imperfections, which are gradually being corrected.

LEVINSON, HARRY. "Employee Counseling in Industry: Observations on Three Programs," *Bulletin of the Menninger Clinic,* Vol. 20 (March, 1956), pp. 76–84.

Discusses the programs of the Western Electric Company, the Prudential Life Insurance Company, and the Caterpillar Tractor Company. Bibliography.

MACK, DAVID. "Function of the Interview in Personnel Administration," *Management Review,* Vol. 39 (March, 1950), pp. 134–38. (Reprinted in PAUL PIGORS and CHARLES A. MYERS [eds.], *Readings in Personnel Administration* [New York: McGraw-Hill Book Co., 1952], pp. 188–93.)

Advises staff interviewers that they must not undercut line officials and that employees in a democratic society must solve their personal problems themselves.

MELCHER, ROBERT D. "Getting the Facts on Employee Resignations: An Exit Interview Program," *Personnel,* Vol. 31 (May, 1955), pp. 504–14.

Highly detailed case study.

WILENSKY, JEANNE L., and HAROLD L. "Personnel Counseling: The Hawthorne Case," *American Journal of Sociology,* Vol. 57 (November, 1951), pp. 265–80.

A critical review and appraisal of Western Electric's counseling program by two sociologists, one of whom worked as a Hawthorne interviewer for three years.

XIV / *Employee Opinion Polls*

ADVANCES in interviewing methods, supplemented with the techniques of psychological testing, have opened up the field of employee opinion polling. By using scientific sampling procedures, polling promises to overcome some of the major limitations of other interviewing programs as communicative devices. Exit interviews, for example, deal only with those individuals who are leaving, and counseling interviews only with those who take personal problems to a counselor.

Whenever the interviewees do not comprise a representative sample, it is difficult for an interviewer to offer management a systematic analysis of his interviewing results. The pollster, however, working with all the employees or with a representative group of them, can secure results that lend themselves to systematic, quantitative analysis. The psychological value of the counseling interview is present to a slight degree in polls—the employees still have an opportunity to "let off steam." But polls do not focus on *individuals;* instead the emphasis is on gathering information about a *group.*

THE DEVELOPMENT OF
EMPLOYEE OPINION POLLING

Employee opinion polls were introduced in the early 1920's, but as late as 1944 the National Industrial Conference Board had difficulty in finding fifty corporations using them.[1] Ten years later, out of four hundred and sixty-nine companies replying to another Board survey, ninety-six (slightly more than 20 per cent) had made use of polls. The percentage was considerably higher among the largest companies (56 per cent) than among the smallest ones (10.6 per cent).[2] One of the pioneering companies has been Aldens, a Chicago mail-order firm, which has conducted polls each year since 1937.

Among the large companies that have conducted polls in recent years are American Potash and Chemical, Armstrong Cork, Carnation Company, Caterpillar Tractor, Cleveland Graphite Bronze, Ford, General Foods, Koppers, *Los Angeles Times-Mirror*, New York Telephone, Owens-Illinois Glass, Pacific Telephone and Telegraph, Standard Oil of California, and Sears, Roebuck. In Great Britain considerable attention has been directed to polling techniques, but in only a few companies (including Esso Petroleum and the Rowntree Works) have polls actually been conducted.[3]

Polls have also been introduced in governmental administration—in cities, counties, and various federal departments.[4] Certainly the most ambitious organizational polling program to date was the one conducted during and immediately after World War II by the United States Army. Two million officers and enlisted men were covered by several hundred polls that dealt with such subjects as combat motivation, postwar morale, attitudes toward the enemy and the people of occupied countries, attitude changes resulting from the army's motion pictures and other indoctrination efforts, the reasons why medical officers would or would not accept Regular Army commissions, enlisted men's preferences in food and clothing, and the opinions of hospital patients about their treatment. The Army's point system of redeployment and discharge was based on the preferences expressed in polls.[5]

Polling has been adopted as a means of administrative communication within a few labor unions to guide union leaders on the opinions of members. Obviously the tenor of questions appearing in union polls differs markedly from that seen in management-sponsored polls.

MAJOR STEPS IN THE CONDUCT OF POLLS

Polling in administration is but a small section of the field of public opinion polling, which also encompasses the federal census, political forecasting, and market research. With the bulk of all polling being done outside industry, employee opinion polling can take advantage of, and must conform to, generally accepted polling methods.

Defining Objectives

It is imperative that the pollster and the sponsoring organization agree on the objectives of a poll before it is undertaken. The imitation of someone else's poll is scarcely more rational than the imitation of someone else's employee handbook.

We noted in the first chapter that management was originally interested in communication along with morale. This accounts for the traditional appellations—"morale survey" and "attitude survey." Employees were queried about their work and pay, working conditions, personal relations with co-workers and supervisors, and the prestige of the organization. These items, and others like them, continue to appear in polls, but they no longer dominate them as they did.

In an increasing number of polls the objective is to measure various aspects of administrative communication—what employees know and how they learned it, what they want to know, and what communicative methods they prefer. The answers to questions in these areas constitute an audit of administrative communication, which is a logical step in any drive for improvement.

Polls are also used to gain other information that does not flow upward with ease, such as suggestions for improvements and employee reaction to proposed changes in policy, procedure, and organization. Polls are used to secure material for management training programs and, in some cases, to stimulate the respondents to think about the items mentioned in the polls. Too often, however, the objectives are not established clearly at the outset, with the surveyors failing to ask themselves what they really want to know. This deficiency later imperils the value or validity of the polling results.

Designing a Poll

Once objectives have been clearly defined, the next step is to design the poll. Every poll has two sections, and many have a third. The first section is limited to factual information about the respondents, such as age, sex, salary, and length of service.

The second section comprises the questions in the specific areas being explored. These questions must be drawn up with great care in order to safeguard the statistical validity and reliability of the responses. It has been rather common practice to provide a third section for comments that the respondents might volunteer. These comments do not lend themselves readily to statistical treatment, but they often give interesting clues to problems not covered by the specific questions. An alert pollster will follow up these clues in preparing questions for his next poll.

A pollster has many types of questions to choose from. The six basic types, however, are shown below, along with examples:

1. *Dichotomous, or Yes-No:* Do you like your work? [Besides a "Yes" or "No" answer, there is frequently provision for a "Don't know" or "No opinion" answer.]

2. *Multiple-Choice:* What do you think about the food in the cafeteria? (Mark the answer you agree with.) Excellent —— Good —— Fair —— Not bad —— Terrible ——.

3. *Check-List:* What were your reasons for choosing our company as a place to work? Salary —— Location —— Friends —— Our reputation —— Training program —— Working conditions —— Things our employment interviewer said to you —— Other reasons ——.

4. *Ranking, or Rank-Order:* Place a number, from 1 to 5, before

each of the following items, according to their importance to you:
— Good wages — Good working conditions — Opportunities for
advancement — Job security — Friendly co-workers. [Some polls
have consisted of only one question of this type.]

5. *Coincidental, Recall, and Recognition:* What was Bulletin 217
about?

6. *Open-End:* What are the things you like least about our company? [This is a typical question for the third section of an employee
opinion poll, with as much as an entire blank page provided for the
response.]

The *free story* is yet another type of questioning technique.
It is used only in a face-to-face interview, where the interviewer alone knows the specific questions for which responses
are wanted. After the conclusion of an extensive and partially
non-directive interview, the interviewer writes down the answers he has elicited.

A variation of the multiple-choice question is used in rating
scales, which, by providing for gradations of intensity in the
answers, afford a degree of flexibility and refinement not normally found in the more conventional forms of questionnaires.
The respondent is offered not a question but a positive statement; for example, "This is a good company to work for,"
with five options ranging from "Decidedly agree" through
"Tend to agree," "Undecided," "Tend to disagree," and "Decidedly disagree."[6] The dividing line between positive and
negative responses can be shifted for each question and in
different applications, and these shifts will not be obvious to
the respondents. If the question "This is a good company to
work for" were asked of clerks in a department store, any
answer except "Decidedly agree" might be regarded as a negative response. But if the same question were asked of coal
miners, all answers short of "Decidedly disagree" might be
regarded as positive.

Every question, no matter of what type, must ask what is
intended and nothing more. This points to the need for pretesting questions, which is discussed below, and for pretesting

the possible replies with management lest they later prove to be unanticipated traps. If management is determined, for example, to operate the plant or office from eight to five, it would be foolish to ask the employees how they like the hours.

Selecting the Sample

One of the most significant contributions of polling to the study of social life is the technique of sampling. Working with a small but representative sample, a pollster can determine, with a high degree of accuracy, the characteristics of the larger group of which the sample is a part. The accuracy of the determination varies from one poll to another, but each successive poll leads to further statistical refinements in sampling methods.

The size of the sample depends on how large the organization is. In relatively small organizations, it is possible to cover all the employees (technically called "the universe"), or all those of certain classes, such as all hourly shop workers. In larger organizations it may be faster and less expensive to use only a sample. The sample for a poll on items of organization-wide implication might include everyone in a few representative departments or locations, while in another case the sample could be extracted from the total population throughout the entire organization.

Pretesting

Polling questions must be pretested to make certain that they will be interpreted as the surveyor intended. It is readily apparent that terms such as "company benefits," "expansion program," "government regulation," and "personnel matters" are susceptible of varying interpretations among employees of differing backgrounds and assignments. Even the arrangement of the options in a check list or in a multiple-choice or rank-order question will affect the replies.

Questions can be pretested in individual interviews or in pilot polls. A pilot poll can be used, also, to pretest the procedures (such as timing, the distribution and collection of questionnaires, and scoring) for the final poll.[7]

Securing Replies

The actual taking of the poll may be carried out in a variety of ways: by individual interviews, by the distribution of questionnaires (to individuals or to assembled groups), or by a combination of these methods. The individual interview is more time-consuming and therefore more expensive per unit, but it has certain offsetting advantages: a respondent can be kept interested longer when an interviewer is working with him than when he is working alone on a questionnaire; the individual interview takes care of respondents who would not understand the written questions; there is no "reading ahead" in an individual interview the way there is with a questionnaire; and a skilled interviewer, through firsthand observation and insight, may get truer and more complete answers than those indicated by a respondent's check mark or fill-in.[8]

The usual practice in the administration of employee polls is to assemble the respondents in a meeting room or cafeteria in groups of as many as a hundred at a time, as seen in the photograph taken during a recent poll at Aldens, Inc. (Fig. 17). It is the task of the interviewer, or proctor, to explain the poll and give instructions and to distribute and collect the questionnaires. At Aldens it is explained to the participants that there are no *right* or *wrong* answers. This is particularly important for persons who are participating for the first time. They are also asked not to discuss the questions with their neighbors, but the company has never observed any interest in copying answers.

The interviewer must assure the respondents of their anonymity by admonishing them not to sign their names and by making it clear that all the questionnaires will be destroyed as soon as they have been tabulated, with only summary tabulations going to the sponsor. He may provide sealed envelopes for the completed questionnaires and perhaps have them deposited in a locked ballot box. The trust which the respondents have in the interviewer is a product of their trust in the management which has employed him and their prior experiences with interviewers.

Analyzing and Presenting Results

The technical processes of polling culminate in the analysis and presentation of the replies. Because neither raw tabulations nor percentages alone tell the story, the pollster must use the most suitable statistical methods and bring to bear on the results a high degree of insight. He must make every effort to avoid statistically unreliable interpretations and unwarranted generalizations. If, for example, only five people respond to a question, even a single response has too much weight, and two responses can markedly influence the results. The same one or two responses in a group of twenty-five or thirty would have much less effect.[9]

No single question in an interview or on a questionnaire will provide the meaningfulness that can come from a number of questions aimed at the same general subject from different angles. In the same way, no one poll will be as enlightening as the comparative results of successive polls in the same organization or parallel polls in comparable units of the organization. The comparison feature, so important throughout administration, can be readily utilized in reporting the results of polls through statistical, narrative, or graphic media, or combinations of them.

Fig. 17.—Personnel at Aldens, Inc., completing their questionnaires in a poll

INFORMATION COMMUNICATED THROUGH POLLS
Facts

The questions asked in polls seek three broad categories of information: facts, knowledge, and attitudes and preferences.

Employee opinion polls always begin with questions that are concerned with census-type factual data—questions on age, sex, marital status, education, years of employment, current earnings, plant or department, and tenure in current assignment. The reason for having these questions is to permit analysis of results in relation to age groups, earning levels, departments, etc. Provision is made for bracketing most answers in ranges; for example, age, 25–30; years of employment, 5–10; weekly earnings, $50–$60. The brackets represent the desired breakdowns for sorting and analysis, and they are drawn to cover not less than twenty or twenty-five persons in each one.[10] Thus, there are enough answers in each category to give a presumably reliable picture, and, at the same time, the respondents are given further assurance of their anonymity. In a poll conducted through individual interviews, the census data can be obtained as well from the organization's personnel files as from the respondents.

Questions which elicit factual answers may also appear in the second section of the poll. Questions regarding the respondent's use of the company's educational and recreational facilities would call for factual answers. Some questions designed to bring out factual replies, however, may be too affected by other conditions to insure entirely objective answers. The factual answer to a multiple-choice question asking an employee how he finds out about changes in policy might be "My supervisor tells me," but a respondent who has not gotten along well with his supervisor may be strongly motivated to fabricate a reply to the question.

What Employees Know

The second broad type of information deals with the respondents' knowledge about the organization. Questions in this area dominate polls concerned with measuring administrative communication. Corson's pioneering work in the Bureau of Old Age and Survivors' Insurance was aimed at finding out the degree to which instructions were remembered and understood, and the same objective underlies the "communication knowledge test" developed at the University of Minnnesota.[11]

Any review of employee opinion polls, including those not pinpointing communication, reveals a number of questions that test the respondents' knowledge about something. Recent polls conducted by the Industrial Relations Section of the California Institute of Technology, for example, have tested employees' knowledge about hospital insurance plans, retirement plans, group insurance plans, suggestion systems, company profits, the number of employees, and the number of stockholders.

Employees' responses to questions about what they know rank second in accuracy to those that call for facts. However, the employees' generalized attitudes toward their superiors and the organization as a whole may lead them to respond inaccurately or untruthfully. Furthermore, in any test of employees' knowledge, some people may be unwilling to reveal their ignorance, leading them to fabricate replies or not reply at all.

Attitudes

It is the third general category of information that has come to have the greatest emphasis—the category of attitudes and preferences. Illustrative are these questions taken from a recent poll conducted by the Standard Oil Company of California.

I feel that my present job is:
—— (1) Very interesting
—— (2) Interesting
—— (3) Of little interest
—— (4) Of no interest
In general, I would rate working conditions on my job:
—— (1) Very good
—— (2) Satisfactory
—— (3) Fair
—— (4) Unsatisfactory
When it comes to getting the cooperation of his employees, I feel
that my immediate supervisor is:
—— (1) Absolutely tops
—— (2) Good
—— (3) Fair
—— (4) Not very effective
As a group to work with, my fellow-employees are:
—— (1) As fine a group as I could want
—— (2) A good group
—— (3) Fair
—— (4) Unsatisfactory

The most difficult polling problems have arisen in the field
of attitude measurement. One is confronted with a succession
of debates about such questions as what is meant by "attitude,"
the relationship of attitudes and opinions, and the relationship
between attitudes, opinions, and behavior.[12] The expression
of an opinion is an overt act and, therefore, the result of the
interplay of a number of potentially active attitudes, some of
which may first cross an individual's mind at the moment of
interrogation. Thus the solicitation of an opinion not only may
fail to bring out the particular attitude sought but may arouse
attitudes which are quite different and apparently unrelated.[13]
The relationship between attitudes, opinions, and behavior is
further complicated by the way in which opinions adapt attitudes to social situations and relentlessly remold them.[14]

Seldom, if ever, in the course of his employment, is an employee asked to comment explicitly on his job satisfaction or
on his boss's competence. When he is suddenly called upon to

express his opinion on one of these subjects, it is reasonable to suspect that he may be stimulated to think about many things related to the specific subject—some directly related, others indirectly related, and yet others only remotely related. Out of this new complex of thoughts and emotions comes the stimulus to mark an X in one or another spot on a questionnaire. And the fact that he marked it that way may fixate his belief accordingly.

Nor can we yet feel certain that an attitude, assuming it is discoverable, is a fixed thing that influences behavior in a direct and predictable manner.[15] In a classic piece of research, R. T. La Piere traveled approximately ten thousand miles by car with a Chinese couple. They crossed the United States twice, and went up and down the Pacific coast. They were provided with sleeping accommodations at sixty-six different places and they were served meals in one hundred eighty-four restaurants. They were refused service only once. After the trip, La Piere sent a questionnaire to all the hotels, inns, and restaurants asking whether they would accept members of the Chinese race as guests. One hundred and twenty-eight replies were received. In startling contradiction to the prior experience, about 93 per cent of the restaurants and about 92 per cent of the lodging places responded "No."[16]

From a practical standpoint, the pollster must constantly re-examine and refine the objectives of his studies, recognizing that it is one thing to determine what the existing opinions are but quite another to uncover the underlying attitudes, to discover why they exist, and to predict behavior.

THE EMPLOYEE OPINION POLL: A NEW MEDIUM

In most public opinion polls the pollster addresses his questions to the respondents, and they reply, thus concluding the relationship. In employee opinion polling, however, the relationship is a continuing one, with the poll another episode in a never-ending series of communicative acts. Administrators must regard respondents as both communicators and communicatees, as people receiving information through the poll, responding to it, and awaiting management's reaction.

Management Communication through Polling Questions

There is no doubt that management, wittingly or unwittingly, communicates something to the respondents through its polls. The mere fact that the poll is conducted indicates that management is interested in the employees' expressions. This interest is verbalized, of course, by the interviewer and in the letter of transmittal which generally prefaces any written questionnaire.

The questions themselves, no matter how barren they appear to be at first glance, are highly meaningful to those among the respondents who are at all perceptive. "Does your supervisor notify you of changes in plans?" suggests to the employee that one of the measures of a good supervisor is whether or not he notifies his subordinates of changes in plans. The authors of the communication knowledge test at the University of Minnesota found that, immediately following the test, "the whole staff became 'communication-conscious.' They rummaged through their desk drawers locating manuals and memoranda and promptly began to 'bone up' and go into huddles with one another to discuss the 'right answers.' "[17]

Some questions are consciously laid out to convey information to the respondents. "We have a medical plan, a hospital plan, a group insurance plan, and a pension plan. Place your check mark in the blank space below preceding the percentage figure that you think states most nearly the company's contribution and your contribution." A question of this sort can be an effective reminder that these various plans are in existence.

Management's Response

In an earlier chapter we noted the need for prompt response to employees who submit suggestions. As already observed, employees are likely to become restive while waiting for the organization's response to their sincere and often, to them, difficult verbalization. The problem of response is quite similar in employee opinion polling.

There are several ways that an organization can reply to the expressions of its employees. One is to report the results of the poll to all the employees through an available medium or through a special publication. A popular method is to reprint the questionnaire with the tabulations of the answers written in. This may be made the subject of a management newsletter, as illustrated in Figure 18, to rush the results to supervisors and other members of the management group. General distribution can follow in the employee newspaper or magazine. The Carnation Company, Cleveland Graphite Bronze Division, and Standard Oil Company of California have issued special and highly attractive booklets, one of which is illustrated in Figure 19.

An organization can also reply by taking action on the subject matter of the poll. Whenever the results—alone or in conjunction with other information—indicate the need for action, it should be initiated as soon as possible. When a poll at the University of Illinois showed how little the employees knew about their retirement and disability benefits, the university's reply was to distribute more information on the subject.[18] When Corson's poll revealed how ill informed his subordinates were about their job instructions, he redesigned the written instructions, giving attention to the location of items on a page, headings, length of paragraphs, and the use of illustrations.[19]

We know of two polls that showed highly negative employee attitudes which produced two entirely different management reactions. In the first situation only 50 per cent of the employees rated the company as "the best place in town to work." This was interpreted to mean that the company had too high a ratio of young men for the "loyalty" it wanted, and gradually the younger men were replaced by older, more mature men.[20] Such a cure may be worse than the disease, for,

MANAGEMENT NEWS LETTER

Issued monthly by
Standard Oil Company of California
to keep management informed
on developments within the corporate family

| Prepared by Personnel Department | December 1955 |

SPECIAL EDITION   OPINION POLL REPORT

The results of the Employee Opinion Poll have been received from Caltech and are now being printed in booklet form. This booklet "Here Again Is Your Opinion," will be mailed in the next few days to the homes of all employees of companies that participated in the poll

In advance, for you, percentage answers are shown below. These results are the composite of answers given by employees in all the companies included in the poll. The poll results for individual departments and operating companies will soon be presented through channels

The answers to the first eight "Personal Information" questions are not shown here as they were obtained primarily to assist in analyzing results.

Total of Employees Eligible to Participate · · · · · · · · · 19,573
Total of Questionnaires Returned · · · · · · · · · · · · · 15,969
Percentage of Eligible Employees Who Participated in Poll · · 81.5%

YOUR COMPANY IN GENERAL. This group of questions relates to how you feel about your company its management its future and your relationships with it.

9. Looking at my company as compared with other companies, I would say that it is:
42.8 ☐ (1) Among the best managed companies
31.0 ☐ (2) Better managed than most companies
21.8 ☐ (3) About as well managed as most companies
2.6 ☐ (4) Not quite as well managed as most companies
0.8 ☐ (5) One of the poorly managed companies
1.0 *No Answer*

10. How do you feel when you tell people what company you work for?
52.3 ☐ (1) Proud
38.6 ☐ (2) Good
7.4 ☐ (3) Just a place to work
0.7 ☐ (4) Not too happy about telling where I work
1.0 *No Answer*

11. How interested do you think your company is in its employees?
55.0 ☐ (1) Very interested
38.8 ☐ (2) Fairly interested
4.8 ☐ (3) Not so interested
0.8 ☐ (4) Not interested at all
0.6 *No Answer*

12. During the next 10 years I think that my company's position in the oil industry will:
84.0 ☐ (1) Improve
14.0 ☐ (2) Remain the same
1.0 ☐ (3) Decline
1.0 *No Answer*

13. Total Company contributions each quarter to the Stock Plan are:
71.3 ☐ (1) Based on the profits of the Company
14.9 ☐ (2) Based on the contributions of the members of the Plan
4.9 ☐ (3) Based on the market price of the stock
8.9 *No Answer*

Fig. 18.—Front page of a management newsletter reporting on an opinion poll at the Standard Oil Company of California.

B. YOUR COMPANY IN GENERAL

In this section you answered a series of questions about facts
you know and opinions you and others have of the Company.

5. I think the reputation our Company has with the
public is:

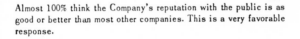

69.0%(1) Excellent
21.5%(2) Better than most other companies
8.6% (3) About as good as most other companies
0.4% (4) Not as good as most other companies
0.0%(5) Very poor
0.5% No Answer

Almost 100% think the Company's reputation with the public is as
good or better than most other companies. This is a very favorable
response.

6. I think the reputation our Company has with the
trade is:

46.2%(1) Excellent
36.1%(2) Better than most other companies
15.4%(3) About as good as most other companies
1.4% (4) Not as good as most other companies
0.0%(5) Very poor
0.9% No Answer

Better than 90% feel the Company's reputation with the trade is as
good or better than most other companies. This, too, is a very
favorable response.

FIG. 19.—Page from a report to employees on an opinion poll at The
Carnation Company.

once employees believe that polling results may be used against them, they will probably lie or refuse to respond in subsequent polls.

The second case concerns a large public utility whose poll revealed that those employees who were college graduates were the least satisfied with their jobs and had the least pride in the organization. This company might have reacted as the first one did by replacing its college graduates. Instead, managers and supervisors were admonished to "be alert to opportunities for assigning to all employees . . . tasks that will be a real challenge to their abilities."

Getting rid of disaffected employees, at one extreme, and eliminating the underlying causes, at the other, illustrate how broad is the range of possible managerial action. Whatever action is taken constitutes a meaningful response to the employees concerned. No action at all is also a response.

The Accuracy of Polls

The technical efficiency of employee opinion polls varies according to the integrity and competence of the surveyors and according to the subject matter dealt with. Polling, like other interviewing, calls for unblemished integrity, for no interviewer dares violate the trust of his respondents. An executive unwilling to observe this limitation will find it difficult if not impossible to employ reputable consultants in the polling field.

Even the most competent pollster suffers from the gaps in polling technique. Of the several types of information communicated in polls, factual data are reported most accurately, although the federal census itself is not without error. What employees know about things ranks next in accuracy, but it must be recognized that an employee's knowledge of an instruction does not necessarily mean that he will comply with it.

Attitude measurements are most vulnerable to error, particularly when they are made by persons without experience and training. Many attitude surveys can be challenged on the grounds that objectives were not clearly defined beforehand, that sufficient insight has not been brought to bear on the results, that single questions have presumed to tell much more than they ever do about management-employee relations, and that there has not been adequate pretesting.[21] Much difficult work is being done to refine the techniques of attitude measurement, and the promise of increased accuracy is great.

One of the potential advantages of questionnaire polls over individual interviews is the elimination of the effect of the interviewer. But, even when anonymous questionnaires are used, the results may vary with the type of interviewer who hands them out. "The respondents perceive something about the interviewer immediately from his mere appearance or behavior, interpret this for some reason in a certain way, and in turn alter their behavior."[22] In practice, of course, the interviewers make introductory speeches, which multiply the chances for them to affect results. In recognition of this problem, the interviewers at Aldens are required to make only the briefest prefatory remarks, answer questions quickly, and be off in a corner within four minutes.

Polls, like several other communicative devices, violate the fabric of superior-subordinate relationships. If polls are used at all, top management should be certain to work with the middle and lower levels of supervision at every step. There is no more justification for using polls to "put the finger" on superiors than on subordinates. Instead, as is already the practice in many companies, the polling results for each location or department should be furnished to the responsible superior, along with the company-wide results, for such action as *he* sees fit.

Selected Readings

BOOKS AND MONOGRAPHS

Experience with Employee Attitude Surveys. ("Studies in Personnel Policy," No. 115.) New York: National Industrial Conference Board, Inc., 1951.

Survey report covering 111 companies.

GRAY, ROBERT D. *Surveys of Employee Opinions—and What To Do with Them.* Pasadena: California Institute of Technology, Industrial Relations Section, 1952.

The methods used by Caltech's polling group. Bibliography.

PARTEN, MILDRED. *Surveys, Polls, and Samples: Practical Procedures.* New York: Harper & Bros., 1950.

Basic text on public opinion polling. Bibliography.

YODER, DALE; HENEMAN, HERBERT G., JR.; and CHEIT, EARL F. *Triple Audit of Industrial Relations.* Minneapolis: University of Minnesota Press, 1951.

Survey techniques used by the Industrial Relations Center of the University of Minnesota.

ARTICLES

ABRAMS, MARK. "Possibilities and Problems of Group Interviewing," *Public Opinion Quarterly,* Vol. 13 (Fall, 1949), pp. 502–6.

A novel experiment with the conduct of attitude surveys in discussion-group situations.

ALLEN, LOUIS A. "Action-oriented Attitude Surveys," *Personnel,* Vol. 29 (September, 1952), pp. 141–52.

The limitations and potentialities of attitude surveys, emphasizing the importance of interpreting results correctly and utilizing them constructively. Based on experience at Koppers Company.

CORSON, JOHN J. "Weak Links in the Chain of Command," *Public Opinion Quarterly,* Vol. 9 (Fall, 1945), pp. 346–49.

Report on a poll that revealed how little a group of administrative employees knew about the instructions they had received.

HAIRE, MASON, and GOTTSDANKER, J. S. "Factors Influencing Industrial Morale," *Personnel,* Vol. 27 (May, 1951), pp. 445–54.

Asserts that the factors in morale are highly interdependent and fluctuate in importance as situations change. Bibliography.

HOLDREDGE, F. E., JR. "Implementing an Employee Opinion Survey," *Journal of Applied Psychology*, Vol. 26 (October, 1942), pp. 428–35.

Adverse employee opinion on a particular activity is a danger signal that management cannot afford to ignore, but this evidence alone should not dictate changes.

HYMAN, HERBERT. "Problems in the Collection of Opinion-Research Data," *American Journal of Sociology*, Vol. 55 (January, 1950), pp. 362–70.

Experiments show that the interviewer and the respondent are each affected by the one's perception of the other; thus interviewing results are affected from both directions.

LOTT, CATHERINE S. "Let's Have an Attitude Survey," *Personnel Administration*, Vol. 15 (March, 1952), pp. 5–11.

A critical appraisal of conventional polling methods. Bibliography.

MACCOBY, ELEANOR E., and HOLT, ROBERT R. "How Surveys Are Made," pp. 581–91 in *Readings in Social Psychology*, ed. T. M. NEWCOMB and E. L. HARTLEY. New York: Henry Holt & Co., 1947. (Reprinted in BERNARD BERELSON and MORRIS JANOWITZ [eds.], *Reader in Public Opinion and Communication* [Glencoe, Ill.: Free Press, 1953].)

Brief description of the essentials in public opinion polling.

McCLANCY, B. F. "Polling Employee Opinions," pp. 12–24 in *Checking the Effectiveness of Employee Communication*. ("Personnel Series," No. 108.) New York: American Management Association, 1947.

Suggests that a poll is a pump-priming device to start the flow of information, and, if properly utilized, it should bring about its own elimination.

ROSE, ARNOLD M. "Attitude Measurement and the Questionnaire Survey," *Scientific Monthly*, Vol. 68 (February, 1949), pp. 97–101.

Summarizes the major problems in devising questionnaires, sampling, securing interviews, and analyzing and presenting results.

WIEBE, G. D. "Some Implications of Separating Opinions from Attitudes," *Public Opinion Quarterly*, Vol. 17 (Fall, 1953), pp. 328–52.

Opinions adapt attitudes to social requirements and become ingredients in the gradual reformation of attitudes.

WORTHY, JAMES C. "Discovering and Evaluating Employee Attitudes," pp. 13–22 in *Influencing and Measuring Employee Attitudes.* ("Personnel Series," No. 113.) New York: American Management Association, 1947.

Sears, Roebuck's combined use of polls and individual interviews.

PART IV / *Horizontal Communication*

Chapter XV   CLEARANCE AND REVIEW

Chapter XVI   THE CONFERENCE PROCESS

Great size and specialization cut down the opportunities for cross-talk while they increase the need for it. Scientific and industrial research depend heavily on prompt and effective interchange of information; without it, work is slowed down and wastefully duplicated. Wherever there is a need for co-ordinated group effort, there is a concomitant need for horizontal communication.

Various methods are used to conduct clearance and review and conferences, the two principal activities primarily concerned with the problem of horizontal communication. Neither of these activities is exclusively horizontal; indeed, all horizontal communication appears to be a by-product of vertical communication.

XV / Clearance and Review

THE MAJOR part of the communication that goes on in any organizaton is either downward and outward or upward and inward. Indeed, the processes of order-giving and reporting are basic in directing an organization and controlling it. But there is a need for co-ordination beyond the scope of order-giving and reporting. This co-ordination, whether a part of the line job or separate from it, is carried out by communication activities that are essentially horizontal in their direction. The two major activities are clearance and review and the conference process. The two are not entirely separable, as we shall note again later, since one of the methods for carrying on clearance is through conferences.

Horizontal communication is a newer and less well-charted field than either upward or downward communication and is largely a by-product of vertical communication. Significantly, it exists only as a by-product of vertical communication. This is well illustrated in Benjamin Makela's description of the sequence of determining a policy and transmitting the resultant instructions. (The parenthetical comments have been added here.)

Somewhere in the organizational structure a man conceived an idea. He probably talked this over with his associates (horizontal communication), tried it out on his subordinates (downward communication), and then passed it along as a suggestion or recommendation to his superiors (upward communication). These superiors may have followed the same pattern and then passed it on up to a higher level in the business echelon. Later, this idea may have been dignified by being the subject of a memorandum or paper sent for comment to the various divisions in the organization (more horizontal communication). At the executive level there would surely have been a conference for the final decision. To implement the decision, it might then be necessary to issue bulletins and handbooks and the like.[1]

In one management survey after another, the findings are that downward communication needs to be improved in certain ways and that upward communication needs to be improved in other ways. But, these findings conclude, the most serious deficiencies are in the area of horizontal communication. Work is needlessly duplicated or inordinately delayed because information available in one department or plant is not available at another work place where it is needed.

THE NATURE OF CLEARANCE AND REVIEW

On frequent occasions, information has to be gathered from various parts of an organization before a decision can be made or action taken. The collection of this information impressed one industrial engineer as being a "county-fair arrangement in which all the people get together and contribute information to a common pool."[2] A variety of techniques is used for clearance and review, of course, in addition to convening the people concerned.

Diverse facts and opinions must be brought to bear on a decision or action as a means of pretesting it or simply to make a number of people familiar with a subject. In the development or revision of policies, procedures, or organizational plans or in the drafting of letters and reports, an organization may have further reasons for using the clearance process. An executive may depend on clearance to resolve differences among his subordinates, so that he can be spared making decisions on subsidiary matters except when the subordinates fail to agree.[3] Clearance may serve also to check compliance with established practices, revealing worthwhile divergences as well as unacceptable ones. Finally, in the process of clearance and review, especially in the development of written instructions, it is often possible to "force" decisions where they were previously difficult to obtain. This is the time when even the most reluctant decision-maker must finally make a decision.

The process of clearance and review might be called into play when, for example, a plant manager drafts a letter to the mayor opposing a pending zoning ordinance. Before the letter can be sent out, it must be sent to the central office for clearance with the public relations director and the general counsel, who may either initial their approval or suggest changes. To cite another example, a safety director designs a new guard for drill presses, but before the plant superintendent can approve its installation, the design must be cleared with the machine-shop foremen, who in turn probably clear it with the assistant foremen and some of the operators.

In the case of the new safety guard, clearance is likely to be personal and relatively unsystematic, with a series of conversations among people who call each other by their first names. Higher in an organization, as in the case of the zoning ordinance, the clearance process becomes more impersonal and planned; face-to-face conversations largely give way to the circulation of papers and files. At the highest levels of business and government, clearances become increasingly complex and important. This was noted by the Hoover Commission when it emphasized the national and international significance of the clearance methods used by the State Department, the Department of Defense, and the White House in acting on cables from our missions and embassies.[4]

CLEARANCE METHODS

It is quite common to find mandatory clearance provisions imposed on activities having legal or public relations implications. Also, some organizations make it mandatory that any new or revised form or written instruction be cleared with a systems and procedures unit or industrial engineering department. Military commanders often require that matters coming to them for signature must first be cleared with all general staff officers and some special staff officers. In the absence of a mandatory provision, officials who initiate actions are free to clear them with others.

Clearance may be carried on orally or in writing. There is a wide variety of written methods, as described in the paragraphs that follow. But all clearances, oral and written alike, are conducted in one of two fashions—sequentially or concurrently.

Sequential Clearance

When an item is to be cleared, the initiator will most often talk to various individuals in turn. Or, if the item is written, he may send it to the various people under cover of a routing or "buck" slip. These mimeographed or printed slips, of which there are as many varieties as there are organizations, show the source of the item and, in the order in which they are to receive it, the names of the recipients. Usually some of the names are preprinted, with blanks provided for additional ones, and the slip bears a caption such as "For Comment or Approval" or "For Your Information." Generally these captions need to be supplemented with more specific instructions, for every recipient should know precisely why an item has been sent to him and what he is expected to do with it. The same clearance action is likely to involve people with different responsibilities and interests. An engineer may be called upon to contribute his ideas on the development of a new product, while the public relations director needs to be informed of progress in its development.

Illustrated in Figure 20 is the clearance and approval form used by the advertising department of Union Carbide Chemicals Company. The original copy of this form is sent out of the department along with the accompanying folder of material. Spaces are provided for the signatures of those who approve;

CHEMICALS
FOR THE
TEXTILE

... for Your Approval

COPY ☐
LAYOUT ☐
DUMMY ☐
PROOF ☒

FOR APPROVAL

FROM
Union Carbide Chemicals Company
ADVERTISING DEPARTMENT
Room 328 - 30 East 42nd Street
New York 17, New York

Date: DEC 5, 1957

PROJECT NO.: P-57-0713   TITLE: CHEMICALS FOR THE TEXTILE INDUSTRY

FOR USE AS: SALES PROMOTION OF UNION CARBIDE CHEMICALS USED IN TEXTILE INDUSTRY

TO APPROVERS: This advertising material is submitted to you so that you may be assured of its factual and technical accuracy and conformity to the interests, responsibilities, or practices of your group. Unless otherwise noted, minor corrections may be made directly on the copy (please print). Extensive alterations should be typed on separate sheets of paper and keyed to the proper location in the advertising material.

If O.K., please sign, date, and pass along to next consecutive number in the order column. Please do not change the order of routing of this material, or send it out of your Department for further action without first discussing it with:

AUTHOR: F.H. McCREADY   PAX: 597

ORDER	APPROVER	LOCATION	RECEIVED DATE	APPROVED	DATE
1 S	ASSISTANT SALES MANAGER	SALES DEPARTMENT Room 331	DEC 6, 1957	J R Pruitt	DEC 9, 1957
2 S	H E HOWE	TECHNICAL SERVICE Room 340	DEC. 9, 1957	H F Howe	DEC 9, 1957
3	F F TYRON	LAW DEPT Room 940	DEC. 10, 1957	F F Tyron	DEC 11, 1957
4	R L AMES	MARKETING V P Room 1621	DEC 12, 1957	R L Ames	DEC 16, 1957
5	W G KENNY	ADV MGR Room 328	DEC 16, 1957	OK to print W G K.	12/16/57
	RETURN TO:				
	F H McCREADY				
	AUTHOR	Room 328 30 East 42nd Street			

S - Multiple copies sent simultaneously to this group.

TO SECRETARIES: If the approver is absent or will not be able to take some action on this within 24 hours, please call the Author so he can arrange alternate approvals.

Form 40,143

RETURN PROMPTLY TO
CHEMICALS
ISING DEPARTMENT
ROOM 328
ST 42nd STREET, N. Y.

FIG. 20.—Clearance and approval form, from Union Carbide Chemicals Company.

disapprovals or other comments are incorporated in memoranda that become part of the file. If, as in the Sears, Roebuck example in Figure 21, the desired comments themselves can be entered in a blank space (e.g., a figure or a date), the clearance and approval form is expanded accordingly.

In the Air Force's Air Materiel Command, the clearance procedure centers on an extra tissue copy of the letter, report, or

BULLETIN APPROVAL SHEET AND DISTRIBUTION INSTRUCTIONS

SUBJECT__________

BULLETIN NO.__________ CANCELS BULLETIN NO.__________

Temporary File, hold until ☐ ________ Permanent File ☐ _____ For Tickler ☐ ________

Check below the Territories and Regions to which bulletin applies:

MIDWESTERN	EASTERN	SOUTHERN	SOUTHWESTERN	PACIFIC COAST
Chicago ☐	Philadelphia ☐	Atlanta ☐	Dallas ☐	L. A. ☐
K. C. ☐	Boston ☐	Greensboro ☐		Seattle ☐
Mpls. ☐		Memphis ☐		

Bulletin applies to: Control Stores ☐ Foreign Stores ☐ (Per attached) Pool Stock ☐ Central Service ☐ List Attached ☐

CONTROL STORE DISTRIBUTION

General Manager . . . . . ☐
Merchandise Superintendent . . . . . ☐
Operating Superintendent . . . . . ☐
Inspection, Dept. 180 . . . . . ☐
Credit Manager, Dept. 153-160 . . . . . ☐
Return and Adj., Dept. 155-157 . . . . . ☐
Traffic Manager, Dept. 154-754 . . . . . ☐
Supply Manager, Dept. 206-806 . . . . . ☐
Order Office Supervisor, Dept. 382 . . . . . ☐
________ ☐

RETAIL STORE DISTRIBUTION

ZONE MANAGER . . . ☐
DISTRICT & GROUP MGR. ☐

	A	B1a	B1	B2a	B2	B3	C
STORE MANAGER	☐	☐	☐	☐	☐	☐	☐
Customer Service Mgr.	☐	☐	☐	☐	☐	☐	☐
Receiving Mgr.	☐	☐	☐	☐	☐	☐	☐
Service Man - Div.	☐	☐	☐	☐	☐	☐	☐
Unit Buying Control.	☐	☐	☐	☐	☐	☐	☐
Personnel Mgr.	☐						
________	☐	☐	☐	☐	☐	☐	☐

All Retail Stores Carrying ________

PARENT DEPT. DISTRIBUTION

Mgr. or Supervisor, Dept.________ ☐
All Parent Departments ________ ☐
Mdse. Controller, Dept.________ ☐
Retail Sales Mgr., Dept.________ ☐
Parent Dept's For Foreign Stores________ ☐

Date scheduled for mailing:

Complete Bulletin consists of pages.

Indicate below the quantity of ATTACHMENTS to be distributed to each type of store.

	Control Stores	Retail Stores A	B1a	B1	B2a	B2	B3	C	Pool Stock	Central Service	List Att.

APPROVALS (Signature and Date): ________

PREPARED BY________

F65322 Rev. 10/5/49

FIG. 21.—Transmittal sheet used for clearance and distribution instruction, from Sears, Roebuck & Co.

other document. The tissue is distinctively colored and pre-printed along the left margin with the titles of the principal line and staff officers (Fig. 22). Each officer in turn initials his approval, and his comments, if any, are added to the file. This clearance copy is retained in the central file against the later

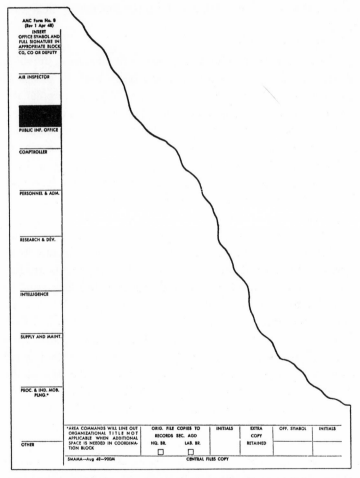

Fig. 22.—Preprinted carbon-copy sheet used for sequential clearance in the Air Materiel Command, United States Air Force.

need to fix responsibility or to make further assignments relating to the same subject.

Where only a few people are involved, where everyone acts quickly, and where the subject matter is not over-complex or controversial, few difficulties are encountered in clearing items sequentially. Where these conditions do not exist, however, it is advisable to use one of the methods for concurrent clearance.

Concurrent Methods

There are several methods of concurrent clearance, in which an item is presented to two or more individuals or offices at about the same time rather than in turn. The most popular device for concurrent clearance, particularly where the subject is a complex or controversial one, is the conference, which is discussed more fully in the next chapter. It is good practice to distribute in advance a conference agenda, describing in detail the item to be cleared. A matter of fair play is involved here because the proponents of one viewpoint may have had a lot more time to prepare their case. It is desirable, also, to seek firm agreement in the conference (having the participants initial the agreed-on changes at the time) and then to distribute copies of the redraft promptly—before the agreements are forgotten. Someone must be assigned to record the discussion as it applies to the subject and prepare and distribute the redraft.

The concurrent clearance of written material requires that, no matter how extensive the material may be, separate copies of it be dispatched at one time to everyone concerned. Each recipient comments independently and returns the item to the initiator or to a central clearance unit. Comments are collated in a redraft which is itself cleared, if necessary, by any of the various clearance methods. Indeed, combinations of clearance methods may be indicated. (Note the combined use of sequential and concurrent clearance in Figure 20.) It is not unusual to find that, after an item has been cleared sequentially, a conference is still required. We have seen one case where the auditing department is notoriously so slow in clearing material that a separate copy must be sent there while one other copy is circulating among the remaining departments in sequence.

CLEARANCE AND REVIEW IN ACTION

Clearance is a promising device for improving administrative communication, but, in actual practice, clearance methods leave much to be desired. Too often there are aggravating delays, and actions are taken either without sufficient facts or on the basis of authority and social relationships without regard to facts.

Delays

Repeated delays and petty bickering frequently accompany the clearance process, and, as the scope of the clearance list is broadened, or the quantity of the material increased, the delays stretch out. Within the central office of one of our best managed corporations, clearances take from two to five weeks. In a large government department that is not so well managed, clearances may take as long as a year.

To avoid delays, officials sometimes clear an item by "walking it through," that is, carrying it from one person to another and getting each one's approval or comments on the spot. Obviously, if everyone were to walk his projects through, the orderly scheduling of other work would suffer. Moreover, it is questionable whether significant comments can be given, or are even wanted, when one is asked to record his views without having time to study the matter.

It is far better to counteract delays by systematizing clearances in much the same way one can systematize reports. It is possible to set up reasonable distribution schedules, to assign suspense dates, and, through the use of a control sheet or card file, to follow up any delinquents. Where clearance becomes a major activity, a central clearance and review unit may have to be set up. If all these devices fail, it will probably be necessary to clear items concurrently through conferences.

Because so much time is spent in securing extensive clearances, officials sometimes curtail them as much as possible. If this is done, however, it is advisable to utilize other devices, such as brief notices of action taken, to prevent the complete cutting-off of cross-talk simply because clearances bog down. Customers (and taxpayers, too) become annoyed, and field personnel get the blame, when a central office acts on a matter without letting the field people know about it.

The Need for Background Material

People cannot take intelligent action on clearances unless they have sufficient background material. The initiator should not assume that his project is self-explanatory, or even interesting, to a number of other people busy with their own work. Preceding a conference the agenda can serve as the vehicle for necessary background material, as already mentioned. When written clearance methods are used, all the relevant material, including explanations of proposals, can be distributed in a manila folder. (Figure 20 illustrates such a folder.) If the current and background material is extensive, it should be arranged in a logical sequence with a table of contents. Concurrent written clearances can become major undertakings when they involve the preparation of separate folders of material for every name on a clearance list.

Routing

In the conduct of business and government affairs, who shares in the clearance action and who acts first may have considerable bearing on the final outcome. Administrators and technicians utilizing clearance processes should seek the smoothest method of handling each type of material. Action on policy matters may require the viewpoints of only a few, while action on procedures may call for extensive clearances extending to the loading platforms and clerical desks in the farthest reaches of the organization. Often, however, there is no clear delineation of the levels of policy determination or of the separation between policy and procedure. Top officials delay clearances while they dot the *i*'s and cross the *t*'s of procedural detail, and subordinates are allowed to flounder over policy matters they know nothing about.

A subordinate may believe it impolitic not to clear what his superior has already cleared. Or just the reverse may happen, with superiors being unduly affected by their subordinates' opinions or reluctant to question them. Concurrent written clearances minimize the effects of superior-subordinate relationships. But is the unbiased thinking obtained through concurrent written clearance more valuable than the interchange of ideas that occurs when successive comments are added one to another? There is no universal answer to this question.

When Clearance Fails

It is true that individuals in specialized positions often lack the knowledge to act outside of a rather narrow sphere. But there is the psychological factor that these same individuals use their formal job descriptions as defenses against assuming responsibility. Thus the official who solicits clearance on a matter may not care about his colleagues' comments so long as they offer initialed evidence of sharing the responsibility for his action. A superior may have already made a decision, but the clearance process affords him a "crutch" to lean on for support. When others in the organization perceive how the clearance processes are being abused, they are likely to refrain from participating. One wartime agency sought to insure the adaptability of its forthcoming instructions by clearing them with the field installations. The field personnel reacted negatively with "You tell us what to do, and we'll do it."[5]

Underlying the use of clearance is an assumption that others share and accept the same organizational purposes. The process is expected to elicit comments that amend or implement but not to arouse a challenge on fundamentals. In some situations, however, individual and group viewpoints are in marked opposition. In such circumstances the clearance process may become a ready weapon, as in the following incident:

> The American general in command of an occupied area after World War II decided to revise all the traditional titles of office in the area and thereby eliminate the symbols of leadership and followership. A staff officer, who disagreed wholeheartedly with the scheme, was given the assignment of preparing new titles for the offices. In spite of his subordinate's objections, the general insisted that the program go forward.
>
> Located in the area was a State Department liaison official with whom major program changes were always cleared. At the very time the staff officer was preparing the new titles, he persuaded the liaison official, who had been a college friend, that the program should never be permitted to go into effect. As a result, when it was submitted for clearance, the liaison official recorded his objections. Failing to secure State Department clearance, the general decided to drop the entire matter.

Others who have had experience in large organizations agree that clearance has frequently been used to undercut unpopular proposals. Often enough such acts stem from honest motives, but they are eloquent testimony to the importance of informal organizations as they affect administrative communication. Co-operation is always a key factor in the success of the clearance process.

In Scientific and Industrial Research

The nature of modern enterprise is such that for nearly everyone—even the chief executive—contact with activities outside his own sphere is limited and remote. Operators and machinists are isolated at their benches, analysts and clerks at their desks, and scientists and engineers in their laboratories. At a time when corporations, medical institutions, and even nations are racing to develop new products, such isolation is not only a luxury—it is an intolerable waste.

One of the ways in which scientific research can be accelerated is through a more efficient gathering and distribution of the information which scientists need. This was stated forcefully by Gerard Piel, publisher of the *Scientific American*, testifying before a congressional committee in 1956:

> Communication is a vital part of research. It is inseparable from research. It is not too much to say that research is communication. New scientific work does not have any existence in this world until it has been communicated from one scientist to another.
>
> Communication goes on at many levels. It is highly subject to disruption, and to frustration, and to tampering. Among human beings it is a difficult thing to achieve at any time.
>
> Today, with our vast number of journals, and even with punch cards and mechanized mediums of communication, the problem that burdens communication is the reverse of that of the nineteenth century. It is the enormous volume of work that must be carried by the channels of communication in science.[6]

What Piel said about pure research is equally true of research and development work in industry. In the words of one engineer:

> The real output of research and development work is not so much a working model or a prototype as it is information on how to make and use a product satisfactorily. This information goes to many places for many purposes and each type of information must match the needs and convenience of the group using it. . . . The importance of this concept is that, in our experience, approximately one-half of the total cost of the research and development activity is incurred in getting information in a form suitable to pass on to other groups in the company after the prototype of a new product is complete.[7]

In order to meet the information needs of scientists at work, some attention is being given to the establishment of a new profession—the information scientist. It would be this specialist's task to procure, sift, route, and file today's vast quantity of scientific information. "The information scientist," according to J. Farradane, writing in the British journal *Research,* should be the *alter ego* of the men at the bench, in the works, or in the office, continually in touch with and understanding their needs and problems, so that not only can he supply the right information to the right man at the right time, but he can anticipate such needs and make fruitful suggestions on the basis of his reading and contacts. . . . The information scientist must be kept fully cognizant of the technical processes being carried out by the firm, of the problems being studied by the research staff, and of the firm's possible objectives.[8]

In the United States, this specialty may very well develop from among the librarians.

The problems of clearance and review are indeed great. But the process is becoming more and more important. Unless information is made available to people, it can be of no use to them. Mistakes can usually be corrected, but it is far better to have means of safeguarding against their being made. By the same token, duplicated effort can be curtailed—or avoided entirely. The questions of what to clear, how, and with whom, are subsidiary to an organization's need for wide sharing of information and broad participation in decision-making.

Selected Readings

BOOKS AND MONOGRAPHS

BERNAL, J. D. *The Social Function of Science*. New York: Macmillan Co., 1939. Chap. xi, "Scientific Communication."

In science, communication takes much of the place of administration in other services.

LEARNED, EDMUND P.; ULRICH, DAVID N.; and BOOZ, DONALD R. *Executive Action*. Cambridge: Harvard University, Graduate School of Business Administration, Division of Research, 1951. Chap. vii, "Communication."

Persons within the management group should be free to consult with one another, provided superiors are kept sufficiently informed.

SHERA, JESSE H.; KENT, ALLEN; and PERRY, JAMES W. *Documentation in Action*. New York: Reinhold Publishing Co., 1956.

Report of a librarians' meeting on information-handling for science and industry.

ARTICLES

ATWOOD, J. L. "Communication within Management," pp. 3–11 in *Building a Balanced Communications Program.* ("General Management Series," No. 170.) New York: American Management Association, 1954.

Horizontal communication, including clearance, is part of every management job.

BURLING, TEMPLE. "Aids and Bars to Internal Communication," *Hospitals,* Vol. 28 (November, 1954), pp. 82–85.

Cites the need for improved horizontal communication in hospital administration.

FARRADANE, J. "Information Service in Industry," *Research,* Vol. 6 (August, 1953), pp. 327–30.

Advocating a new type of position—information scientist—to collect, collate, organize, and disseminate scientific and technical information.

XVI / *The Conference Process*

THE CONFERENCE is a form of horizontal communication. Meetings that are convened simply to express opinions, transmit reports, or issue orders are not conferences. The elements that identify a conference are its purposefulness, the presence of a leader and a small group, member participation and interchange, and the absence of speeches.

If understanding is the goal, the conference will be informational or instructional, with a relatively high percentage of leader participation. If acceptance is sought, the conference will be developmental, problem-solving, or policy-making, with the leader stepping aside and the conferees becoming the chief contributors. In the first type—the so-called guided conference —the leader is quite like a teacher or seminar leader. In the other type—the unguided or open conference—the leader may even be a novice with respect to the discussion topic, but he uses his skill as a leader to help the members of the group arrive at their own conclusion.[1]

THE CONFERENCE IN ADMINISTRATION

Among the Greeks and Romans were those who felt that the way to solve a problem was to subject it to intensive public discussion. In America we have had experience with "cracker-barrel" discussion groups and New England town meetings. Identification of group discussion with the democratic process is so strong that democracy has even been defined as "government by talk."[2] In this tradition there has arisen recently a philosophy of "multiple management," centering largely on the provision for intraorganizational discussion or conference.[3]

260

Great Britain is experiencing the development of a quite similar movement under the name of "joint consultation."

As long ago as 1918, Mary Parker Follett advocated a system of industrial management that would, while preserving the rights of individuals to express differing opinions on how work should be done, "integrate" their differences in a common denominator of acceptance. "Functional authority, pluralistic responsibility," in the words she used to describe her system, "requires conference as its method."[4] She was against compromises, which, she felt, leave everyone less than satisfied. She was also against majority rule, which leaves in its wake an unco-operative minority.

The conference process made its most significant entrance into administration as a training technique. Charles Allen is credited with first using the conference for foreman-training when he introduced it in the Du Pont organization during World War I.[5] By the time another war descended on the country, the conference process had become the most popular method for supervisory training. During World War II the Labor-Management Division of the War Production Board encouraged labor-management conferences to improve morale, to reduce strikes and absenteeism, to strengthen the quality of supervision, and to increase the flow of suggestions from employees. The conference—particularly as an informational medium—continued in popularity after the war.

Courses on conference leadership are multiplying throughout industry and government, and the conference process continues to enlist supporters, although it is also losing some. Staff conferences and committee forms of organization are being widely used as devices for intramanagement communication.

Group dynamics, embracing the conference process as well as role-playing and other combinations of group demonstration and discussion, is regarded by its ardent advocates as a prerequisite of sound administration. Since 1955 there has been great interest in "brainstorming." This variation on the conference process was developed by Alex Osborn as a method of stimulating ideas for advertising and marketing. But today brainstorming is being used widely in many other activities.

The use of conferences and committees has come under particular attack, due to the "leveling effect" of these mediums, which influences people to believe and say only what they think others will find acceptable.[6] Doubtless some executives put such a high premium on agreement that the result is abject conformity. There have been cases in which this condition became so acute that the conference process was abandoned. Such a remedy, however, is superficial; conformity exists throughout an organization and is never a phenomenon unique to the conference room.

THE NATURE OF THE CONFERENCE PROCESS

The oral interchange of a conference increases understanding and acceptance where these might not otherwise be possible. Key elements are the interactions that occur between individuals, between individuals and groups, and between groups and groups. Experimental findings have demonstrated that the mere fact of close physical grouping—even where no discussion takes place—affects the behavior of the individuals involved.[7] Conferences differ from either conventional interviews or lecture meetings in the quantity and extent of interaction among individuals. Any audience is, in a sense, a group, but in a lecture room the primary interaction is between the speaker and individual listeners.[8]

Group discussion affords a means of relieving tension, sometimes—because of the feeling of group support—more effectively than does a personal interview. Successes with group psychotherapy testify to the value of discussion for discussion's sake.

In administration the conference is more important as a medium for sharing knowledge and securing effective action. Although an individual alone may think more profoundly, he cannot normally develop the variety of ideas that grow out of group interchange. The conference draws together bits of information and experience from many limited positions and puts the data into broad organizational perspective.

By definition, conferences are not the means for one-way transmission of orders and reports; they are used successfully when they precede, parallel, or follow such transmissions. Studies of learning, perception, and motivation indicate that lectures may be as effective as conferences for *teaching* something, but no method surpasses the small-group discussion for producing action.[9] This does not mean that action is an inevitable result of discussion. But when an alert leader and conscientious conferees finally do achieve a decision, action can be more confidently expected than it would be following a lecture, an interview, or the issuance of a written directive. The interaction that takes place in a small group is a dynamo, and, with competent leadership and participation, much of its power can be harnessed to increase administrative efficiency.

The Conference Leader

The most important person in a conference is the leader, or chairman, "who steers the bark of discussion—stimulates the desire to speak, encourages the timid, quiets the unduly loquacious, quells the unruly, humorously dissolves acrimony, guides the discussion into profitable channels."[10] The mere presence of a designated leader markedly affects a conference group's efforts. Maier and Solem demonstrated this with groups solving an elementary arithmetic problem. The leaders were so restricted in their roles that they hardly led—and still they affected the results.[11]

Theoreticians enamored of the tremendous potential of group work sometimes suggest that leadership arises spontaneously, that it is unnecessary to teach conference leadership, and that a person learns quickly enough from actual experience how to perform the leader's job. In a classroom or a women's club there may be time for leadership to develop unaided, but such a process is uneconomical in administration. The social and psychological aspects of group discussion may indeed be important, but we are primarily interested in the conference as a method of administrative communication. No business should have to develop conference leaders by trial and error, any more than it would train drill-press operators or stenographers in such a fashion.

Eleven talents and personality traits appear to be desirable in a successful conference leader:

1. Mental alertness.

2. Sensitivity and perception. (The leader is concerned not only with what people say but why they say it and the overtones of meaning in the way they say it.)[12]

3. Language facility.

4. Impartiality.

5. Tact.

6. Poise and self-restraint. (The ability to maintain deliberate composure under pressure. These qualities are prerequisite to a sense of timing, often as necessary in conference leadership as on the stage.)

7. Patience.

8. Friendliness and good will. (The leader who dislikes the conferees or is disliked by them cannot accomplish anything in a conference.)

9. A sense of humor.

10. Interest. (The ability to maintain his own interest and to stimulate interest among others. The listening ability of the interviewer fits well the listening requirements of the conference leader.)

11. Fairness. (The willingness to let others make decisions

and to accept what they decide. The willingness, also, to do some of the unpleasant work.)

These qualities of personal conduct—or qualities substantially like these, since there is no single formula that will fit everyone—are not entirely separable from the techniques of conference leadership. Whether these personal qualities can be acquired along with the techniques is questionable.

The success or failure of a conference depends largely on the leader. Although some people find conference-leading rather easy, it still requires skill. The current interest in increasing productivity through group participation in decision-making may hurry managers into calling conferences. But if the leaders are unskilful, their conferences will probably fail.[13]

Preparing for the conference.—The leader must make plans well in advance of the conference itself. His first consideration is the kind of conference he needs, as determined by the purpose of the meeting—to discuss for discussion's sake and thereby relieve tension, to disseminate facts and supplement the knowledge of each participant, or to reach a decision leading to a course of action.[14] If, for example, a managerial decision has already been made in some detail, it would be a mistake to plan a purely developmental conference.

The type of conference decided on will determine the nature of the conference outline, in which the leader lists the key points that he hopes to see developed and typical discussion questions that he may be able to use in developing these points. Sample conference outlines are illustrated in several of the standard writings on conference leadership. Integral to the planning and preparation is a consideration of the physical facilities—the size and kind of room, chairs and tables and their arrangement, ashtrays, light, heat, and ventilation, facilities for displaying visual aids, and protection from interruption.

It may be useful to distribute the agenda in advance, thereby giving the conferees an opportunity to equip themselves for participation. Advance distribution may be inadvisable, however, if the agenda items are going to be seized upon to mobilize factions for or against a discussion item.

Getting the conference under way.—The second phase of the leader's job occurs after the group has assembled and necessary introductions have been made. The leader must advise the conferees of the extent of participation that is invited (this may vary for different items on the agenda) and advise them further about time limits and about the limitations of scope and authority established for the leader and the group. (Are they to decide something or are they simply to express opinions?) The type of conference will determine the way in which the leader and the conferees share in introducing and defining each discussion topic, with the conferees having an increasing share as the conference moves from the informational to the developmental type.

The body of the discussion.—During the next phase, the leader steps into the role of moderator, leaning heavily on the use of questions. "Is there anyone who has had experience with personnel policy manuals and can tell us something about them?" (an undirected lead-off question). "Why do some people say that manuals do more harm than good?" (an undirected provocative question). "Mr. Brown, your question sounds interesting. Would you be willing to offer a tentative answer to it yourself?" (a reverse follow-up question). "Mr. Jones, how would the type of manual just described by Mr. Smith fit our company?" (a directed follow-up question). Actually, in the last case (of a directed question), the leader should be somewhat more verbose and thereby give Mr. Jones a little more time to gather his thoughts for an answer.

There has been considerable debate regarding the extent to which the leader should contribute positively to the discussion and not just indirectly through questioning. We concur in Miller's experimental findings that, once the participants reach a point where they need additional knowledge, the leader must supply it or expect a conference failure.[15] A substitute technique is to have in attendance a "resource person" who is able to furnish necessary factual information. Obviously, facts are not the products of collective ignorance, no matter how lively the discussion.

The leader's job is to keep the discussion on the track (allowing for some digressions), to sharpen and clarify the members' thinking and speaking, to encourage participation, to protect the group from its more troublesome members, to check frequently for comprehension and acceptance, to resolve conflicts, to take notes, and to summarize periodically.

Concluding the conference.—As the conference approaches its windup, the leader must guide the conferees into agreement, summarization, and decision. At this point some leaders invoke majority rule, putting decisions to a vote. A strong case is presented against the voting procedure, however, by those who prefer to have the group agree without voting. Mary Parker Follett wrote:

> The vote is a deceptive business altogether. How often we used to see a tiny child driving with his father made happy by being allowed to hold the reins. The vote makes many people happy in the same way; they think they are driving when they are not. . . . Everyone talks today of co-operation, but there is no way of making consent spell co-operation.[16]

If the vote is used at all, it should be used only to settle what the group agrees are minor issues.[17]

As a final step the leader must carry the group's action from the conference room to the organizational world outside. A conference group may have concluded, for example, that six important factors should be evaluated in a semiannual performance report. The group must be told what happens next. Will top management adopt their findings immediately and revise the performance rating forms and procedures accordingly? Or is the leader going to merely present the group's findings as recommendations or advice? If the latter, when and how will the group be informed of the superior's decision? The nature of these final actions by the leader depends to a great extent on the initial presentation of the discussion topic. If the group was called on at the outset to develop an actionable decision, the leader dares not suggest to the group, in conclusion, that he will "pass along" the group's "advice and comments."

The Conference Group

Although the leader occupies a vital position, the conferees, individually and collectively, are also important. There is little a leader can do to keep a discussion moving forward if the group is hostile, truculent, subservient or otherwise passive, grossly unlettered, rigidly doctrinaire, or completely uniform in its thinking. People tend to emphasize conference leadership; too little attention is given to conference participation.

Group size.—The optimum size of a conference group has been the subject of both discussion and experiment. There has been no precise agreement, as evidenced in the following tabulation of recommended minimum, maximum, and optimum group sizes:[18]

Authority	Minimum	Maximum	Optimum
Watson	3	10	**10**
Bales	4	7	**5**
Jaques	6	12	**9**
Coon and others ("Brainstorming")	3	15	**12**

Elliott Jaques, justifying his figures, explained that

in groups larger than 12 . . . either fission occurs, with simultaneous conversational or silent subgroups in different parts of the room, so that each group member misses much of what is going on, or else audience formation ensues, with one person holding the floor and the rest merging into a relatively homogeneous whole. On the other hand, in groups smaller than six, individual personalities seem to emerge too sharply, making it difficult to retire easily and say little if that is one's desire at a given moment.[19]

Another variable affecting optimum size is the degree of skill possessed by the leader. Greater skill is required when the group is either extremely large or extremely small.

Since it is not always feasible to set up a number of entirely separate small-group sessions to deal with a problem, one can use the "buzz" technique originated by J. Donald Phillips. A large group is first convened in a meeting, where one or more speakers make formal presentations. The audience is then broken up into small units to discuss an assigned subject turning on the lecture material or a particular aspect of it. The small groups organize themselves, choosing their own chairmen and recorders. After they have held their own brief conferences, they report their decisions—generally orally—to the large group. Further action is taken under the leadership of the large-group chairman, or, as an intermediate step, a small group, which has not itself conferred earlier, is called to summarize and synthesize the various small-group findings.[20]

Composition.—In bringing a conference group together, one must consider its composition in terms of rank, competence, and diversity of opinion. There is a general tendency to include in one conference only people at the same or neighboring levels. The presence of a superior of markedly higher rank is quite likely to produce a situation in which the extent of participation may be only "Yes, sir."[21] Any superior in a conference with subordinates must, for the sake of frank discussion, divest himself of his halo of authority. This is never easy, but it is least difficult when only neighboring levels of rank are involved.

The members of the group should also be of relatively equal competence. If the level of discussion must be held down for those who react slowly, others will lose interest.

There must be some diversity of opinion among the conferees and an awareness of the diversity. If there is complete agreement, or appears to be, there is no stimulus for discussion.[22] If, on the other hand, the differences of opinion are too great and too rigid, there is little chance for profitable discussion, and what was scheduled as a conference will degenerate into a debate. If the sales manager and the advertising manager each knows beyond all doubt that he is right and the other wrong, a conference will probably do nothing more than align the conferees behind the leaders of the opposing forces. In such a situation a discussion has exactly the opposite of the effect desired; not only has there been no increase in understanding and acceptance, but the divergences are fixed more

Heinrich Kannegieszer

GROUP MEMBERS AS THE LEADER SEES THEM

1. THE QUARRELSOME TYPE	6. THE NEGATIVE TYPE
2. THE POSITIVE TYPE	7. THE THICK-SKINNED UN-
3. THE KNOW-IT-ALL	INTERESTED TYPE
4. THE TALKATIVE TYPE	8. THE HIGHBROW
5. THE SHY TYPE	9. THE PERSISTENT QUESTIONER

resolutely than before.[23] In an office or a factory, under the pressure of work that must be done, irreconcilable disagreements must be resolved by a superior. One might say that this represents a conference failure, but perhaps just such action is evidence of a successful adaptation of the conference process to modern management.

Conference participation.—A successful conference requires certain personality traits and talents in the conferees just as it does in the leader. We have already mentioned that the participants must have sufficient factual knowledge, but they must also be able—and, above all, willing—to express themselves freely. They must be open-minded, withholding judgment until all facts are in. They should interest themselves in what others say, more in order to gain understanding than to secure ammunition for refutation, and, in like manner, speak with the objective of making the group endeavor successful. Contributions should be impersonal and objective, yet not lacking in vigor and enthusiasm; brief and not too frequent; and explanatory rather than expostulatory—not only setting forth the contributor's position but also explaining and justifying it.[24] Conferences suffer when the conferees are special pleaders whose medium is more properly the debate or lecture. Experts are often poor conferees and are likely to regard the conference process with contempt.[25]

The word "participation" has come to have an unpleasant connotation, with a caricature of the boss pointing an accusing finger at a cowering conferee and ordering him to "participate!" A better word today is "involvement." A person may be actively involved in the purpose and content of a discussion without taking part verbally; or the reverse may happen, with a person taking part verbally without really being involved.[26] As everyone knows, the quantity of talk is no measure of its quality.

Brainstorming

Brainstorming differs from other conference techniques in several major respects. The participants address themselves to a particular question (e.g., "What can we do to improve our passenger service?"), but there is no discussion in the conventional sense of the word. The emphasis, instead, is on the spontaneous production of as many ideas as possible, regardless of their merit. Free association in a permissive group setting produces a great quantity of ideas; and if the quantity is great enough, a few of the ideas will presumably be good ones. (The same presumption exists in the field of suggestion systems, to wit, receipt of a great quantity of suggestions increases the chances of there being one or several important suggestions.)

The role of the leader or chairman in a brainstorming session is that of moderator. He enforces the strict prohibition (during the session, not afterwards) against negative comments of any kind. He also designates the contributors in turn from among those who have raised their hands. In doing so, he gives priority to those who want to amplify ("hitch-hike" or "piggyback" are the terms used) an idea mentioned by a previous contributor. The chairman asks undirected provocative questions whenever the ideation process needs stimulation.

The expressed ideas are recorded stenographically or through tape recording. They are then typed and distributed, therby stimulating the brainstormers to add more ideas to the list. The expanded list, edited by the chairman, is passed along to one or a committee of his colleagues for grouping into logical categories and for evaluation.[27]

No one can gainsay the reported successes of brainstorming. In case after case, a hundred or more ideas have been produced in a half-hour session, with another twenty to fifty added the next day. Yet there are critics of the process, particularly of its usefulness in connection with complicated subjects.[28]

Another criticism has been mentioned earlier as a criticism against all conferences, to wit, that too much emphasis is put on "group thinking" to the detriment of individual thought.

TOWARD BETTER CONFERENCES

Despite its actual and potential advantages, many executives and subordinates look on the conference process with disdain. In businessese a conference is "a place where conversation is substituted for the dreariness of labor and the loneliness of thought" or "a group of people who individually can do nothing but who meet collectively and agree that nothing can be done." A committee, it has been said, "is a group that keeps minutes and wastes hours."

The Time Factor

According to many executives, conferences would be used more often if they took up less time. In comparisons between conferences and lectures and between conferences and decisions by one person, conferences are always said to be slower. But it is unfair to compare the development of a decision in a conference with a decision announced by one person using a lecture platform, a public-address system, or a written release. The enunciation of a one-man decision is usually the outcome of extensive conversations, research, and clearance and review—including conferences. The hours spent in preparing and distributing a message, or in clarifying it later, are not added up. On a net-time-spent basis, it might be shown that many important matters could benefit from more conference hours instead of fewer.[29]

It is necessary, also, to distinguish between time spent and time wasted.[30] Without skilful leadership and competent participation there will no doubt be a substantial amount of time and effort wasted. The time factor does militate against using conferences in emergencies, but crisis administration, whether a product of the circumstances or of poor planning, is not the only situation in which to judge the conference process.

The Organization's Response and Follow-Up

If a group is invited to reach a decision on a subsequent action, the organization must comply with that decision. If a group is invited to comment, the organization must recognize the comments. To violate faith with the group will alienate the members and possibly vitiate the usefulness of conferences indefinitely. The leader is responsible initially for making clear the scope of his and the group's authority, but there is always the danger that his superiors will let him down.

The pattern of authority in an organization determines when and what types of conferences can be used. If top management issues detailed and highly inflexible instructions, there is no opportunity for a decision-making conference; and conferences to elicit comments can be used only if the superiors really want comments, including adverse ones.

Conferences suffer from the impermanence inherent in any oral process. The action decided upon may not persist, or the ideas gained may fade from the participants' minds, unless the results of the conference are tied into the organization's written informational and instructional materials. As a rule, verbatim minutes are too full of extraneous matter to be useful. Newsletters and memoranda can be employed to capture the high points of informative interchanges, up-to-date conference outlines can preserve the essence of training conferences, and the prompt issuance or revision of written instructions or reports can effectuate conference decisions.

Training for Conference Participation

Certainly no one can make people co-operate in a conference. The best that can be done by management in general, and by a conference leader in particular, is to create a situation favorable to co-operation, and what happens after that is up to the conferees themselves.[31] However, in recognition of the fact that conferring is not easy or natural behavior for most employees, management should institute training for better conference participation.

Today the principal training for participation comes through training in conference leadership, for it has been found that people trained as leaders make excellent conferees.

Another method is seen in the practice followed by some agricultural extension workers in their conferences with farm groups. Before each meeting the participants are instructed in their roles. They are told, for example, to speak freely, to listen thoughtfully to others, and not to monopolize the discussion.[32] Briefing of this sort seems suitable for groups that meet only infrequently, perhaps once or several times a year.

Some organizations have employed consultant-observers who interview leaders and conferees to ascertain whether they feel that their discussions have been effective and satisfying and, if not, why not. The consultant may detour an unsuccessful conference group from its substantive work in favor of discussing some aspect of the conference process, such as the general nature of misunderstanding and disagreement. Once they master themselves, the participants are better equipped to master their substantive problems.[33]

A final way to train participants is through frequent participation under leaders who have a conscious desire to improve the quality of participation. Such leaders look beyond the immediate conference and—largely by indirection—train the conferees for future conferences. Conference sessions are interrupted from time to time by the leader, and good and bad aspects of the participation are tactfully identified. The leader may take the group into his confidence periodically, pointing out that he performed in a certain manner because of something that was happening in the session. He may refer members to various readings on the conference process, such as those listed in the "Selected Readings" at the end of this chapter. A person is often willing to read objectively what he would resent or misconstrue as a personal comment. It is difficult, for example, for a leader to lecture a group on courtesy when everyone knows that the remarks actually apply to one person among them.

The President's Commission on Higher Education has said that one of the objectives of general education is "to understand the ideas of others and to express one's own effectively." This objective has been elaborated in part as follows:

> Developing the skills of communication is perhaps the least debatable of the objectives of general education. Without free, clear, and distinct communication a true meeting of minds does not occur, and understanding and co-operation are retarded if not prevented. And to communicate easily and well with one's fellows one must be able to write and to read, to talk and to listen.[34]

The development of communication skills has barely begun to find its way into the curricula of the schools and colleges that furnish most of the clerks, machine operators, professional people, and administrators. The conference process offers management a great opportunity to promote "a true meeting of minds" through the exchange of ideas. If, as often happens, the ability to exchange ideas is lacking, it must be fostered by offering training opportunities in specific communication talents and also by maintaining an atmosphere favorable to free and clear communication.

These demands on educators and managers have dimensions far greater than those of the conference process or of any other single communication activity. Indeed, everyone in modern industrial society must share in meeting these demands. In the words of Crawford H. Greenewalt, president of the Du Pont Company:

The great problem, the great question, is to develop within the framework of the group the creative genius of the individual. It is a problem for management, for public education, for government, for the church, for the press—for everyone. The stake is both the material one of preserving our most productive source of progress and the spiritual one of insuring to each individual the human dignity which is his birthright.[35]

Selected Readings

BOOKS AND MONOGRAPHS

COOPER, ALFRED M. *How To Conduct Conferences.* 2d ed. New York: McGraw-Hill Book Co., 1946.

Widely used description of the conference process in its many applications.

[FOLLETT, MARY PARKER.] *Dynamic Administration: The Collected Papers of Mary Parker Follett,* ed. HENRY. C. METCALF and L. URWICK. New York and London: Harper & Bros., 1942. Chap. viii, "The Influence of Employee Representation in a Remoulding of the Accepted Type of Business Manager."

Superiors using the conference method must be communicative rather than secretive, must explain rather than command, must make of differences a unifying rather than a disrupting force.

FOWLER, GLORIA M. *The Art of Exchanging Ideas.* (Bulletin No. 24.) Pasadena: California Institute of Technology, Industrial Relations Section, 1953.

———. *Frustrations in Conferences.* (Circular No. 22.) Pasadena: California Institute of Technology, Industrial Relations Section, 1955.

Intimate observations on individual and group behavior in a conference-leadership training course.

HANNAFORD, EARLE S. *Conference Leadership in Business and Industry.* New York: McGraw-Hill Book Co., 1945.

Step-by-step procedures in conference leadership.

JAQUES, ELLIOTT. *The Changing Culture of a Factory.* New York: Dryden Press, Inc., 1952.

Report of a three-year analysis of the social functioning—including communication—in a British factory operating under a system of multiple-committee management.

LEE, IRVING J. *How To Talk with People.* New York: Harper & Bros., 1952.

A semanticist's view of the problems of group discussion, based on several years' work as a consultant-observer of conferences in administration.

MCBURNEY, JAMES H., and HANCE, K. C. *The Principles and Methods of Discussion.* New York: Harper & Bros., 1939.

College text, with sections on development, techniques, and desirable forms of conduct for leaders and participants.

UTTERBACK, WILLIAM E. *Group Thinking and Conference Leadership.* New York: Rinehart & Co., 1950. Chap. xiii, "Discussion in Industry."

The different types of business conferences, with a brief statement of techniques. Bibliography.

ARTICLES

BALES, ROBERT F. "In Conference," *Harvard Business Review,* Vol. 32 (March–April, 1954), pp. 44–50.

Report on studies of committee behavior at Harvard's Laboratory of Social Relations.

BENSON, BERNARD S. "Let's Toss This Idea Up . . ." *Fortune,* Vol. 56 (October, 1957), pp. 145–46.

What can be accomplished in a group discussion can be accomplished as well or better by an individual, especially in technical fields.

BERWITZ, CLEMENT J. "The Work Committee: An Administrative Technique," *Harvard Business Review,* Vol. 30 (January–February, 1952), pp. 110–24.

The committee method of solving business problems, an excellent example of the conference as horizontal communication.

BRADFORD, LELAND P. "Who Has a Question?" *American Journal of Nursing,* Vol. 55 (February, 1955), pp. 181–84.

Techniques that can be used to stimulate discussion.

COON, ARTHUR M. "Brainstorming—A Creative Problem-Solving Technique," *Journal of Communication,* Vol. 7 (Autumn, 1957), pp. 111–18.

Brief and laudatory description of brainstorming.

JENNINGS, EUGENE E. "Agreement or Compromise? The 'Leveling Effect' in Group Discussion," *Personnel,* Vol. 31 (July, 1954), pp. 66–71.

How the pressures for conformity foster agreement at the expense of a full and free expression of individual viewpoints.

LEE, IRVING J. "Procedure for 'Coercing' Agreement," *Harvard Business Review*, Vol. 32 (January–February, 1954), pp. 39–45.

Report on a procedure for getting a full hearing for everyone in a conference.

LEVINE, JACOB, and BUTLER, JOHN. "Lecture vs. Group Decision in Changing Behavior," *Journal of Applied Psychology*, Vol. 36 (February, 1952), pp. 29–33.

A research project in an industrial setting demonstrating the greater effectiveness of group decision over the lecture method of training. Confirms Lewin's earlier findings (below).

LEWIN, KURT. "Group Decision and Social Change," pp. 330–44 in *Readings in Social Psychology*, ed. T. M. NEWCOMB and E. L. HARTLEY. New York: Henry Holt & Co., 1947.

Exposition by a founder of "group dynamics" on the attainment and effectiveness of a group decision.

MAURER, MERRYMAN. "Management by Committee," *Fortune*, Vol. 47 (April, 1953), pp. 145–47, 192 ff.

The committee method, already strong, needs more experimentation and refinement.

TAYLOR, DONALD W.; BERRY, PAUL C.; and BLOCK, CLIFFORD H. "Does Group Participation when Using Brainstorming Facilitate or Inhibit Creative Thinking?" *Administrative Science Quarterly*, Vol. 3 (June, 1958), pp. 23–47.

Experiment at Yale concluding that brainstorming inhibits creative thinking.

Acknowledgments for the Second Edition

Acknowledgments for the Second Edition

FRIENDS and colleagues throughout the country have generously provided worthwhile data, and from these persons came a variety of illustrative material and commentary. In a few instances we have had to use the material anonymously in deference to the confidential nature of the sources.

Many other persons—some in industry, others in government, and still others on the staffs of universities and professional associations—have been generous contributors. At the risk of omitting names that should be here, I wish to acknowledge my indebtedness to the persons and organizations listed below:

Kenneth E. Boulding, University of Michigan; Ralph L. Carl, Corning Glass Works; Mary Cassidy, United States Bureau of the Census; H. H. Cherry, Jr., Cherry-Burrell Corporation; Dale Cox and Edmund Lieberman, International Harvester Company; Warren Donnelly, Atomic Energy Commission; John G. Gray and Malcolm Macurda, Pacific Telephone and Telegraph Company; Robert D. Gray, California Institute of Technology; S. A. Halgren, Carnation Company; W. G. Ingraham, Standard Oil Company of California; Fred Lesieur, Massachusetts Institute of Technology; Edith P. Lewis, *American Journal of Nursing;* Everett J. Livesey, Dime Savings Bank of Brooklyn; R. J. Mardle, *Labour and Employment Gazette* (New Zealand); H. C. Marmaduke, Illinois Central Railroad; Elizabeth B. MacLatchie, California Department of Social Welfare; Eric Moonman, British Institute of Management; George B. Moynahan, Union Carbide Corporation; Murray R. Nathan, New York State Department of Health; Hal E. Nourse, United Air Lines, Incorporated; William J. Olivey,

Remington Rand Division (Elmira); Carl E. Osteen, *New York Times;* James Osterburg, New York City Police Department; Bryant W. Ruthven, Tennessee Valley Authority; William Sansone, United States Veterans Administration; Charles T. Schrage and J. George Schoener, Jr., New York Telephone Company; Douglas S. Sherwin, Phillips Chemical Company; Jack C. Staehle, Aldens, Incorporated; Herbert L. Sutton, Pacific Mutual Life Insurance Company; Ralph Thornton, *Minneapolis Star and Tribune;* L. C. Volling, Green Giant Company; William B. Warren and Carmella Macaluso, Port of New York Authority; Warren Weaver, Rockefeller Foundation; H. Ashley Weeks, University of Michigan; James C. Worthy, Sears, Roebuck and Company; and Hollis Wyman, Chas. Pfizer and Company.

My special thanks go to Melva Weber and Iona J. Thornton for their invaluable assistance in the editorial preparation of this book.

I reaffirm my great debt to these people and their organizations but burden none of them with responsibility for what I have written.

Notes

Notes

Chapter I INTRODUCTION

1. Chester I. Barnard, *The Functions of the Executive* (Cambridge: Harvard University Press, 1938), p. 226.

2. Claude E. Shannon and Warren Weaver, *The Mathematical Theory of Communication* (Urbana: University of Illinois Press, 1949), pp. 98–99.

3. Kenneth E. Boulding, "Notes on the Information Concept," *Explorations* (University of Toronto), No. 5 (July, 1955), pp. 103–12.

4. Carl I. Hovland, "Social Communication," *Proceedings of the American Philosophical Society*, Vol. 92 (1948), p. 371; Richard Braddock, "An Extension of the 'Lasswell Formula,'" *Journal of Communication*, Vol. 8 (Summer, 1958), pp. 88–93.

5. Edward Sapir, "Communication," *Encyclopaedia of the Social Sciences* (New York: Macmillan Co., 1937), Vol. 4, p. 78; Jurgen Ruesch and Weldon Kees, *Nonverbal Communication* (Berkeley: University of California Press, 1956).

6. Everett C. Hughes, "Dilemmas and Contradictions of Status," *American Journal of Sociology*, Vol. 50 (March, 1945), p. 356.

7. Earl Planty and William Machaver, "Upward Communications: A Project in Executive Development," *Personnel*, Vol. 28 (January, 1952), p. 316.

8. Gordon Allport and Leo Postman, "The Basic Psychology of Rumor," in *The Process and Effects of Mass Communication*, ed. Wilbur Schramm (Urbana: University of Illinois Press, 1955), pp. 146–53.

9. A. C. Leyton, "Operational Definition in Communication," *British Management Review*, Vol. 12 (October, 1954), pp. 269–70.

10. Alex Bavelas and Dermot Barrett, "An Experimental Approach to Organizational Communication," *Personnel*, Vol. 27 (March, 1951), pp. 366–71; Dallis Perry and Thomas A. Mahoney, "In-plant Communications and Employee Morale," *Personnel Psychology*, Vol. 8 (Autumn, 1955), pp. 339–46.

11. T. M. Higham, "Basic Psychological Factors in Communication," *Occupational Psychology*, Vol. 31 (January, 1957), pp. 4–5.

Chapter II WHAT ADMINISTRATIVE COMMUNICATION DEALS WITH

1. Vincent P. Connolly, "Procedures and Systems from the Ground Up," *Systems and Procedures Quarterly*, Vol. 6 (August, 1955), p. 17.

2. E. H. Conarroe, "Preparation and Use of Office Manuals," *Bulletin of the National Association of Cost Accountants*, Vol. 24 (June 1, 1943), p. 1196; Geneva Seybold, *Written Statements of Personnel Policy* ("Studies in Personnel Policy," No. 79 [New York: National Industrial Conference Board, Inc., 1947]), p. 3.

3. Peter F. Drucker, "The New Philosophy Comes to Life," *Harper's Magazine*, Vol. 215 (August, 1957), pp. 37–38.

4. "New Horizons for Closed Circuit TV," *Management Review*, Vol. 45 (November, 1956), p. 958; "Sears Launches New Magazine To Inform Execs, Cut Turnover," *Wall Street Journal*, September 16, 1957.

5. "Boss & Worker: Better Communications between Them Boosts Output, Companies Find," *Wall Street Journal*, October 13, 1955.

6. "Survey Shows Growth," *Stet*, No. 200 (May, 1957), pp. 1–5.

7. "Management Looks at Reading Racks," *Management Review*, Vol. 45 (January, 1956), pp. 13–14.

8. "More Firms Take Pen in Hand To Report to Workers, Kill Rumors," *Wall Street Journal*, April 30, 1957.

9. "Boss & Worker: Better Communications between Them Boosts Output, Companies Find," *loc. cit.*

10. *Ibid.*

11. Melville Dalton, "Unofficial Union-Management Relations," *American Sociological Review*, Vol. 15 (October, 1950), pp. 611–19.

12. "Sears Launches New Magazine To Inform Execs, Cut Turnover," *loc. cit.*

Chapter III SOME GUIDING PRINCIPLES

1. Lloyd Frankenberg, "How Clear Is Clarity?" in *Highlights of Modern Literature*, ed. Francis Brown (New York: New American Library, 1954), p. 40.

2. Stephen E. Fitzgerald, "Literature by Slide Rule," *Saturday Review*, Vol. 36 (February 14, 1953), pp. 15–16, 53–54; Herbert C. Morton, *Putting Words To Work* (Hanover, N.H.: Dartmouth College, Amos Tuck School, 1955), pp. 9–10.

3. S. R. Neuberger, "The Concept of Readability," *British Management Review*, Vol. 12 (October, 1944), p. 298.

4. Robert F. Lockman, "A Note on Measuring 'Understandability,'" *Journal of Applied Psychology*, Vol. 40 (June, 1956), p. 195.

5. Leonard Schatzman and Anselm Strauss, "Social Class and Modes of Communication," *American Journal of Sociology*, Vol. 60 (January, 1955), pp. 329–38.

6. W. V. Machaver and W. A. Borrie, "A Reading Improvement Program for Industry," *Personnel*, Vol. 28 (September, 1951), pp. 123–30.

7. William H. Whyte, Jr., and the Editors of *Fortune, Is Anybody Listening?* (New York: Simon & Schuster, Inc., 1952), pp. 48–50.

8. Paul and Faith Pigors, *Understanding as a Condition for Success in Order-giving* (Cambridge, Mass.: Industrial Relations Associates, Inc., 1945), p. 19.

9. William F. Whyte, "Semantics and Industrial Relations," *Human Organization*, Vol. 8 (Spring, 1949), pp. 4–10.

10. Pigors and Pigors, *op. cit.*, p. 5.

11. Robert C. Hood, *Communications: A Dynamic Factor in Emergency Management* ("Management Reports," No. 105 [Berkeley: California Personnel Management Association, Research Division, 1951]), p. 8.

12. Reginald O. Kapp, *The Presentation of Technical Information* (London: Constable and Co., Ltd., 1949), p. 46.

13. *Ibid.*, pp. 44, 93.

14. Norbert Wiener, *The Human Use of Human Beings* (Garden City: Doubleday & Co., 1954), p. 123.

15. Donald M. Sloat and Robert M. Creaghead, "Foreman's Manual Answers All His Questions," *Factory Management and Maintenance*, Vol. 102 (October, 1944), p. 104.

16. Chester I. Barnard, *The Functions of the Executive* (Cambridge: Harvard University Press, 1938), p. 177.

17. Albert Somit, "Andrew Jackson as Administrator," *Public Administration Review*, Vol. 8 (Summer, 1948), p. 189.

18. Helen Baker, J. W. Ballantine, and J. M. True, *Transmitting Information through Management and Union Channels* (Princeton: Princeton University, Industrial Relations Section, 1949), p. 126.

19. Lent D. Upson, "Principles of Administration Applicable to Health Departments," *American Journal of Public Health*, Vol. 31 (January, 1941), pp. 39–44.

20. N. J. Haase, "Introducing Procedural Changes Is a Ticklish Business: Here Are Some Ideas That Have Worked," *Journal of Accountancy*, Vol. 87 (June, 1949), p. 492.

21. T. T. Paterson, "The New Profession of Management," *Listener*, December 6, 1956, pp. 921–22.

Chapter IV TELLING OTHERS WHAT TO DO

1. V. W. Oubridge, "Delegation of Authority in the Medium-sized Company," *British Management Review,* Vol. 12 (July, 1954), p. 200.

2. J. K. Galbraith, "The Business of Business Is Business," *Reporter,* Vol. 6 (May 13, 1952), p. 36.

3. Albert Somit, "Andrew Jackson as Administrator," *Public Administration Review,* Vol. 8 (Summer, 1948), p. 192.

4. J. J. Jenkins, "Communication Structures" (Paper delivered at a meeting of the Minneapolis–St. Paul chapter of the National Office Management Association, unpublished transcript), pp. 6, 8.

5. William E. Henry, "The Business Executive: A Study in the Psychodynamics of a Social Role," *American Journal of Sociology,* Vol. 54 (January, 1949), p. 290.

6. Ernest Dale, "Contributions to Administration by Alfred P. Sloan, Jr., and GM," *Administrative Science Quarterly,* Vol. 1 (June, 1956), p. 36.

7. *Ibid.,* p. 46.

8. Lawrence A. Appley, "A Body of Management Know-How," *Management News,* Vol. 28 (March, 1955), p. 8.

9. Winston S. Churchill, *The Second World War: Closing the Ring* (Boston: Houghton Mifflin Co., 1951), pp. 487–89.

10. Barrett McGurn, "Guards Aid Refugees To Cross Line," New York *Herald Tribune,* November 26, 1956.

11. Oubridge, *op. cit.,* pp. 199–201.

12. Donald M. Sloat and Robert M. Creaghead, "Foreman's Manual Answers All His Questions," *Factory Management and Maintenance,* Vol. 102 (October, 1944), p. 104.

13. *Ibid.,* p. 103.

14. Paul and Faith Pigors, *Understanding as a Condition for Success in Order-giving* (Cambridge, Mass.: Industrial Relations Associates, Inc., 1945), p. 22.

15. *Dynamic Administration: The Collected Papers of Mary Parker Follett,* ed. Henry C. Metcalf and L. Urwick (New York and London: Harper & Bros., 1942), pp. 58 ff.

16. H. B. Maynard, "Installing a Methods Program," *Advanced Management,* Vol. 11 (June, 1946), pp. 57–61.

17. Pigors and Pigors, *op. cit.,* pp. 22–23.

18. Sir Geoffrey Vickers, "Human Communication," *British Management Review,* Vol. 12 (January, 1954), p. 72.

Chapter V ORAL OR WRITTEN INSTRUCTIONS?

1. Stephen E. Fitzgerald, *Communicating Ideas to the Public* (New York: Funk & Wagnalls Co., 1950), pp. 91–92.

2. *New York Times,* February 11 and 12, 1951.

3. John J. Corson, "The Role of Communication in the Process of Administration," *Public Administration Review,* Vol. 4 (Winter, 1944), p. 15.

4. A. N. Colby and Joseph Tiffin, "The Reading Ability of Industrial Supervisors," *Personnel,* Vol. 27 (September, 1950), pp. 156–59.

5. Fitzgerald, *op. cit.,* p. 95.

6. Lillian M. Gilbreth and Alice R. Cook, *The Foreman in Manpower Management* (New York: McGraw-Hill Book Co., 1947), p. 22.

7. Paul and Faith Pigors, *Understanding as a Condition for Success in Order-giving* (Cambridge, Mass.: Industrial Relations Associates, Inc., 1945), p. 26.

8. *Ibid.,* pp. 26–27.

9. Geneva Seybold, *Written Statements of Personnel Policy* ("Studies in Personnel Policy," No. 79 [New York: National Industrial Conference Board, Inc., 1947]), p. 5.

10. Thomas L. Dahle, "Transmitting Information to Employees: A Study of Five Methods," *Personnel,* Vol. 31 (November, 1954), pp. 243–46.

11. "On Saying What You Mean," *Royal Bank of Canada Monthly Letter,* March, 1954.

Chapter VI INDIVIDUAL MESSAGES AND CIRCULARS

1. L. Urwick, *The Elements of Administration* (New York and London: Harper & Bros., 1943), p. 70.

2. Herbert C. Morton, *Putting Words To Work* (Hanover, N.H.: Dartmouth College, Amos Tuck School, 1955), p. 2.

3. W. S. Harris, "Selecting a Medium for Written Instructions," *Public Administration Review,* Vol. 2 (Autumn, 1942), p. 326.

4. Donald M. Sloat and Robert M. Creaghead, "Foreman's Manual Answers All His Questions," *Factory Management and Maintenance,* Vol. 102 (October, 1944), p. 101.

Chapter VII MANUALS

1. Eileen Ahern, *How To Prepare and Maintain a Supervisors' Policy Manual* ("Research Reports," No. 11 [New York: American Management Association, 1947]), p. 23.

2. Leslie Matthies, "Systems as a Channel of Communications," in *Ideas for Management: Papers and Case Histories Presented at the Ninth Annual International Systems Meeting* (Cleveland: Modern Office Procedures, 1957), Sec. I, pp. 29–40.

3. E. H. Conarroe, "Preparation and Use of Office Manuals," *Bulletin of the National Association of Cost Accountants,* Vol. 24 (June 1, 1943), p. 1204.

4. Ahern, *op. cit.,* pp. 15–23.

5. *Ibid.,* p. 43.

6. *Ibid.,* p. 65.

7. Donald M. Sloat and Robert M. Creaghead, "Foreman's Manual Answers All His Questions," *Factory Management and Maintenance,* Vol. 102 (October, 1944), p. 101.

8. Lenore P. Nelson, *Employee Handbook Printing Practices* (University of Minnesota, Industrial Relations Center, Research and Technical Report 3 [Dubuque, Iowa: Wm. C. Brown Co., 1950]), pp. 1–9.

Chapter VIII HANDBOOKS AND EMPLOYEE HANDBOOKS

1. J. J. W. Neuner and B. R. Haynes, *Office Management and Practices* (2d ed.; Cincinnati: South-Western Publishing Co., 1947), p. 610.

2. J. H. MacDonald, *Office Management* (rev. ed.; New York: Prentice-Hall, Inc., 1946), pp. 399–400.

3. Geneva Seybold, *Company Rules—Aids to Teamwork* ("Studies in Personnel Policy," No. 95 [New York: National Industrial Conference Board, Inc., 1948]), pp. 1–2.

4. *Preparing an Employee Handbook* (London: Institute of Personnel Management, 1947), p. 5.

5. *Ibid.,* pp. 6–7.

6. Seybold, *op. cit.,* pp. 35–55.

7. W. B. Dominick, "The Employee Handbook: A Training Aid," *Personnel Administration,* Vol. 4 (May, 1942), pp. 1, 3–5.

8. "What Worries New Workers?" *Management Review,* Vol. 42 (May, 1953), p. 260.

9. Burleigh B. Gardner, *Human Relations in Industry* (Chicago: Richard D. Irwin, Inc., 1945), p. 211.

Chapter IX EMPLOYEE PUBLICATIONS

1. *Operation Tapemeasure,* ed. Henry B. Bachrach (Akron, Ohio: International Council of Industrial Editors, 1956), p. 3.

2. *Ibid.,* p. 3.

3. *Information Sheet: Annual Awards Program* (Akron, Ohio: International Council of Industrial Editors, 1957).

4. *Operation Tapemeasure,* p. 15.

5. *Ibid.*

6. *Ibid.,* pp. 4, 15.

7. *Ibid.,* pp. 9, 13.

8. *Ibid.,* pp. 4, 6, 16.

9. *Ibid.,* pp. 10, 13.

10. *Ibid.,* p. 13.

Chapter X COMMUNICATION AND CONTROL

1. Douglas S. Sherwin, "The Meaning of Control," *Dun's Review and Modern Industry,* Vol. 67 (January, 1956), p. 46.

2. Kenneth E. Boulding, *The Organizational Revolution* (New York: Harper & Bros., 1952), pp. xxviii–xxix.

3. Sherwin, *op. cit.,* p. 46.

4. L. Urwick, *The Elements of Administration* (New York and London: Harper & Bros., 1943), p. 102.

5. Edward H. Litchfield, "Notes on a General Theory of Administration," *Administrative Science Quarterly,* Vol. 1 (June, 1956), pp. 12–20.

6. Sherwin, *op. cit.,* pp. 46, 84.

7. John M. Pfiffner, "The 'Third Dimension' of Organization," *Personnel,* Vol. 28 (March, 1952), p. 391.

8. Sherwin, *op. cit.,* p. 83.

9. Richard L. Waddell, "Communications: Pushbutton Control," *Challenge,* Vol. 4 (August–September, 1956), p. 14.

10. Sir Geoffrey Vickers, "Initiative and Control," *The Listener,* Vol. 55 (January 19, 1956), p. 93.

11. Sherwin, *op. cit.,* p. 84.

Chapter XI ADMINISTRATIVE REPORTING

1. Lent D. Upson, *Letters on Public Administration: From a Dean to His Graduates* (Detroit: National Training School for Public Service, 1947), p. 27.

2. James Hart, *The American Presidency in Action: 1789* (New York: Macmillan Co., 1948), p. 135.

3. Marshall E. Dimock, *The Executive in Action* (New York: Harper & Bros., 1945), p. 153.

4. C. Aubrey Smith and Jim G. Ashburne, "Internal Blueprint: The Controller Reports to Top Management," *The Controller,* Vol. 19 (December, 1951), p. 559.

5. *Ibid.*, p. 562.

6. Burleigh B. Gardner, *Human Relations in Industry* (Chicago: Richard D. Irwin, Inc., 1945), p. 32.

7. Robert D. Gray, "What Your Boss Wants To Know," *Oil and Gas Journal*, Vol. 53 (August 30, 1954), pp. 84–87. (Reprinted in *Effective Communication on the Job*, ed. M. Joseph Dooher [New York: American Management Association, 1956].)

8. Paul Appleby, *Policy and Administration* (Birmingham, Ala.: University of Alabama Press, 1949), p. 75.

9. C. C. James, "Principles of Organization and Operation," *Advanced Management*, Vol. 10 (April–June, 1945), p. 51; A. E. Werolin, "Effective Controls for Top Management," *Advanced Management*, Vol. 12 (September, 1947), p. 123.

10. Werolin, *op. cit.*, p. 123.

11. Richard F. Neuschel, "Strengthening and Simplifying the Structure of Management Reports," *Improving Office Reports, Manuals and Records* ("Office Management Series," No. 141 [New York: American Management Association, 1955]), pp. 3–12; and Richard F. Neuschel, "What Top Management Needs To Know About Electronic Data Processing," *Improved Techniques for Administration and Control* ("General Management Series," No. 187 [New York: American Management Association, 1957]), pp. 28–42.

12. "Speeding Up Reports for Executive Control," in *The Prentice-Hall Business Ideas Handbook* (New York: Prentice-Hall, Inc., 1949), chap. ix.

13. Helen Baker, J. W. Ballantine, and J. M. True, *Transmitting Information through Management and Union Channels* (Princeton: Princeton University, Industrial Relations Section, 1949), p. 127.

14. Heinz Linge, "I Saw Hitler Die," *New York World-Telegram & Sun*, November 16, 1955.

15. R. H. Crawford, "Why Occupations Decline," *Military Government Journal*, Vol. 2 (Fall, 1949), p. 3.

16. Paul Pigors, *Effective Communication in Industry* (New York: National Association of Manufacturers, 1949), pp. 19–20.

17. Eugenia Sheppard, "Inside Fashion," New York *Herald Tribune*, October 28, 1957.

18. Dimock, *op. cit.*, pp. 51–52.

19. Burleigh B. Gardner and William F. Whyte, "The Man in the Middle: Position and Problems of the Foreman," *Applied Anthropology*, Vol. 4 (Spring, 1945) (special issue), pp. 4–5.

20. Sir Frank Tribe, "Efficiency in the Public Service," *Public Administration*, Vol. 27 (Autumn, 1949), p. 165.

Chapter XII communicating suggestions and
complaints

1. L. Keith Caldwell, *The Administrative Theories of Hamilton and Jefferson* (Chicago: University of Chicago Press, 1944), pp. 91–92.

2. Alex Osborn, *Your Creative Power* (New York: Charles Scribner's Sons, 1948), p. 276.

3. L. J. Alger, "Suggestion Statistics," *Getting and Using Employees' Ideas* ("Production Series," No. 165 [New York: American Management Association, 1946]), p. 11.

4. J. A. Donaho, "Employee Suggestion Systems in the Public Service," *Public Personnel Review*, Vol. 6 (October, 1945), p. 231.

5. "Suggestions Pay Heavy Dividends," *New York Times*, February 20, 1955.

6. V. M. Yeager, "Is Management Paying Enough for Suggestions?" *NASS Quarterly*, Vol. 5 (December, 1949), p. 5A.

7. Alger, *op. cit.*, p. 11.

8. Christian Steenstrup, "Leadership and the Development of Ingenuity," *NASS Quarterly*, Vol. 5 (December, 1949), pp. 15–16.

9. F. J. Roethlisberger, *Management and Morale* (Cambridge: Harvard University Press, 1941), pp. 58–59.

10. Herman W. Seinwerth, *Getting Results from Suggestion Plans* (New York: McGraw-Hill Book Co., 1948), pp. 38–40.

11. *NASS Annual Statistical Report for the Year 1956* (Chicago: National Association of Suggestion Systems, 1957), *passim*.

12. J. J. Morrow, "Is Management Paying Enough for Suggestions?" *NASS Quarterly*, Vol. 5 (December, 1949), p. 2A.

13. *American Business*, Vol. 55 (November, 1955), p. 42.

14. "Maytag Recognizes Supervisors for Work Simplification," *NASS Quarterly*, n.v. (Spring, 1956), p. 15.

15. Ernest Dale, *Greater Productivity through Labor-Management Cooperation* ("Research Reports," No. 14 [New York: American Management Association, 1949]), pp. 63–65.

16. Joseph N. Scanlon, "Adamson and His Profit-sharing Plan," *Planning and Administering Effective Incentives* ("Production Series," No. 172 [New York: American Management Association, 1947]), pp. 10–12.

17. Russell W. Davenport, "Enterprise for Everyman," *Fortune*, Vol. 41 (January, 1950), pp. 55–59 ff.

18. George P. Shultz, "Worker Participation on Production Problems," *Personnel*, Vol. 28 (November, 1951), p. 210.

19. Clare M. Cotton, "Dogs in Glass Houses Could Watch in Rain, Says Corning Employee," *Wall Street Journal*, November 29, 1954.

Chapter XIII INTERVIEWING

1. F. J. Roethlisberger, *Management and Morale* (Cambridge: Harvard University Press, 1941), p. 40.

2. Norman R. F. Maier, *Principles of Human Relations* (New York: John Wiley & Sons, 1952), p. 393.

3. Lillian M. Gilbreth and Alice R. Cook, *The Foreman in Manpower Management* (New York: McGraw-Hill Book Co., 1947), p. 16.

4. Earl G. Planty and Carlos E. Efferson, "Counseling Executives after Merit Rating or Evaluation," *Personnel,* Vol. 27 (March, 1951), pp. 384–96.

5. "What Pensioners Really Think and Do about Retirement," *Factory Management and Maintenance,* Vol. 110 (May, 1952), pp. 84–89.

6. Jeanne L. and Harold L. Wilensky, "Personnel Counseling: The Hawthorne Case," *American Journal of Sociology,* Vol. 57 (November, 1951), p. 275.

7. Harry Levinson, "Employee Counseling in Industry: Observations on Three Programs," *Bulletin of the Menninger Clinic,* Vol. 20 (March, 1956), pp. 76–79.

8. Wade E. Shurtleff, "Is Management Listening?" *Personnel,* Vol. 28 (September, 1951), p. 103.

9. F. J. Roethlisberger and William J. Dickson, *Management and the Worker* (Cambridge: Harvard University Press, 1939), pp. 189–91.

10. Levinson, *op. cit.,* p. 78.

11. Burleigh B. Gardner, *Human Relations in Industry* (Chicago: Richard D. Irwin, Inc., 1945), p. 244; Wilensky and Wilensky, *op. cit.,* p. 268.

12. James D. Weinland and Margaret V. Gross, *Personnel Interviewing* (New York: Ronald Press Co., 1952), pp. 201–2.

13. Maier, *op. cit.,* p. 397.

14. James C. Worthy, "Discovering and Evaluating Employee Attitudes," *Influencing and Measuring Employee Attitudes* ("Personnel Series," No. 113 [New York: American Management Association, 1947]), p. 16.

15. Wilensky and Wilensky, *op. cit.,* p. 268.

16. *Ibid.,* pp. 275–77.

17. John M. Pfiffner, *The Supervision of Personnel: Human Relations in the Management of Men* (New York: Prentice-Hall, Inc., 1951), p. 365.

18. Leonard E. Himler, "The Counseling Interview," in *Readings*

in Personnel Administration, ed. Paul Pigors and Charles A. Myers (New York: McGraw-Hill Book Co., 1952), p. 169.

19. Herbert Hyman, "Interviewing as a Scientific Procedure," in *The Policy Sciences,* ed. Daniel Lerner and Harold D. Lasswell (Stanford, Calif.: Stanford University Press, 1951), p. 214.

20. Edward Gross, "Social Science Techniques: A Problem of Power and Responsibility," *Scientific Monthly,* Vol. 83 (November, 1956), p. 243; L. J. Henderson, "Creative Listening," in *Readings in Personnel Administration,* ed. Pigors and Myers, p. 186; Roethlisberger, *op. cit.,* p. 43.

21. Weinland and Gross, *op. cit.,* p. 16.

22. John A. Wilson, *The Burden of Egypt* (Chicago: University of Chicago Press, 1951), p. 93.

23. Clifford E. Erickson, *The Counseling Interview* (New York: Prentice-Hall, Inc., 1950), p. 11.

24. Hyman, *op. cit.,* p. 214; Maier, *op. cit.,* p. 408.

25. Paul Pigors and Charles A. Myers, *Personnel Administration: A Point of View and a Method* (2d ed.; New York: McGraw-Hill Book Co., 1951), p. 82.

26. Rue Bucher, C. E. Fritz, and E. L. Quarantelli, "Tape Recorded Interviews in Social Research," *American Sociological Review,* Vol. 21 (June, 1956), pp. 359–64.

27. Levinson, *op. cit.,* p. 77.

28. Wilensky and Wilensky, *op. cit.,* pp. 273–74.

29. Levinson, *op. cit.,* p. 77.

30. Pfiffner, *op. cit.,* pp. 321–25.

31. Herbert Hyman, "Problems in the Collection of Opinion-Research Data," *American Journal of Sociology,* Vol. 55 (January, 1950), p. 365.

32. Stuart A. Rice, "Contagious Bias in the Interview: A Methodological Note," *American Journal of Sociology,* Vol. 35 (November, 1929), pp. 420–23.

33. Walter V. Bingham, "Halo, Invalid and Valid," *Journal of Applied Psychology,* Vol. 23 (April, 1939), pp. 221–28; W. J. E. Crissy and James J. Regan, "Halo in the Employment Interview," *Journal of Applied Psychology,* Vol. 35 (October, 1951), pp. 338–41.

34. Gardner, *op. cit.,* p. 241.

35. Robert N. McMurry, *Handling Personality Adjustment in Industry* (New York: Harper & Bros., 1944), p. 104.

36. King MacRury, "Employee Morale: Analyses of Absence Records and Opinion Polls," *Industrial and Labor Relations Review,* Vol. 21 (January, 1949), pp. 241–42; Pigors and Myers, *Personnel Administration,* p. 110.

37. William J. Giese and H. W. Ruter, "An Objective Analysis of Morale," *Journal of Applied Psychology,* Vol. 33 (October, 1949), pp. 421–27.

38. Alfred J. Marrow and Gilbert David, "The Turnover Problem—Why Do They *Really* Quit?" *Personnel Administration,* Vol. 14 (November, 1951), pp. 1–6.

39. Neil W. Chamberlain, review of Alexander R. Heron's *Why Men Work,* in *Advanced Management,* Vol. 13 (September, 1948), pp. 134–35.

40. Mark Abrams, "Possibilities and Problems of Group Interviewing," *Public Opinion Quarterly,* Vol. 13 (Fall, 1949), pp. 502–6; Walter Gellhorn and William Brody, "Selecting Supervisory Mediators through Trial by Combat," *Public Administration Review,* Vol. 8 (Autumn, 1948), pp. 259–66; Margaret Chandler, "An Evaluation of the Group Interview," *Human Organization,* Vol. 13 (Spring, 1954), pp. 26–28.

41. Worthy, *op. cit.,* pp. 15–16.

Chapter XIV EMPLOYEE OPINION POLLS

1. *Experience with Employee Attitude Surveys* ("Studies in Personnel Policy," No. 115 [New York: National Industrial Conference Board, Inc., 1951]), p. 7.

2. *Personnel Practices in Factories and Offices* ("Studies in Personnel Policy," No. 145 [New York: National Industrial Conference Board, Inc., 1954]), *passim.*

3. *Communication in Industry,* ed. Cecil Chisolm (London: Business Publications Ltd., 1955), p. 147.

4. C. N. Cofer and E. B. Cohen, "Job Attitudes of a Hundred and One Federal Employees," *Public Personnel Review,* Vol. 4 (April, 1943), pp. 96–102; *Employee Attitude Survey, Civil Service Employees of San Diego County, February 15, 1949* (County of San Diego, Civil Service Commission, n.d.); Sidney Selzer, "Studying Job Satisfaction among Hospital Attendants," *Public Personnel Review,* Vol. 11 (January, 1950), pp. 26–29; Bill N. Taylor, "We Found Out What Our Municipal Employees Want," *American City,* Vol. 64 (March, 1949), pp. 101, 129.

5. Samuel A. Stouffer *et al., Studies in Social Psychology in World War II* (4 vols.; Princeton: Princeton University Press, 1949–50).

6. Arthur Kolstad, "Employee Attitudes in a Department Store," *Journal of Applied Psychology,* Vol. 22 (October, 1938), pp. 470–79; Lewis M. Nixon, "Techniques of Surveying Employee Attitudes," *Public Personnel Review,* Vol. 10 (January, 1949), pp. 23–27.

7. Mildred Parten, *Surveys, Polls and Samples: Practical Procedures* (New York: Harper & Bros., 1950), pp. 56–58.

8. Herbert Hyman, "Interviewing as a Scientific Procedure," in *The Policy Sciences,* ed. Daniel Lerner and Harold D. Lasswell (Stanford, Calif.: Stanford University Press, 1951), p. 209.

9. Louis A. Allen, "Action-oriented Attitude Surveys," *Personnel,* Vol. 29 (September, 1952), p. 148.

10. Robert D. Gray, *Surveys of Employee Opinions—and What To Do with Them.* (Pasadena: California Institute of Technology, Industrial Relations Section, 1952), p. 13.

11. Harry B. Funk and Robert C. Becker, "Measuring the Effectiveness of Industrial Communications," *Personnel,* Vol. 29 (November, 1952), pp. 237–40.

12. Parten, *op. cit.,* p. 193.

13. Ellsworth Faris, "The Concept of Social Attitudes," in *Social Attitudes, ed. Kimball Young* (New York: Henry Holt & Co., 1931), pp. 3–15.

14. G. D. Wiebe, "Some Implications of Separating Opinions from Attitudes," *Public Opinion Quarterly,* Vol. 17 (Fall, 1953), p. 333.

15. Herbert Hyman, "Problems in the Collection of Opinion-Research Data," *American Journal of Sociology,* Vol. 55 (January, 1950), p. 366.

16. Eugene L. and Ruth E. Hartley, *Fundamentals of Social Psychology* (New York: Alfred A. Knopf, 1952), p. 549.

17. Funk and Becker, *op. cit.,* p. 239.

18. Gerald Carter, "Employee Attitudes at the University of Illinois," *Journal of Applied Psychology,* Vol. 31 (October, 1947), pp. 463–68.

19. John J. Corson, "Weak Links in the Chain of Command," *Public Opinion Quarterly,* Vol. 9 (Fall, 1945), pp. 346–49.

20. B. F. McClancy, "Polling Employee Opinions," *Checking the Effectiveness of Employee Communication* ("Personnel Series," No. 108 [New York: American Management Association, 1947]), p. 16.

21. Parten, *op. cit.,* p. 194.

22. Hyman, "Problems in the Collection of Opinion-Research Data," *op. cit.,* p. 366.

Chapter XV CLEARANCE AND REVIEW

1. Benjamin R. Makela, "Communication in Management" (a book review), *The Controller,* Vol. 22 (March, 1954), p. 128.

2. Joseph M. Juran, *Bureaucracy: A Challenge to Better Management* (New York: Harper & Bros., 1944), p. 32.

3. Joseph D. Cooper, *Procedural Coordination: Principles and Practices* (Washington, D.C.: Federal Security Agency, 1948), p. 67.

4. Commission on Organization of the Executive Branch of the Government, *Task Force Report on Foreign Affairs* (Washington, D.C.: Government Printing Office, 1949), Appendix H, p. 201.

5. Ray Miller, "Evolution of a Wartime Procedure Manual," *Public Administration Review*, Vol. 6 (Summer, 1946), p. 233.

6. Gerard Piel, "The Dangers of Secrecy in Science," New York *Herald Tribune*, October 18, 1957.

7. Hugh F. Colvin, "Controls for Research and Development," *Controls and Techniques for Better Management* ("General Management Series," No. 176 [New York: American Management Association, 1956]), p. 27.

8. J. Farradane, "Information Service in Industry," *Research*, Vol. 6 (August, 1953), p. 328.

Chapter XVI   THE CONFERENCE PROCESS

1. H. LeRoy Marlow, "Does the Conference Leader Talk Too Much?" *Management Review*, Vol. 44 (July, 1955), p. 462.

2. William E. Utterback, *Group Thinking and Conference Leadership: Techniques of Discussion* (New York: Rinehart & Co., Inc., 1950), p. 10.

3. Charles P. McCormick, *Multiple Management Up to Date* (New York: Harper & Bros., 1949).

4. *Dynamic Administration: The Collected Papers of Mary Parker Follett*, ed. Henry C. Metcalf and L. Urwick (New York and London: Harper & Bros., 1942), p. 175.

5. Esso Training Center, *Conference Leadership* (New York: Esso, Inc., 1947), p. 4.

6. Eugene E. Jennings, "Agreement or Compromise—The 'Leveling Effect' in Group Discussion," *Personnel*, Vol. 31 (July, 1954), pp. 66–71.

7. C. Arnold Anderson, "An Experimental Study of 'Social Facilitation' as Affected by 'Intelligence,' " *American Journal of Sociology*, Vol. 34 (March, 1929), pp. 874–81; J. F. Dashiell, "An Experimental Analysis of Some Group Effects," *Journal of Abnormal and Social Psychology*, Vol. 25 (July–September, 1930), pp. 190–99; Herbert Gurnee, "A Comparison of Collective and Individual Judgments of Fact," *Journal of Experimental Psychology*, Vol. 21 (July, 1937), pp. 106–12; Charles C. Peters, "Effect of Membership in Groups," *Review of Educational Research*, Vol. 7 (February, 1937), pp. 26–35.

8. Kurt Lewin, "Group Decision and Social Change," in *Readings*

in Social Psychology, ed. T. M. Newcomb and E. L. Hartley (New York: Henry Holt & Co., 1947), p. 336.

9. Jacob Levine and John Butler, "Lecture vs. Group Decision in Changing Behavior," *Journal of Applied Psychology,* Vol. 36 (February, 1952), pp. 29–31.

10. Joseph F. O'Brien, "A Definition and Classification of Forms of Discussion," *Quarterly Journal of Speech,* Vol. 25 (April, 1939), p. 236.

11. N. R. F. Maier and A. R. Solem, "The Contribution of a Discussion Leader to the Quality of Group Thinking," *Human Relations,* Vol. 5 (August, 1952), pp. 277–88.

12. Irving J. Lee, *How To Talk with People* (New York: Harper & Bros., 1952), pp. 162–68.

13. Kurt Lewin, "Frontiers in Group Dynamics," *Human Relations,* Vol. 1, No. 1 (1947), p. 36.

14. Irene Bennett Needham, "The Uses and Limitations of the Discussion Method," *Journal of Home Economics,* Vol. 27 (October, 1935), p. 514.

15. Delbert C. Miller, "An Experiment in the Measurement of Social Interaction in Group Discussion," *American Sociological Review,* Vol. 4 (June, 1939), pp. 345–46.

16. *Dynamic Administration: The Collected Papers of Mary Parker Follett,* p. 171.

17. Clement J. Berwitz, "The Work Committee: An Administrative Technique," *Harvard Business Review,* Vol. 30 (January–February, 1952), p. 121.

18. Goodwin B. Watson, "Do Groups Think More Efficiently than Individuals?" *Journal of Abnormal and Social Psychology,* Vol. 23 (October–December, 1928), p. 336; Robert F. Bales, "In Conference," *Harvard Business Review,* Vol. 32 (March–April, 1954), pp. 44–50; Elliott Jaques, "Interpretive Group Discussion as a Method of Facilitating Social Change," *Human Relations,* Vol. 1, No. 4 (1948), p. 540; *"Brainstorming" in General Foods* (White Plains: General Foods Corp., n.d.), p. 6; Arthur M. Coon, "Brainstorming—A Creative Problem-Solving Technique," *Journal of Communication,* Vol. 7 (Autumn, 1957), p. 113; Willard A. Pleuthner, "Brainstorming in Action," *Manpower Management* (White Plains: General Foods Corp., 1955), p. 22.

19. Jaques, *op. cit.*

20. Louis A. Allen, "How To Get the Most Out of Your Conference," *Advanced Management,* Vol. 16 (October, 1951), pp. 15–16.

21. Alfred M. Cooper, *How To Conduct Conferences* (New York: McGraw-Hill Book Co., 1946), pp. 112–13.

22. Arthur Jenness, "The Role of Discussion in Changing Opinion Regarding a Matter of Fact," *Journal of Abnormal and Social Psychology,* Vol. 27 (October–December, 1932), pp. 279–96.

23. Floyd H. Allport, *Social Psychology* (Boston: Houghton Mifflin Co., 1924), pp. 305–6; Harvey A. Carr, "The Law of Effect," *Psychological Review,* Vol. 45 (May, 1938), p. 191.

24. Lyman S. Judson, *A Manual of Group Discussion* (Illinois Agricultural Experiment Station Circular 446 [Urbana: University of Illinois, 1936]), pp. 53–57; James H. McBurney and K. G. Hance, *The Principles and Methods of Discussion* (New York: Harper & Bros., 1939), pp. 87–112.

25. Eduard C. Lindeman, "The Place of Discussion in the Learning Process," *Journal of Home Economics,* Vol. 27 (June–July, 1935), p. 351.

26. Leland P. Bradford, "Who Has a Question?" *American Journal of Nursing,* Vol. 55 (February, 1955), p. 181.

27. Coon, *op. cit.,* pp. 113–16.

28. Bernard S. Benson, "Let's Toss This Idea Up . . ." *Fortune,* Vol. 56 (October, 1957), pp. 145–46.

29. Lee, *op. cit.,* p. 9.

30. *Ibid.,* p. 147.

31. McBurney and Hance, *op. cit.,* p. 93.

32. *Discussion Leader's Guide* (containing materials used at the New York State Rural Youth Conference, February, 1950) (Ithaca: New York State College of Agriculture, 1950), p. 12.

33. Lee, *op. cit.,* pp. 51–59, 128–30, 157–59.

34. *Higher Education for American Democracy* (Washington, D.C.: Government Printing Office, 1947), Vol. 1, p. 52.

35. Crawford H. Greenewalt, "Is the 'Uncommon Man' in Peril?" *Management Review,* Vol. 45 (June, 1956), p. 466.

Index

Index